X

DATE DUE
Fecha

Good Morning, Mr. Zip Zip Zip

BOOKS BY RICHARD SCHICKEL

RICHARD SCHICKEL

Good Morning, Mr. Zip Zip Zip

MOVIES, MEMORY, AND WORLD WAR II

Ivan R. Dee

CHICAGO 2003

GOOD MORNING, MR. ZIP ZIP ZIP. Copyright © 2003 by Richard Schickel. All rights reserved, including the right to reproduce this book or portions thereof in any form. For information, address: Ivan R. Dee, Publisher, 1332 North Halsted Street, Chicago 60622. Manufactured in the United States of America and printed on acid-free paper.

Library of Congress Cataloging-in-Publication Data:
Schickel, Richard.
    Good morning, Mr. Zip Zip Zip : movies, memory, and World War II / Richard Schickel.
        p. cm.
    Includes index.
    ISBN 1-56663-491-1 (alk. paper)
    1. Schickel, Richard. 2. Film critics—United States—Biography. 3. Motion pictures—United States. 4. World War, 1939–1945—Motion pictures and the war. I. Title.

PN1998.3.S347 A3 2003
791.43'092—dc21
[B]   2002031399

For Frances, Georgia, and Lily

with love from GP

. . . in case you ever get to wondering

Contents

Prologue: Wartime Lies

WHEN I WAS a very little boy, in the years before most of the events recalled in this book took place, my father used to sing me a little song after he and my mother had tucked me into bed at night. Standing in the doorway of my room, his hand on the light switch, he would warble this chipper little ditty:

> Good morning Mr. Zip Zip Zip,
> With your hair cut just as short as mine.
> Good morning Mr. Zip Zip Zip,
> You're surely lookin' fine.
> Good morning, good morning, good morning,
> Mr. Zip Zip Zip.

That was it, though there is, I have lately discovered, more to the song, which appears to be a novelty tune dating back to World War I, something like Irving Berlin's "Oh, How I Hate to Get Up in the Morning" if much less famous.

Sometimes my father would vary his concert, either substituting for or adding to *Mr. Zip Zip Zip* another song that rang equally silly in my ears:

> If you want to be a Badger,
> Just come along with me,
> Just come along with me,
> By the bright shining light of the moon.
> By the light of the moon, by the light of the moon,
> By the bright shining light of the moon.

This song, dating to the turn of the nineteenth century, is one people used to sing—probably still sing—at the University of Wisconsin in Madison, which my father briefly attended, and from which I would later graduate. Because of that connection this little tune, with its sweet but easily ignored sexual innuendo—what must a girl do in the moonlight if she wished to become a fully initiated Badger?—entered that peculiar stream of consciousness along which burble hundreds of lyric fragments that pop into my head at odd moments, some with poignant or ironic appropriateness, some for no discernible reason. Later on I would sing the Badger song to my own daughters, usually to relieve the boredom of long drives, and they would laugh and join in.

The persistence in memory of *Mr. Zip Zip Zip* is a little more mysterious to me. I suppose my father chose both these songs precisely because they were entirely free of meaning to a child, therefore could not in any way disturb his imminent slumber. They posed questions so profoundly—or so shallowly—unanswerable that a kid would simply consign them to that vast, dim world that adults seemed to get around in quite comfortably, and which you imagined one day you would too. But not for a while. Not until you were ready for it.

Here are some questions that occur to me now about *Mr.*

Zip Zip Zip. The most obvious of them is that it is inappropriate to its hour. It is clearly meant to be a bouncy wake-up call, not a good-night tune; it is meant to stir, not relax. But skip that and think of that silly name—whoever heard such a moniker in the real world. And then there's that business about his hair being cut just as short as mine. I had no reference for that whatsoever. You can see now that it refers to military haircuts. But the army's buzz cuts, administered with electric clippers and a central humiliation of basic training in World War II, were as yet generally unheard of.

No, it's obvious that Dad did not think much about the questions the song raised. He correctly counted on the goofy play of the words to delight. He surely did not count on them lingering in some obscure corner of memory until, in the process of writing this book, they suddenly reappeared.

With, naturally, an adult meaning conveniently attached. *Mr. Zip Zip Zip* is obviously, metaphorically, me being awakened to understanding. And, if the reader will forgive the cliché, beginning the long process of losing my innocence—a process that is, I am bound to admit, still incomplete. (I am constantly amazed at the amount of mysterious, seemingly motiveless, malignity that surrounds us all.)

I cannot say that I yearn for the innocence of that little boy chortling sleepily at his father's rendition of a nonsense song. Yet the song, and the sweet circumstances in which I heard it, is in some ways emblematic of the childhood I had—or, to put it more precisely, the childhood those adults responsible for it wanted me to have, and worked so dutifully to provide.

MEMOIRS THAT RECOUNT tales of childhood abuse or adult addiction, and the writer's conquest of these afflictions, are the fashion nowadays. This is not, as I'm sure is already obvious, a book of that kind—more's the commercial pity, I suppose.

All right, it does chart the growth of one addiction—moviegoing. But that was, on balance, a benign one; it may have been life-shaping, but it was scarcely life-threatening. Most basically, I suppose my book can be read as an attempt to explain—first of all to myself—why I surrendered a great deal of my imaginative self, more than a half-century ago, to the movies, that most immediate and potent—though certainly not the most subtle—narrative instrument our society has yet created.

That addiction arose initially because the serene and placid little world I inhabited as a kid was so lacking in romantic and heroic adventure. I wanted not just to hear but to inhabit stories of a grander, more melodramatic kind than any I perceived in my immediate vicinity.

At the time I did not see that to be the case. Movies and movielike narratives (the radio, comic books, boy's books) were unconsciously chosen pastimes. They were omnipresent, and I heedlessly, passionately embraced them—more so, I'm convinced, than most of my contemporaries, who seemed able to take them or leave them much more dispassionately. I have come to believe that I was driven by an unacknowledged need that transcended a mere longing for dashing alternatives to my comfortable reality.

For a long time, when people asked me about my childhood, I responded with a wry shrug. It was, I said, "pleasant" or "nice." There was no point, I thought, in looking at what seemed to me a largely contented and uneventful past for clues to such torments as adulthood held for me.

But when I became involved with the movies as a critic, began writing books and making television programs about their history, I began to see that I was wrong about that. I began to sense that I had used pop narrative not merely as a way of adding a touch of glamour to my routine little life but as a means of escaping from certain failures my family was prone to but that I did not wish to admit—sad failures of ambition, more subtle failures of love.

In time I became a participant in some of these failures. Taken together they formed a story of dreams deferred and denied, of small, safe pleasures embraced, of larger passions unexpressed. It was, above all, an incomplete story in which the fiction of uninterrupted, unimprovable middle-class standards of culture, politics, and morality was at all costs maintained.

A lot of the drama in my young life was covered in silence, duplicity, misdirection. We were, after all, Midwestern WASPs, to whom confession and confrontation are anathema, to whom, in the time I am talking about, heroic therapeutic interventions in aid of happiness or "wholeness" were largely unknown and always disapproved.

The happy middle-class fiction by which we lived evaded the harsher facts of life as most Americans endured them. This fiction consisted of three elements. First, there was our immediate culture: our parents, our schools, our churches, and our Cub Scout packs were teaching us to be content with our non- if not downright anti-heroic, lives. We were supposed to be good-natured, helpful, not particularly competitive. We were not supposed to stand out from the crowd—unless, of course, we were high school sports heroes. It was okay to bask for a moment in that sort of fame, since the unspoken understanding was that you would soon enough sink back into obscurity and your father's real estate business.

Second, there was the popular culture, to which I have already alluded. It was largely devoted to showing us the world's fantastic possibilities—of wealth, wit, sexiness, and, of course, melodramatic adventure. The art in this material lay in rendering these implausibilities plausible, attainable by the likes of us, however firmly the adults surrounding us (vaguely disapproving, without quite disowning, popular culture in its many cheesy manifestations) insisted on maintaining their simple, small-town values and tried their best to impose them on us.

Finally there was World War II. I did not fully realize, until I started writing this book, how it raised to a flashpoint the conflict between our stoutly defended ordinariness and the extraordinary exertions of our fighting men in places few of us had heard of until they appeared in the headlines.

In the fictions of the war—which were, of course, part of an overall megafiction—our soldiers were always presented as profoundly normal human beings. You know the clichés: guys getting a dirty job done as quickly as possible so they could return to their girlfriends, their mutts, Mom's apple pie. It occurred to none of us that you cannot be a hero in wartime (or a success in peacetime) and maintain the fiction of ordinariness. Moreover, maintaining this lie required the culture to sustain other lies that were in some ways more devastating.

For example: During World War II, in the midst of my burgeoning life, I was surrounded—as we all were—by death on a scale unprecedented in human history. Yet it was constantly lied about. In the movies particularly, tragedy was almost always subsumed in triumphalism, mortality in broadly hinted suggestions of heroic immortality.

But something like 55 million people died in World War II, for the most part passing like extras in a movie battle scene, their unparticularized sacrifices acknowledged, at most, by some equivalent of a movie's inspirational and slightly insincere voice-over. Sometimes, in the movies, they lived on as helpful ghosts, whispering advice to the young men who had replaced them in the cockpit or the foxhole.

But no one we cared about in these fictions ever died in vain. Or absurdly. Or stupidly. Or as a coward. They died nobly. In defense of "our way of life." Naturally I believed that. Just about everyone—a few pacifist cranks aside—believed that.

This is a lie that has returned, revitalized, in the "greatest generation" fantasy. Each generation is obliged to play the cards that fate—in the form of metapolitics, metaeconomics, metaculture—deals it. It may play them well or poorly, but since the American "experiment" has not yet come to an end, we are perhaps entitled to see ourselves, crudely speaking, on a permanent winning streak. "Progress is our most important product," as the old advertising slogan once went. But it does not seem to me that the generation that survived the Great Depression and won World War II particularly distinguished itself in those efforts.

It did about as well as might be expected. As in any war, there were many acts of heroism and self-sacrifice. But even within my childish ken—and often enough within my very sight and hearing—there were acts of pettiness, selfishness, meanness that were anything but great. And American racism and anti-Semitism continued largely unabated. I am by no means alone in my resistance to Tom Brokaw's big think; many men and women who were adults during the war, I find, look askance at his claims.

Putting it simply, the greatest generation responded to the challenges of its times pretty much within the limits imposed on it by the spirit of those times, which was more dutiful than glorious. Those who went beyond those limits, who found within themselves the good stuff that enabled them to transcend the conventional wisdom of their moment were, as ever, few and perhaps rather lonely in their righteousness.

I continue to believe that World War II was a necessary war, that both the Germans and the Japanese were practicing evil on a scale unprecedented in human history. But I have come to believe that, for the most part, we engaged in that war more or less blindly, that it was not until a point very near its end, when, for instance, the concentration camps were liberated, or the few survivors of the Bataan death march began telling their stories, that we generally began to perceive the well-organized enormity—we're not talking about the isolated atrocities that every war produces—of the crimes our enemies perpetrated against humanity.

Grappling with these horrors, grappling as well with my childish ignorance of war's devastating reality, I found this book beginning to veer occasionally toward meditations on the vast, slippery realms of ontology. That is to say, in various passages it ceases to be a memoir at all or a book about how the groundwork for my future as a professional moviegoer was laid down. I don't apologize for that. As with old movies, so with my old life; I am revisiting my childhood as a man on the cusp of old age, bringing to bear on my innocence, my generation's innocence, a critical sense of the past.

I suppose if I had done otherwise—if I had attempted to write a book in which the viewpoint resolutely remained that of a child, groping dimly for understanding amidst the patriotic uproar of the time—I would have written a smoother, more shapely book. But then I would have had to leave out many of the things that are, at least in my opinion, the best part of the mature me, an individual who values, in art and in life, the randomness of existence—its incongruities, indeterminacy, absurdities, ambiguities, paradoxes, and ironies (above all, the last). Variously blended and adapted, they are what I have in the way of a philosophy.

I suppose it is the application of those qualities that accounts for the tolerant, not to say bemused, attitude I take toward the people who shared and shaped my boyhood. Our families and our local institutions were doing the best they could to raise useful, optimistic, good-hearted little citizens. You can't blame them for hiding the more dangerous and bitter truths from us. Especially since in those days these truths were not necessarily obvious to complacent adulthood either.

Indeed, it is possible to argue that only very recently—since the events of September 11, 2001—has it finally become completely clear to everyone that we are no longer safe in our daily lives, that terror of the kind that the rest of the world has lived with for centuries can happen here, inevitably will again happen here. We have not really been safe behind our ocean barricades for several decades, but now that is at last clear to everyone, and the complacencies that for so long sustained us, even in the midst of world war, are permanently shattered. The ludicrous "American Century" is now Europeanized, and we have to recognize that the bomb in the café—all right, the Starbucks—is a real possibility.

One obviously cannot blame wartime adulthood for failing to imagine a permanently insecure "homeland." On the other hand, about the larger institutions that manipulated them during World War II—the government, the mass media—I am less forgiving. I do believe they knew more than they were telling (and selling), that they deliberately distorted much of what they put forth in those days in order to keep us bent pliantly to their will. I think it may even be possible that I became what I became—a critic—out of some dimly felt desire to help set this errant record straight.

That, though, is a claim I don't advance very confidently. A lot of the time, at the movies, I am as complicit in their genial and saving lies as I was when I was a boy. One is, after all, an American, thus often not as vigilant as one might be when out on cultural patrol.

In this book, however, I am being alert. I am calling to account these institutions and, above all I hope, my all too innocent self, attempting to identify at least some of what we missed or were misled about. I do not traffic much in nostalgia, a fraudulent emotion I despise. It covers memory with a softening and forgiving mist, places rose-colored glasses on our historical gaze, and then, at last, cranks up a sentimental ballad on the CD player, drowning out our attempts to tell the truth about the past in straightforward fashion. It is authentic recall's most insidious enemy.

THE LOST PAST was not golden. It was all right in some respects, not all right in others. But I haven't the slightest desire to return to it. I only want to understand it. And me as a part of it. That doesn't make me a tough guy. It makes me a realist, someone trying to look back in honesty.

This is particularly true of the movies that remain, for me, a significant part of the past. They are fairly easily recovered memories. You can find them on television, on videotape, even sometimes in certain theaters. Since this is so, I was determined not to write about any of the films I saw as a child without confronting them anew. This seems to me an elementary (though often shirked) duty for the movie historian. It's not just that memory often plays tricks on us when we try to recall the details of old movies. It's that our relationship to them—and our opinions of them—are bound to change with the passing years. It makes me crazy when people pretend otherwise, speak and write—usually with moronic fondness—about old movies as if they are forever fixed as they were when we first glimpsed them as easily impressed children or adolescents.

So . . . with a few clearly marked exceptions, all the movies discussed in this book are movies I saw during the years it covers; all of them I have seen at least once more for the purposes of this book. False naiveté is no more in my range than is false nostalgia.

I don't know if the balance of this book makes any sense to anyone but myself—conventional reminiscence, critical considerations of movies almost everyone else has forgotten, a certain contempt for the false pieties and hypocrisies of our old public culture. It makes for some odd juxtapositions, some odd shifts in tone too. But, to borrow one of my favorite James Cagney lines, "That's the kind of hairpin I am."

R. S.

Los Angeles
September 2002

Good Morning, Mr. Zip Zip Zip

1

City of Homes

WE LIVED, during the war (and for many years thereafter) in a place called Wauwatosa.

Wauwatosa. Something inescapably comic in that soft tumble of vowels. But it was a serious place: a suburb of Milwaukee where many of the people who soberly, responsibly tended the larger city's business lived.

The name is a corruption of a word borrowed from some local Indian dialect. I don't know its literal meaning. In high school the joke was that it meant "strong middle class with delusions of grandeur." Delusions of stability would be more like it— a dream of seamless continuity between past, present, and future. Writing brilliantly about another kind of suburb—newer, rawer, Californian—D. J. Waldie observed, "The necessary illusion is predictability."

In our case this was based in part on the fact that, unlike other suburbs, this little city had not been created whole cloth out of some developer's dream. It had a history of organic growth that appeared to be logically extensible into the future. It had been founded as a rural trading center in the nineteenth century. Whittaker Chambers's grandmother was born there in its early days—to my mind one of the most interesting facts about Wauwatosa. Its whole point was not to produce, or have any truck with, characters like Whittaker Chambers, to pretend that impassioned figures of his sort—tortured souls desperately certain that history was a tragic drama—did not exist. "Well, he certainly didn't get that from his grandmother," people would have said had they known of his roots.

Eventually the little city grew to a point at which it and Milwaukee shared a border—the big city ended on the east side of Sixtieth Street, the smaller one on its west side. Along this street (and on other major thoroughfares leading in and out of it) the town had erected signboards. They were fashioned of metal and hung from weathered wooden posts. The top was a cutout silhouette of little trees and houses. Below them you were welcomed with these words:

CITY OF HOMES
GOOD SCHOOLS
ARTESIAN WATER

After which the current population (around 25,000 in those days) was noted. All those boasts were as reliable as the census figures that followed.

IT WAS NEVER explained to me why my mother and father decided to move to Wauwatosa from Milwaukee's East Side in 1937 or '38. It was one of those matters that people in those days did not feel a need to discuss with their children.

I'm sure "Good Schools" had a lot to do with it, since I was arriving at kindergarten age. And "Artesian Water" was not to be entirely overlooked. Milwaukee's drinking water, drawn from Lake Michigan, had to be treated chemically and tasted distinctly unfresh. But it was, I think, that "City of Homes" slogan that sealed their bargain.

For this was a town that believed in free-standing dwellings and serious zoning. Our house was a swollen, yellow stucco bungalow, more spacious than it looked from the outside. It had a second floor we never knew quite what to do with and a garage under the house, which kept the car warm on cold winter nights, though the extra long curve of the driveway required to reach it demanded prodigies of shoveling in a blizzard's aftermath.

Our address was 1721 North 68th Street. This was in the historic heart of the town, a grid of streets running five long blocks north and south, something like twenty blocks east and west, all of them richly canopied by elms and maples. The houses, set well back from the street, seemed as deeply rooted as the trees. They were the products, I suppose, of the first intensive wave of suburban building that began around the turn of the century, predominantly colonial in design, generously proportioned, often with a side porch or sunroom added.

These were sober houses, not built to create an overwhelming first impression but to endure. The last time I looked, in the fall of 2001, when I returned for my fiftieth high school reunion, they were all still there. There were other districts in town, of course, one or two richer than ours, one or two poorer. We were right in the middle, socially as well as geographically, of this middle-class community.

OUR TOWN'S CENTER was called "The Village." It nestled in a curve of the Menominee River, where several streets, running on downhill diagonals, came together near the railroad station. The weekly newspaper's office was there, also the volunteer fire department (which sounded a noon whistle every workday, a shriek that carried for miles) and a police station (at my grandfather's urging, the chief, a Masonic lodge brother, once opened his coat to reveal his holstered gun).

The major building, located on a triangular plot where all the streets converged, was an old-fashioned dry goods emporium, dark and musty. It was called Lefeber's. Its toy department, in the basement, was nearly always closed—a slat with a bit of mournful black oilcloth tacked to it barring your way. If you wanted to examine its rather good stock of lead soldiers, you had to apply to a clerk, usually a middle-aged spinsterish woman, who would grudgingly precede you down the stairs, flip on the light switches, and impatiently await your selection. On the store's second floor the city rented a large room where the town council met.

Among The Village's other shops were a dime store, a hardware store, two drugstores, each with a marble soda counter, and a shoe store with an x-ray fitter, in which you could observe your own wiggling toe bones as you tried on your new footwear while your mother and the salesman peered through other viewers, judging the fit. Everyone was unaware of the carcinogenic danger to which they were being exposed.

All these buildings were flat-faced and functional. But as you climbed the hill you passed the little-used bandstand; St. Bernard's, the Catholic grade school; and the Underwood Hotel, where my grandparents lived, and came, three blocks from Lefeber's, to the library. It stood on another triangular plot, a stone building, steeply eaved, whimsical in design—like a fairy-tale building, I thought. It had a children's alcove with a long cushioned seat beneath a large stained-glass window. My mother would take me there on rainy summer afternoons when I was small, and I would spend a sweet hour in that hushed, cozy place, leafing through the picture books, trying to puzzle out the few words they contained.

Later the library, which was just six blocks from our house, was the savior of many a restless summer day. It could always be relied on for the latest from F. Van Wyck Mason, a now forgotten fictioneer, who wrote a series of spy novels featuring a James Bond precursor called Colonel North as well as seafaring historical novels that seemed to me racy—lots of girls in piratical jeopardy. The library also offered the collected works of P. G. Wodehouse, which somehow made me laugh out loud despite the fact that I knew nothing of the lost Edwardian world he was satirizing.

ABOUT THE VILLAGE there was something of a country town improbably clinging to life in the midst of a heavily industrialized metropolis. It wasn't self-consciously quaint; preservationism had not yet been invented. Neither did it exert quite the centrifugal force of a main street in a rural county seat; downtown Milwaukee was too near. But it hinted at something about the character of our community—a sort of unexamined traditionalism, a passive but weighty resistance to change.

Sinclair Lewis just two decades earlier had described an old-fashioned American main street as "the climax of civilization," and something of that sense of unimprovable completion had now passed to suburbs like ours.

Sober civic-mindedness was a shared value—men who wished the community's respect were expected to join the service clubs, teach Sunday school, participate in organizations like the PTA. Women were supposed to be Cub Scout den mothers and run white elephant sales at the church.

Every six weeks on winter Saturday nights there was "Minuet." This was a dancing club that met at the Women's Club ballroom, the men in tuxes, the women in long dresses. There were always cocktail parties before the dance. On Sunday morning my father was sometimes hung over, and there was talk of others observed "feeling no pain." Liquor excused the flirtatiousness of these occasions, observable (if not nameable) by me when my parents hosted one of the predance parties. Everyone was just a little more sparkly than usual.

Wauwatosa voted Republican overwhelmingly. In 1940, in a straw vote in my classroom, only three or four of us raised our hands for Roosevelt. Four years later I raised a solitary hand for Norman Thomas and was greeted with cries of outrage—justifiably so, since it was a reaction I was seeking, not a principle I was advancing.

Everyone went to church dutifully—the Protestant denominations mainly, though there was a substantial Catholic minority. There were to my knowledge only two Jewish families in town: the Feldmans, who ran a somewhat deracinated delicatessen where we bought cold cuts and rye bread for our Saturday soup and sandwich dinners; and the Grosses, who were rumored to have a background in raffish show business, though no one ever discovered its details. They possessed the town's only private swimming pool and kept rather to themselves.

These families were tolerated but not embraced. I went to school with children from both of them and often met Larry Gross—a soft-spoken, self-contained boy—on the way to school and walked with him. But I was only rarely invited to his home, and vice versa.

Needless to say, there were no black residents. In fact, there was an ordinance on the books that prohibited blacks from being on our streets after 10 p.m. Most people did not know of this law.

It came to light sometime in the fifties when a black man, a chef in a local restaurant, was arrested for breaking it as he waited for a streetcar to take him home after work. A scandal arose, and the law was rescinded. But I cannot honestly say that in the thirties or forties, had we known of this ordinance, we would have thought it untoward.

I cannot say, either, that my parents were not in some corner of their souls attracted to living in this essentially WASP enclave, so free of disturbing othernesses. They had their prejudices. Everyone I encountered growing up did. These were not virulent. They were expressed as muttered distrust, mild patronization. But never, of course, to anyone's face. That would have been a violation of the politesse on which the town relied for its smooth functioning.

IT WAS THE SAME with money. Those who had it were expected not to flaunt it. Of those who seemed to be doing well, we said only, "They're comfortable." It was a nice, vague, all-encompassing term that embraced virtually everyone we knew, and people worked hard to attain and maintain that state of things.

In the winter you would start clearing your sidewalk as soon as the snow stopped falling. In the spring the bare patches in the lawns were always reseeded as soon as the threat of freezing was over. In the summer the grass was cut and watered once a week. In the autumn the leaves were raked into neat piles on the same schedule.

You were allowed to jump into the leaves if you promised not to scatter them. Eventually they would be gathered in bushel baskets for collection by the trash men. But sometimes they would be burned. No reason not to; in those days the greenhouse effect was, like x-ray shoe fitters, one of a thousand perils as yet unknown. We were entirely free to enjoy the minor drama of the flame struggling to catch in leaves that were often wet, the cloud of gray smoke curling upward, your father warning you to stay a safe distance upwind.

There was something ritualistic about all the puttering, tidying, sprucing-up chores with which little boys were encouraged to assist (we were all equipped with child-sized rakes and shovels). They were repayment on the unspoken obligation we owed to the masculine enigma. Pestering, yet quickly bored, we were learning the tricks of the grown-up trade, certain deftnesses and patiences that were not taught in books. In the process we were also discovering and paying the interest on the other unspoken debt that could never be fully discharged—the upkeep we owed to the city of homes and the social compact our parents had made with it.

The little city was perhaps less socially homogenous in truth than it is in memory. Just south of our house, where the land sloped down to the river valley, was a working-class district— neat little bungalows in carefully tended yards. North of us were other such areas, while further west were sections of newer homes, spacious enough but not yet fully settled into their land-scapes of newly sodded lawns and young trees.

Across the street from us, the Highlands began. These were a set of low hills with curving streets following their contours. Many of the houses there were quite grand, several of them near to showy. There the "rich" (as we judged them to be) lived. It seems to me that the people there were less neighborly and mixed less in the life of the town than others did, which may be, come to think of it, why the Grosses, in their mysterious, faintly glamorous prosperity, abided there.

Whatever he did, Mr. Gross at least did not sell real estate or life insurance, which is what everyone else's father seemed to do. I exaggerate. Those of them who did not work in white collars in Milwaukee's factories were in the professions or had small businesses of their own. But no one was an airline pilot. Or an FBI agent. No one went off to the war, when it came, in some heroic or secretive capacity.

Our mothers, for the most part, did not hold jobs. Mainly they shopped, made dinner, kept house, and tended their children. They were alert to our needs, but—my own nervous mother aside—not oppressive in their concerns. They didn't need to be, for we were entirely unthreatened. There were no bad neighborhoods in Wauwatosa, few latchkey children, and, of course, no drugs and no guns other than hunting weapons, which were handled by adults with a great show of respect.

"Juvenile delinquency" was a postwar concept and concern. I suppose there must have been "dysfunctional" families pretending to function in this benign environment, but divorce and alcoholism were rare. Spousal and child abuse were virtually unheard of.

Virtually. A friend of my mother's, someone with one of those plain, sensible names—Esther or Margaret or Clara—did separate from her husband. Then one night her home was invaded by an unidentified intruder and she was severely beaten. The story made the front page of the *Milwaukee Journal's* second section (where the local news was carried), and it was I who read it first and brought it to my mother's attention. She immediately suspected the estranged husband. Everyone did. But no arrest was made. A few weeks later, after supper one night, he dropped by our house. People did that all the time. It was called "visiting." He was all smiles. As if nothing had happened.

But something had. The strain between my parents and this man was palpable. He soon departed. Later he left town—or at least our part of it—not to be seen again. It is more than possible that his battered wife covered up for him. We know now how common that is. We did not know it then.

We even had outright sex scandals. Curiously, both involved high school teachers. In the first case the teacher was charged with statutory rape when a student who worked with him after school in the student finance office became pregnant. Although no one mentioned it at the time, there was an odd disconnect between the dull, bookkeeperish activities of that office—it collected involuntary contrbutions (five or ten dollars a year) from each student and disbursed this money to the school paper, yearbook, and other extracurricular activities to help defray their expenses—and the sad, hot passion that occurred within the office's prim confines. The teacher, of course, went to jail, the girl in the case went away. Her younger brother was my classmate all through school.

The second case was more spectacular. We had a high school basketball coach, a bland, round-faced man who taught shop and was married to an extremely atttactive girls' gym teacher. He coached a rather daring run-and-shoot style of basketball. This was a disconnect of another kind—between his personality and his rather harum-scarum teams. Somehow, though, some talent aggregated around him, and the team won the state championship the first year I was in high school. It continued going to the state tournament three more years, though it never again won the title. Then, a year or two after my class graduated, the coach was caught in a raid on a whorehouse operating just across the county line. Because he was a famous coach, the story made headlines. He was, of course, instantly dismissed from his job. Within the week, like some Sherwood Anderson character, he killed himself.

Much sympathy was extended to his widow. But later on I

came to wonder about her. The girls' gym program was run by an obvious lesbian. Perhaps this woman shared that taste. Perhaps the cathouse was the only release available to her mate. I don't know.

People made as little of these incidents as possible. They were treated as inexplicable anomalies, sudden, unpleasant deviations from the placid flow of our town's narrative. We put them behind us as quickly as we could. We found no instruction in them.

WE WERE implicitly urged to find no instruction in anything that seriously disturbed our placidity. I don't entirely understand why I was not absorbed—perhaps drowned is a better word—in it. Almost everyone with whom I grew up was taken in by it, happily so.

Restlessness is ever a mystery. Why is one kid afflicted by it, the rest not? That's especially so when one thinks back on this time and place. For if it could be said to have a collective imagination, it was cast comfortably backward, not excitingly forward.

We are talking about a time between three and four decades after the turn of the nineteenth century. My father was born two years before it, my mother three years after it. All our parents were of this generation. All looked nostalgically back on their beginnings.

Many of the old ways of doing business, which they had known since childhood, reassuringly persisted. When we moved into our house, we shared our telephone line (BLuemound 7728) with another party. The milkman from Gridley's Dairy still made his rounds in a horse-drawn wagon. The iceman came in a motorized truck, but it still carried twenty-five- or fifty-pound blocks of ice packed in sawdust. Responding to a card in our front window, which specified the weight we wanted, the iceman would hoist one of these huge cubes to his padded shoulder with his tongs and carry it to the wooden icebox in our kitchen. He would chip off slivers of the ice with his pick and hand them to kids on a hot summer's day.

Two or three times each winter the coal truck would pull up to our curb, a metal chute would be arranged over the basement window above the coal bin, and the men from the truck would carry the coal in canvas bushels on their shoulders and dump it into the chute. I remember the blackness of their hands and faces, the rumble of the coal as it tumbled downward, the clouds of dust that arose from that passage.

Tending the furnace was a householding ritual I particularly liked: watching my father lift the latch on its small cast-iron door—too hot to touch—with the edge of his shovel; the blast of heat after the door was nudged open; studying him as he studied the bright orange glow inside, judging just how to spread fresh fuel on it; admiring his craftiness with the shovel; wondering what exactly went into his calculations as he poked thoughtfully at the fire, banking it properly so that it would live through the night.

People did not cling unreasonably to the old ways. We got a single-party phone line sometime during the war. When Gridley's replaced horses with smart little trucks, only a few nostalgic words were spoken about the animals' disappearance from our streets. My parents were proud when they exchanged the icebox for a Norge refrigerator—friends dropped by to inspect this marvel—and delighted to replace the furnace and the coal bin with an oil burner, reclaiming their basement from shameful soot.

Thus did the hummings of modernity enter our house. But never the harsher cacophonies of modernism. My mother and father had grown up free of its taints. They implicitly believed that music must carry a tune, that a picture should represent reality as the eye naturally beheld it. They thought all worthwhile stories had innocent beginnings, logically soluble middle passages, and agreeable, morally instructive endings.

They believed, of course, that history was just such a narrative. They must have heard the far-off echoes of discordancies—who living through the depression as adults did not?—but Wauwatosa, their chosen place, tacitly supported the coherent, old-fashioned story they wished to live. Neither they nor, so far as I could see, anyone else in town was going to let anything disturb that coherence—not even war, when it came.

2

"It's Only a Movie"

ONE SATURDAY in the spring of 1938, not long after I had turned five, supper was served early, and there was a not-quite-suppressed air of excitement in my parents' manner. As we ate they asked me if I'd like to go to the movies with them and see *Snow White and the Seven Dwarfs*.

I had heard of the picture. And I imagine I had begun to wonder what the experience of moviegoing was like. As we drove to the theater—it was, I still recall, the Parkway, a neighborhood house on Milwaukee's North Side, somewhat off our beaten path—my father, obviously having heard of screaming children being removed from the theater when the witch got really scary, told me that if I got frightened I should remember that what we'd be seeing on the screen were "only drawings."

"I know," I replied rather impatiently—though I'm not certain I really understood the difference between animation and live action. Or why drawings would necessarily be less alarming than real people. I felt somewhat put down by his concern that I would not be able to handle anything the hag might dish out.

This was typical of him: he would encourage me to test the unknown but warn me of its untoward possibilities. In this case his concern was unnecessary. I watched the movie fearlessly. And, I'm sure, raptly. Sneezy, Dopey, Doc, and the rest of the dwarfs, plus Snow White, took up residence on a maple knickknack shelf in my bedroom in the form of little hard-rubber models.

I'm not sure they took up such prominent residence in my imagination. Snow White and almost all its animated successors remain rather weightless to me. I remember best the discovery of the sleeping Snow White by the dwarfs—they were memorably cute in their consternation—the queen-witch transformation, the wonderful sequence of the dwarfs and the forest denizens racing to warn Snow White of the poisoned apple.

Or maybe I don't. Maybe they are the result of later exposures to the film. I'm sure the rotoscoped heroine, with her too-classy singing voice and her too-wooden prince, seemed palpably inauthentic to me. There was simply something kinesthetically wrong about them.

I don't think my second movie, *The Wizard of Oz*, worked any better for me. Of course I liked the tornado, and I remember thinking it was neat the way the workaday people of Dorothy's farm life were transformed into the Cowardly Lion, the Tin Woodman, the Scarecrow, the good witch, and the altogether excellent bad witch.

But Dorothy—I don't know. It was hard for a little boy of that era to get fully behind a heroine who was supposed to be just a little older than he was. Maybe that's why the picture failed at the box office on its first release. Surely that's why it has remained a little-girl favorite—including, lately, both of my older granddaughters—and an object of patient indulgence for males.

So it went with me. I enjoyed some later Disney movies like *Dumbo* and *Bambi* without quite taking them fully to heart. The adults in your life expected you to adore them, and you did your best to oblige their expectations of enchantment. But, even without anything much to measure them against, these movies didn't quite seem like movies to me.

The major exception to this reaction was *Pinocchio*. I identified with that prevaricating puppet who turns human, doubtless because at the time I tended to exaggerate my own modest adventures. The images of the carriage in the rain as Pinocchio is abducted to Pleasure Island, the whole terrifying business of being swallowed by Monstro the whale, haunt me still—dark high points of classic Disney animation,

As for my own Pinocchio-like moments, I remember making up a wholly imaginary trip west to a dude ranch, which I reported in rich detail during the inevitable school period devoted to what we had done on our summer vacations. Later I pretended that my father was a newspaperman, which seemed more adventurous to me than his actual job as an ad man. I almost got caught out in the lie. I was rescued by a kindhearted teacher—pretty, red-haired Miss Arnell—who knew the truth but also apparently understood my need to glamorize it.

I was also fond of *The Reluctant Dragon*. I liked Robert Benchley bumbling about the Disney studio, learning how animation was accomplished. It was the first film that made me aware that movies were, among other things, a complicated technological process. The picture also contains a nice little sequence, at what is supposed to be Benchley's house, where he's lying on an inflatable raft in his swimming pool, taking potshots at a rubber ducky with his air gun.

I have no idea why that silly moment permanently entered my memory. Or maybe, come to think of it, I do. Benchley, for all his whiny cluelessness, was at least human, someone whose many befuddlements were akin to my own. You could take him to heart, as you could not a stiffly drawn princess or even a flying elephant.

In truth, I have had trouble with fantasy and fairy tales all my life. In grade school we were expected to read and report on five books a semester, selected from such categories as fiction, biography, history, poetry, and, yes, fantasies and fairy tales. I swept through the first four categories and struggled with the last: The Brothers Grimm, King Arthur and his Round Table left me unmoved, restless, impatiently skimming.

It's the same, now, with Tolkien or the Harry Potter books. I appreciate their artfulness, as I appreciate the skill of Disney's animators, but most of the time I don't get involved.

IF MY FIRST MOVIES somewhat puzzled me, I did like the little flurry they caused in our house—that early, hasty dinner, that car ride filled with anticipation, the entrance into the theater, dim and mysterious, the search for the best remaining seats, the sweeping musical fanfares that introduced even the previews and newsreels. It is sometimes said of me, as a reviewer, that my "love" of movies shines through my writing about them. I find that rather patronizing, but I admit to this: I love going to the movies. And this affection begins in childhood. Very simply, and despite their ready and inexpensive availability, they were an event in my little life, something bigger, grander than little me. Radio and kid books were okay. They were better than nothing, and a lot better than reality. And so they remain.

Something in the shimmer and sheen of movies hypnotized my eye as no other spectacle—then or later—ever did. The silver nitrate stock, on which all prints were then made, imparted a sparkle to those movies that, I now see, cannot be imparted to the safety stocks that replaced them after the war. I suspect, without being able to prove it, that they may have exploited some physiological anomaly—unshared by the general population—in those of us who became, in *Time*'s famous neologism, cinemaddicts.

My parents were not particularly devoted to the movies. My father sometimes spoke affectionately of the smart, stylish women of 1930s romantic comedy—Myrna Loy, Irene Dunne, Jean Arthur—but I don't know when he saw their pictures. My mother, I would discover during the war years, had a taste for period musicals. But their interest was dispassionate. For them, taking me to the movies was a way of giving me a nice treat now and then. If that also included an introduction to the "finer things" (like the Disney films, the artfulness of which attracted much favorable comment at the time) or a convenient way of providing moral instruction, so much the better.

Legally speaking, the movies were still regarded as "common shows," like carnivals and circuses, which denied them their First Amendment rights, enabled localities to censor them, and underlay the massive prudery of the industry's self-censoring Hays office, the day-to-day business of which was conducted by a Catholic layman, Joseph Ignatius Breen, overseeing a staff composed largely of his coreligionists.

About Breen's activities my parents were indifferent. I guess if you'd asked them they would have said that the movies naturally ought to be careful about what they showed, but they probably would have added that they had never been offended by anything they saw on the screen. Risqué jokes—so long as they were "cute"—were not unknown to them.

But if they weren't stuffy about the movies, they did not

think of them as an art form, either. Almost no one did. Gilbert Seldes was unknown in our house. James Agee, writing anonymously in *Time*, under a byline in *The Nation*, was equally unheard of.

By 1940 my parents were starting to select movies for us to see together that had a certain narrative complexity, pictures that did not have children as their prime audience. They had found the magic button. Real toads in imaginary gardens. Or was it real gardens with imaginary toads? Anyway, movies that confused fantasy and reality instead of firmly segregating them the way Disney did.

The confusion was—still is—delicious. And seductive. In his way my father tried to warn me about that too. "Remember, it's only a movie," he would say—as whose father did not in those days?

Again I nodded impatient agreement. But he could not have gone beyond that vague warning if I had asked him to. He was an ad man, not an aesthetician. Besides, the movies were so potent in their glamour that I would not have believed anything disillusioning about them anyway.

ON MY SEVENTH BIRTHDAY my father took my birthday party—five or six schoolmates—to a matinee of *Rulers of the Sea*. It was about the first transatlantic crossing by steamship. Will Fyffe, the Scots comedian, played the steam-power visionary, Douglas Fairbanks, Jr., the young sailing ship seafarer who comes to share his vision. There is a race with a clipper ship. The sailing vessel passes Fyffe-Fairbanks when their ship develops engine trouble. Much hooting and hollering. There followed what seemed to me a terrible (and memorable) explosion in the engine room. It costs the Fyffe character his life. But then the sailing ship is becalmed, and the steamer wins the race. More hooting and hollering.

It was disappointing to reencounter the film recently. Although it was made in the United States, it has the pokey, under-populated air of an English film of the time. And the explosion isn't much more than a pop and a whistle—nothing like the shattering blast I remembered.

But in 1940 it was wonderful enough to me. What I saw in the film was the triumph of a new technology over an outmoded one. It was like the fast trains I was sometimes taken to the station to see thunder past—the Milwaukee Road's Hiawatha, the Northwestern's 400 (so called because that was the number of minutes it consumed in its passage from Chicago to Minneapolis–St. Paul)—evidence of benign and irresistible progress.

The fact that the new rulers of the sea were Englishmen was not lost on us either. We understood—especially in our Anglophilic family—that our cousins across the water were hard-pressed just then—with Dunkirk and the Blitz soon to press them harder. It was good to see their pluck and know-how triumphant.

Knute Rockne, All-American was awesome in a different way. The eponymous protagonist was, of course, a little-boy legend—the great coach who had led his backwater Notre Dame football team from obscurity to greatness, only to die in an airplane crash at the height of his career. The movie was for the most part chipper, often comedic, as it recounted Rockne's rise.

According to the movie, he invented the scandalous forward pass in the course of a summer spent fooling around with a football on the beach with Gus Dorais. The befuddling Notre Dame shift was inspired by some choreography the coach—who was played with appealing bonhomie by Pat O'Brien—observed some chorines doing while on a trip to Chicago.

By these means he more or less turned the game from one of brute strength into one of brains and quickness. This was a subject much on my mind just then. For football was in the process of making another great lurch forward. A coach named Clark Shaughnessy had invented the T-formation at Stanford and had brought his innovation to the Chicago Bears. Led by Sid Luckman—a quarterback who was a National Football League rarity in that he was both an Ivy League graduate and a Jew—the Bears employed the new system to crush the Redskins in the 1940 NFL championship game by the astounding score of 73-0.

But the Rockne film, for all its good spirits, was not unshadowed by doomy portent. How could it be otherwise, since everyone knew, going in, of the coach's untimely demise? That motif was enhanced by the famous story of Rockne's relationship with feckless, gifted George Gipp, who was, of course, played with his frat boy's ease and good humor by Ronald Reagan.

Gipp died even younger than Rockne, but not before urging "Rock" to use his story to inspire the boys to "win one for The Gipper" sometime when they were going down to defeat. This he does with a tearful, rallying speech during a halftime when the Fighting Irish are trailing Army in the big game.

That this inspirational tale was a fiction made up by Rockne and spread by Grantland Rice, the mythomaniac sportswriter, was unknown at the time. I snuffled uncontrollably at it. And Rockne's death in an airplane accident put me away. The movie ends with him grinning boyishly down from the heavens as Notre Dame marches onward to victoreeee.

It would be too much to say that this was the first time I "contemplated" death. I was too young to "contemplate" anything at the time. But it was my introduction to it as a subject that could be represented artistically—a word that is also perhaps too grand for a sentimental little Warner Bros. feature.

Be that as it may, it didn't seem too bad to me. I learned from this movie that with hard work, good values, and a winning spirit (in both senses of the word) it could be transcended.

Soon thereafter I was given a boy's biography of Rockne, written by one of his "Four Horsemen" (another Rice conceit), Harry Stuhldreher, who was then the mediocre head coach at the University of Wisconsin. I found it remarkable that a football coach could write a book. Maybe he didn't. Maybe it was ghosted. I didn't care.

The Great Dictator was infinitely more problematical. Probably it was a mistake to take a seven-year-old to see it. But Charlie Chaplin was a favorite of my mother and father from their younger years. They spoke familiarly and enthusiastically of him, doing their best to prepare me for something they probably suspected would largely befuddle me.

The universal regard in which all the best intellectual circles held Chaplin had, I'm sure, leached through to them, buttressing their own less complicated affection. He was among the finest of the finer things they wished to lead me to.

What I took away from *The Great Dictator* was Charlie, as an artillery man in World War I, aiming his Big Bertha cannon at the Notre Dame Cathedral and hitting an outhouse instead. Also a scene in which peaceful haymows suddenly open up and tanks roll forth from this, to me, incredibly clever camouflage. And a moment when Chaplin, playing a version of Hitler, kisses a baby and the baby wets his uniform.

I'd like to think the movie's greatest scene, in which the

Hitler figure dances with a globe, tossing it in the air and catching it until it bursts like a balloon, made an impression on me. But it probably did not.

The movie's central conceit—it's a mistaken-identity comedy in which Chaplin plays both Hynkel, the dictator of a mythical country, and a Jewish barber who looks just like him—didn't particularly appeal to me. Its concluding speech, an endless plea for universal tolerance, fell on deaf ears. Which was true of more sophisticated critics as well.

One has to acknowledge that Chaplin alluded powerfully to Nazi anti-Semitism in the film, and considering the general silence on that point in the movies of the time, this was no small thing. It was, indeed, a much bigger thing than I understood.

But I have to confess that it took me a long time fully to appreciate Chaplin. He belonged to other people's childhoods. And to that realm of the purely poetic and fantastic to which I was—perhaps still am—so stubbornly immune. It is only lately, when I was asked to make a documentary film about him and had a chance to study his work closely, over a short time span, that I have come to (belatedly) admire his genius—the patience and brilliance of his long, intricate gag sequences, the astonishing grace and subtlety of his pantomime, and, above all, the way he tempers sentiment with the transgressiveness of his Tramp character. I remain dubious about his later work—including much of *The Great Dictator, Monsieur Verdoux, Limelight, The King in New York*; his inability to sustain the Tramp when both he and the world grew too old for him to live on was a disaster for him. Yet there are surprising felicities in those films too, and the great longer silent comedies have an uncanny freshness about them when you encounter them now. It's as if they were made yesterday.

But back then he compared, in my mind, most unfavorably with—forgive me—Abbott and Costello. They made four movies in 1941. All but one of them were service comedies. All but one of them were hilarious. (The flat exception was *In the Navy*, which had far too many musical numbers.) I saw them all. They were to me everything Chaplin was not—low, fast, and, in the interaction between the saturnine Abbott and the childlike Costello, comedically comprehensible to a kid.

War was made to seem curiously weightless in all these movies. Chaplin seemed to say it could be avoided entirely by a fine speech, Abbott and Costello that its largest dangers were KP and the awkward squad. In *Caught in the Draft* in 1941, Bob Hope played a cowardly movie star. He faints at the sight of fake blood on the set of a war movie. He is rendered woozy by the sound of exploding shells. He is seen jumping from a piano, trying to flatten his feet before he takes his Selective Service physical. But in the end he succeeds as a soldier and gets the girl (the commanding general's daughter) without betraying his essentially worthless nature.

I thought him every bit as funny as Abbott and Costello. I still treasure his badinage with Bing Crosby in *Road to Morocco*. What was singular about all their Road pictures was the way they would break their realistic frames and make jokes about what was going on in the movie, making us complicit in the moviemaking process.

AT THIS TIME, the social histories tell us, most Americans believed we would inevitably be drawn into the European war but there was much resistance to that idea too. My grandfather, our resident geopolitician, deplored the America First movement. But I certainly overheard, here and there, talk of once again having to "pull England's chestnuts out of the fire."

But wherever you stood on the question of intervention,

there was little desire for heroic sacrifice. Rather, there was a sort of weary dutifulness in what I overheard. And a faint, continuing hope that somehow we could avoid being drawn into war.

The movies of 1939–1941 played to that spirit. They proposed the inescapability of the military necessity. But they also implied that if war came, it might not be so bad this time. For adults these movies were, I suppose, the very definition of escapist fare.

It was *Sergeant York* that suggested to me, for the first time, there might be another dimension to this question. It was released just before Pearl Harbor. And my father insisted we see it. For men of his generation, Alvin York was one of the two unquestioned heroes of World War I. The other was Eddie Rickenbacker.

York was a Tennessee mountain boy whose sharpshooting and woodcraft made him, potentially, an ideal soldier. The trouble was that he was a determined conscientious objector. What the movie provided was a convincing backstory for his heroic defection from that principle.

It introduced York as a feckless, hard-drinking young man who, riding home on a mule—drunk, in a storm—is almost killed when lightning strikes his long rifle. This leads to a religious conversion. He joins a sect whose principles prohibit killing.

When war comes he is, despite protests, drafted. On the firing range his talent with a rifle is noted, but he continues to insist that he will not employ it to take lives. A kindly officer advises him to take a furlough to think through this potential insubordination.

Back home, wearing a uniform, carrying a Bible, and accompanied by his faithful hound dog, he retreats to a crag, high in the hills, to wrestle with his conscience. Another storm arises, there is great heavenly crashing and flashing, a monstrous swell of Max Steiner's music, and we find the wind has opened Alvin's Bible to the page that advises one to render unto Caesar that which is Caesar's, unto God that which is God's.

This resolves York's conflict. Later in France, when the Germans have his unit pinned down, he circles behind them to get a good firing position. We have seen, at a prewar turkey shoot, that he can produce an excellent gobbling effect, causing the bird to poke his head up so it can be more easily shot. He uses the same sound—strange, of course, to European ears—to get the Germans to do the same.

So effective is his fire that the enemy believe themselves surrounded by a superior force. More than two hundred of them surrender to him. There is a funny bit when York and a couple of comrades march them to the rear and a harassed officer, sorting out POWs, cannot believe how many captives York has in his charge. When he later receives his *Croix de Guerre* he is amusingly embarrassed by the ceremonial kiss bestowed on him by a French officer.

Asked why he did what he did, York justifies his actions by claiming that, on balance, he saved more lives than he took. The officer to whom he haltingly explains himself says that this rationale is more astonishing than his deed itself. This would later become the argument that rationalized many of our military actions, including the use of the atomic bombs on Japan.

But the movie doesn't linger long on that point. It hurries on to show York's reward for his bravery—a piece of the good bottom land for which he has all his life yearned, and a pretty little house where he and his girl friend can settle down—thanks of a grateful nation.

Cooper's reward for this portrayal was his first Academy Award. His hillbilly accent was rather strained, but there was, of course, an unquestionable authenticity about his capacity persuasively to embody brave, simple men struggling to make hard choices.

I had not seen him before, was unaware of his previous work in this line, and I'm pretty sure it was the first time I had heard of the Oscars. But I thoroughly approved the Academy's choice. Cooper became one of the heroes of my boyhood, symbol and repository of large virtue anti-heroically presented.

The movie is an uncharacteristic Howard Hawks film—no male group bickering their way forward to an agreed-upon goal, no Hawksian woman wisecracking her way along with them. When I made a television film about Hawks many years later, he said he had done it—and talked Cooper into doing it—because it was a project Jesse Lasky had in hand. The sometime head of production at Paramount had come upon hard times, and, since he was an old friend, Hawks felt he and Cooper owed him some help.

Sergeant York can be understood as the story of a man abandoning high principle in order to embrace a lesser one. Rendering unto Caesar can't hold a candle to Thou Shalt Not Kill as a moral imperative. But at that moment, with the America Firsters in full cry, and the general desire to avoid struggle and sacrifice a grumbling motif in daily life, this movie had uses that I only dimly perceived. Its very obvious metaphorical message was that it was time to stop idling about pacifistically, time to be up and doing, ready to kill or be killed, on behalf of threatened democracy.

That, of course, is how we read the film when we come across it now. But at the time, curiously, what was stressed to me was York's refusal to capitalize on his heroism. He didn't take endorsement money. He didn't run for office. He lived out the remainder of his hero's life unheroically. When the movie appeared there were pictures of him in the paper—a slightly rumpled figure, with nothing Gary Cooperish about him—looking puzzled as he blinked in the light of the flash bulbs.

Was he meant as a model for similarly reluctant young men, soon to find themselves in roles like his? I'm sure that's so. But I also know that men of my generation still speak admiringly (and surprisingly often) of this movie and of how our fathers took us to see it almost as a moral obligation.

3

Youth Wants to Know

IN 1941, peacetime's last year, I was eight years old and in the third grade. I could read, write, and reason a bit. I was coming to some kind of consciousness about the world beyond my front yard.

I was leading a sort of double life. Sociability was the predominant value in our town. Kids were expected to join the neighborhood gang at their games. Also to join the Cub Scout pack. And to relate happily with one's schoolmates. Clever, busy little boy that I was, I conformed to this ideal. I was liked. I may even have been "well liked."

Yet I was also more deeply immersed in media story-telling—better call it story-receiving—than most of my friends. My family, of course, was ever eager to instruct me in good behavior—telling the truth, being a gracious winner and a manly loser, that sort of thing. But what glamorized, even ennobled, those topics was what I learned about them from books, the radio, the movies.

Why was I so susceptible to "the media," as no one called

them in those days? Partly, I think, because I was often absent from school, down with a sinus condition that gave me colds and sore throats at least once a month. There were long empty hours at home to fill somehow.

Sick or well, I was denied almost nothing the commercial culture had to offer. My parents—and my grandfather, our ever-present, always indulgent patriarch—did not see that culture as the threat it has since become. It was as an educational opportunity. It caused me to ask questions, pursue interests I might not otherwise have entertained.

I think they were somewhat awed by that potential. So much of what was available to me had not been available to them when they were my age—radio, talking pictures, all sorts of cheap reading material. Contemplating an airplane or even a fast train, grandpa would shake his head and say, "It's a great age we live in." To him, all technological progress was an unalloyed blessing.

As it was for me in those days. I was like a modern kid dealing with the Internet. Since I had never known a world without, say, the radio, I calmly accepted it as one of life's good, entirely unthreatening givens.

As for my reading—the thing that most obviously set me apart from my contemporaries—I derived obvious fringe benefits from it. My parents and grandparents frequently bragged to other grown-ups about how "Dick always had his nose stuck in a book." This flattered me. I found out, too, that one could hide behind a book, avoiding certain household chores and social obligations.

Responding to my one authentic precocity, my family ignored the fact that I was a poor speller, hopeless at arithmetic, and the last kid in class to learn to tie my own shoes. Indeed, they perceived me as "advanced" for my age and plagued my childhood with gifts—a chemistry set, a microscope—I was too young to master.

But since I was lavishly praised for my reading ability (and latterly my writing), both at school and at home, I shrewdly concentrated on those gifts and overdeveloped them at the expense of other forms of knowledge and expression. Doubtless the source of my profession is to be found here, in very early boyhood. Maybe that's all anyone needs to know about me.

BUT NO. That does not quite explain me to me. The English novelist Jenny Diski recently observed that when you read, "you make it clear that you have withdrawn your attention from those around you. Perhaps your interest and concern. Who can tell? You are not available."

That's more like it. As the only child of only children, too much anxious—often merely fussy—concern was focused on me. My mother and my grandfather were convinced that I was in constant, probably mortal, danger from which they were determined to defend me. My father—who loved sports—and I had to struggle for my right to roughhouse.

Neither my mother nor her parents, for example, knew how to swim. It was sufficient for them not to go near the water. And to warn me not to, either. My father prevailed on a purely precautionary basis. What if, someday, I accidentally fell into a lake or river?

So on certain summer afternoons, when I was eight or nine, I found myself paddling stark naked around the YMCA pool downtown, being yelled at by a loudmouthed instructor, embarrassed by the comparison between my little wee-wee and those of the big guys horsing around in the pool. Those YMCA jokes I began to hear later always made sense to me. But I did learn to keep myself joylessly afloat.

It was our only victory. My grandfather, for example, prevailed on the question of a street bike. I was not allowed one, which eliminated me from many kid activities as I grew older and reduced me to tears of anger and frustration. I could not understand—do not understand—why I plodded back and forth from school, from sports practices, from friends' houses while everyone else whizzed past me.

Nor was I allowed to have bindings on my skis. My grandfather was certain they were invitations to a broken ankle. As a result, I landed in a heap halfway down every slope while the rest of the kids sailed whooping to the bottom. Later I had to battle every autumn to go out for football. One year, conspiring with my mother, the family doctor flunked me when I took the very modest physical exam the school required.

I needed to escape all that. To be there but not be there. To hide in plain sight. Also, of course, to lose myself in improbable fictional adventures since I was barred from so many of the more probable ones all around me.

Late in her life, my children thought to ask my mother, as I never had, why she had waited so long to have me—she was over thirty when I was born—and why she had had only one child. She told them that she had endured several miscarriages before my birth and wondered if she would ever carry a baby to full term. I guess my safe arrival seemed a miracle to her, one that needed to be defended.

That explains her anxiety about me—and her father's—but it does not entirely excuse it. I should have been permitted my broken arm or mild concussion. I was far from frail. More important, we lived in a quiet, safe, coddled, conscientious world.

No kids became dangerously ill or seriously injured or died in Wauwatosa. That was one reason we lived there.

MY "DOTING" GRANDFATHER was named Claude J. Hendricks. He was an attorney, specializing in real estate law, and also a Mason rising in that organization's ranks and often lost in its mysterious doings. But most nights, until I left home for college, he passed the evenings with me, his only grandchild. He was a reliable source of indulgences, not just for me but for my mother as well. He was in competition—entirely unacknowledged, of course—with my father for our affections.

It was an unfair fight. My dad was an amiable and affectionate man, but grandpa was a force—a well-read, firmly opinionated man, utterly domineering of his tiny patriarchy. He set our agenda, and we abided by it.

I suspect that my parents—certainly my father—harbored the unspoken hope that in their new house, far from the East Side neighborhood where mom and her family had always lived, we would have time and space unambiguously our own. But my grandparents followed us to Wauwatosa less than a year after we moved there. They took a small apartment—two cramped rooms—at the Underwood Hotel that was supposed to be temporary accommodations until they found something more suitable. They never did.

Most of their furniture was placed in storage, and once a year, when I was little, my mother, grandmother, and I would visit their furnishings in the warehouse where they were stored. They would be set out for her inspection on the floor of that vast dark cavern, almost like a stage set waiting for actors to inhabit it—the stuff of a ghost life my grandparents had abandoned.

I'm sure the sight of my grandfather striding confidently up our block, having enjoyed his brisk constitutional from his new apartment, must sometimes have chilled my father's ever-forgiving spirit. Would he never be free of this rival? Would he ever be allowed to be anything but grateful for the generosity that supposedly redeemed his more subtle graspings?

ONCE A MONTH, for many years, my grandfather brought a check made out to my mother. The amount was small, perhaps twenty-five dollars. It was meant to buy her small luxuries she could not otherwise afford. He always left it on a table in our living room, no comment made.

One night, however, my father picked it up and handed it back to him. "We won't be needing this any more, dad," he said. I felt, I think, my father's edgy resolve. I caught a flash of anger in my grandfather's eyes. Or perhaps he was startled. He was not used to having his habits challenged.

A moment of awkward silence followed. I must have sensed significance in it—understood that a gesture of independence was being made. Perhaps I recall it so vividly because I feared the implicit threat to our family's apparently seamless comity.

But my grandfather shrugged. "That's fine, Eddie," he said—only he and my grandmother ever used the diminutive in addressing him—and my father said something about appreciating all his help.

The moment passed. Probably someone turned on the radio. Or perhaps we simply turned back to it. The gesture remained only a gesture. A full-scale declaration of independence did not follow.

To a degree, my grandfather insured our dependence through his gifts—the second car, the summer place we all shared, the "advantages" he bestowed on me. "After all he's done for you . . . ," my mother would say when I complained about my plans conflicting with his—which happened more often when I took up the impatient agendas of adolescence.

When she was in her nineties my mother said she regretted her failure to diminish her father's presence in our day-to-day lives. By then she could see what her acquiescence had cost. She and my father remained "the kids" (or in direct address, "you kids") until they were middle-aged. Grandpa treated them more as siblings than as man and wife.

They never claimed for themselves a life that was fully their own, a life in which they made their own decisions on matters large and small. Always they had to consider Claude J. Hendricks's opinion.

They did not become fully autonomous grown-ups until he was very old. By which time my father was sunk in immobilizing depression—at least partly the result, I believe, of a lifetime's acquiescence in other people's plans. Absent her father, my mother succeeded to unilateral control of their destinies.

WHEN I WAS very small, before we moved to Wauwatosa, grandpa's nightly appearances were the climax of my day, an eagerly awaited and unambiguous benison. Usually he would read to me from the "Green Sheet"—a four-page section, printed on green paper, where the *Milwaukee Journal* segregated its comic strips and light features. We liked "Our Boarding House," a single-panel cartoon that featured Major Hoople, the ne'er-do-well husband of the hardworking woman who ran the eponymous institution. "Fap," he would say when someone awakened him from one of his many snoozes, and I would laugh when grandpa read out that word. I was also fond of "Chester the Pup," a feature that consisted of a single drawing of the title dog and a few paragraphs of prose in which, in the first person, he wryly recounted the doings of "the boss" and other human members of his family.

Often on Sundays my grandfather would take me for a long ride on the public transportation system, an intricate voyage involving many transfers, from bus to trolley, from this route to that. Sometimes we would end up at the zoo. Sometimes we would simply ride to the end of a line.

The vehicles were sparsely populated on the holiday, and there was little traffic to impede them. You sailed smoothly along, looking down on a world that, in memory, is always green, silent, languid. The world through a window, its cries and whispers muted, distanced—a preference for a vantage point slightly removed from reality and its unstructured, irresolute hubbub, was perhaps created in me in those days.

Later my grandfather became my best source of special treats: the Ringling Bros. circus at the lakefront every summer; the Shrine circus in the winter at the Milwaukee Auditorium; the annual visit to the state fair in West Allis, where, farm boy that he had once been, he saw to it that we spent most of our time at the livestock pens, as little of it as possible on the trashy, seductive midway.

If I expressed an interest in anything—photography, a drum set, stamp collecting—it was usually my grandfather who equipped and supplied me. But it was with gifts of a casual but habitual kind that he shaped me.

For he almost never arrived at our house without reading matter of some kind. By the time I was ten he was bringing over periodicals like the *Saturday Review of Literature*, *Newsweek*, *Life*, the Sunday *New York Times*. My subscription to the *New Yorker*, unbroken to this day, began as a gift from him. Sometimes he would bring a book for me. "I was in Des Forges [Milwaukee's leading bookstore] today, and I thought this was something you could use in your business," he would say, handing over, perhaps, a boy's life of Lincoln or General MacArthur.

He was a Book-of-the-Month Club member too, and when I was ten or eleven he started bringing over its newsletter and encouraging me to make a selection from it. Usually it was a historical novel, but during the war it might be something like *They Were Expendable* or one of Bill Mauldin's or Ernie Pyle's books.

Grandpa's taste ran to history and biography. He almost never read fiction and could occasionally be heard to fulminate against "this damned sex stuff," which he understood to be rife in contemporary literature. That aside, he didn't care what I read.

GRANDPA never suggested that writing was a trade I might someday want to follow. He didn't have to. I simply absorbed his romantic regard for "the written word" and made it my own.

I suspect he harbored the thought that he might have become a writer himself had the course of his life run differently. For he took pride in his own prose, which was clear, lawyerly, rather formal in the nineteenth-century manner, but adorned with the occasional rhetorical flourish.

He too derived "consolation" from the world's buffetings by escaping into books. He used that word in a little essay about reading that he wrote and had printed as a bookplate which he pasted on the inside front cover of all twenty-four volumes of the Americana encyclopedia—it came in its own bookcase—that he gave me on my seventh birthday. The encyclopedia stood essentially untouched for years until I started cribbing from it for papers in junior high. But not unappreciated; none of the other kids had anything like it.

I learned another, equally valuable skill—that of a certain

kind of self-assertion—from my grandfather. Bald, erect in his carriage, brisk in his movements, he had a thin, straight nose and lips and wore wire-rimmed glasses. There was something stern about his natural expression, and people deferred to him.

This was more than a matter of appearances. He despised small talk—"twaddle," he called it—but he was full of opinions, moral and ethical, political and aesthetic. Because he was well read, and perhaps because he was a lawyer, a profession that in those days still enjoyed uncomplicated respect, he backed these ideas with citations from history and from the press—existential case law, you might call it—and people seemed to fall back in the face of his authority.

From this I gathered that it was all right to advance your ideas forcefully. It seemed to bring you attention and respect and, occasionally, the excitement of argument. So probably I became a writer because of my grandfather's regard for the craft, and became the kind of writer I am—someone who deals mainly in opinion, in critical argument—because I took a style from him.

You could say that he "spoiled" me—concern on that point was often expressed when I was a kid—and surely he is the source of my dauntless self-centeredness, my sense of entitlement, especially to my own opinions and to their flaunting.

These are not necessarily attractive qualities. But they are essential to a writer. Someone, somewhere along his early way must rescue him from that ordinariness for which everyone else is being prepared, make him believe that he is qualified for what is, if nothing else, an unusual—an elite—calling.

MY GRANDFATHER'S intense presence in our lives was an un-questioned part of our normalcy. People often commented, with sentimental approval, on his closeness with me, as if it were an ideal they wished they had attained in their families. No one seemed to see anything odd or intrusive in his constant attendance on me. I was surprised to discover, as I grew older, that other families were not organized as ours was.

Maybe it was not odd; maybe it was only old-fashioned. We are frequently, approvingly reminded, now that families are so fragmented, that in earlier times several generations often lived together on family farms like the ones where my grandparents grew up. Possibly my grandfather wished merely to sustain that tradition.

But that explanation is too innocent. "They were a tense and peculiar family, the Oedipuses," Max Beerbohm immortally wrote. Not that a Freudian explanation of our family's way would have enlightened grandpa. He had read an article somewhere that claimed psychiatrists eventually grew as mad as their patients, and that became part of his received—and often propagated—wisdom.

I would become, as a man, an odd combination of my father and my grandfather. Humorous, tolerant, easy to get along with, like the former; yet also literate, stern, unforgiving, and, yes, difficult, like the latter. The drama of my life has been the attempt to resolve this conflict.

NATURALLY THAT DRAMA was only dimly perceived when I was a child. But surely avoiding it helps account for the way I lost myself in "ephemera." Or, to call a spade a spade, trash. At the most basic level there were the comics, available for a dime at Mr. Meyer's drugstore on the corner, where, crankily, chronically suspicious, he kept his eye on browsers, not permitting you to spend too much time making your choice. Mostly I liked superhero

comics, though that phrase was not yet used to describe them—
Superman, Batman, Captain Marvel.

I was also drawn to Big Little Books, available in the dime
stores. At some point the publisher changed their name to "Better Little Books," but no one ever called them that. They were
"big" in the number of pages they contained (424) but "little" in
page size (2-1/2 by 3-1/2 inches).

They were printed (in nearby Racine, by the Whitman Publishing Company) on pulpy paper, text on the left, a comic-style
black-and-white illustration opposite. They often featured
comic-strip characters (Mandrake the Magician, Terry and the
Pirates), though some of them starred real-life pop heroes like
Frank (Bring 'Em Back Alive!) Buck, who was a big-game hunter
supplying zoos and circuses, and Clyde Beatty, the animal
trainer.

Eventually I owned something like 125 of these little volumes. I know, because one rainy afternoon I catalogued them.
The first professional writer I ever met was a young woman—I
think she was married to some cousin of my mother's—who
wrote Big Little Books. I was impressed by her achievement, and
she seemed flattered by my interest. Her attainment as an author
was a little bit like mine as a reading whiz—not much by absolute standards, but not nothing either, given the standards of
our time and place.

In those days "real" books—bound in boards and wrapped
in dust jackets—were available from Grosset and Dunlap for
forty-nine cents. Mostly they were series adventures—Don
Winslow of the Navy, and the X Bar X boys (both of which I was
partial to) for boys, Nancy Drew mysteries for girls. From the
same source, for a similar price, you could get Ellery Queen and
Perry Mason mysteries, intended for adults but easily readable
by me.

Once a week my mother and grandmother made a shopping expedition to Schuster's department store. In the summers and after school I often accompanied them. Generally I could work them for the requisite forty-nine cents and start reading my new book in the store while they tried on hats or dresses.

Paperbacks began to appear in the early forties. This lowered the cost of adult reading material to twenty-five cents. I especially liked those in the Pocket Books line. To give the covers an attractive sheen they had a thin coating of plastic. This could be peeled back as you read. Absorbed in mysterious narrative, you could also enjoy a pleasure akin to picking at a scab, but without the bloody consequences.

I RECENTLY ATTENDED an evening with Susan Sontag, at which she was interviewed about her work. The twit posing questions to her asked about "influences," and she surprised him—and charmed me—by mentioning first the Bobbsey Twins—obviously her equivalent to the X Bar X Boys—and Richard Halliburton's travel books. She said they had doubtless "scored" her mind in some way she could not analyze.

Certainly Halliburton scored my mind. He was a handsome adventurer who had wandered the world, writing about what he saw for young people. He disappeared at sea in the course of one of his journeys, never to be seen again. This imparted to his works a sort of doomy glamour. I still have my childhood copy of his *Book of Marvels*, and it remains quite readable—a clear, concise evocation of places I still have mostly not seen and probably never will.

Sontag also mentioned Poe, whom I too read at an early age—in an attractive boxed edition, illustrated with woodcuts. I still have the book, and my grandfather's inscription shows he gave it to me when I was eleven. I responded to the eerieness and ironies of Poe's tales. Sontag, apparently, caught the precursive hints of modernism in them.

She did not mention Sir Arthur Conan Doyle. I need to. I also still own my old Doubleday edition of Sherlock Holmes's complete adventures. I had been turned on to him by the radio series that starred Basil Rathbone and Nigel Bruce, whose interpretations of the detective and his bumbling companion, Dr. Watson, remain for me definitive. It is a book I asked for one time when I was sick, and I spent an impatient day waiting for my father to bring it home to me.

I tore through it in a couple of weeks—4 novels and 57 short stories—1,323 thin, closely printed pages. London fogs, gas lamps, hansom cabs: Holmes's pipe, violin, depressions, and casually presented cocaine habit; Mrs. Hudson, the landlady; Holmes's even brainier brother, Mycroft; the often befuddled Scotland Yard detective, Lestrade; and, of course, Holmes's evil doppelganger, Professor Moriarty.

Perhaps, above all, I responded to the fact that Holmes's adventures were, by his own admission, stirred by his need to escape "ennui." Bored by the routines of his life, he was ever eager to meet the strangers whom Mrs. Hudson conducted up the stairs to his sitting room, always hopeful that when he picked up his sword cane and ventured forth he would be—all ratiocinations aside—obliged to use his weapon against some miscreant.

That spirit spoke to me. As did Holmes's persuasively realistic, plausibly exotic world, a place in which you could completely lose yourself. I returned to it again and again.

Other books offered similar pleasures: John R. Tunis's superbly atmospheric sports novels—read by Philip Roth (talk about mysterious influences), who was born the same year as

Sontag and me—in which the hero did not necessarily win the big game, but which taught excellent lessons about diversity and tolerance; the "Shoes" series by the English writer Noel Streatfeild—*Circus Shoes, Tennis Shoes, Ballet Shoes.* Best of all was her *Secret of the Lodge*, about some English kids rescuing the boy prince of a Graustarkian country who was being kept prisoner (for political reasons) in an outbuilding on their evil uncle's estate.

Eventually I owned all these books. For if I liked something I found in a library, I wanted to read it over and over again, and my family indulged me. I'll bet I read *The Secret of the Lodge*, or Tunis's *The Iron Duke* (it was about a kid—get this agreeable pun—named Wellington who came from Waterloo, Iowa, and became a track star at Harvard) at least twenty-five times each. It was a good deal. I was quiet and content, and the harm that mom and grandpa saw threatening me from every street corner could not reach me as I sat in the living room reading.

When I was ten or eleven I moved on to weightier matter—historical novels by Walter D. Edmunds and Kenneth Roberts. It was a movie that got me started on them, a re-release of the John Ford movie based on Edmunds's most famous book, *Drums Along the Mohawk.*

It was about Indian warfare in New York state during the American Revolution, and it was a good, lively film. It featured a run through the woods by its hero, played by Henry Fonda. He races to bring soldiers to relieve a besieged fort, where his wife and neighbors are trapped by Indians. Three savages pursue him, one of whom runs full tilt while his comrades lope easily behind him. When the lead runner tires, one of the others moves up and turns on the speed—while Fonda, of course, must go full speed, full time. I thought this strategy demonically clever of the savages. It was, of course, a miracle that he outraced them. Or perhaps a tribute to the inherent superiority of the Anglo-Saxon race.

I soon owned all of Edmunds's titles. Many of his tales were of ambitious provincial lads—Chad Hanna, Young Ames—who leave home to find adventure and success further afield.

Kenneth Roberts had, perhaps, a more interesting historical imagination. One of his books was a sympathetic portrait of Benedict Arnold. Another told the tale of the Revolution from the viewpoint of Americans who remained loyal to England.

For a long time—until very recently, in fact—I was plagued by a recurring dream. In it, our house on Sixty-eighth Street was surrounded by Indians. Our little family was fighting them off, but they always penetrated the ground floor as we retreated up the stairs. I always woke up, terrified, before the final slaughter.

Not long ago AMC ran *Drums Along the Mohawk*, and there was the scene, forgotten, buried deep in my unconscious, that was the source of that dream. It is a sequence in which the Indians penetrate Edna Mae Oliver's impressive home. Childlike, they don her finery, break her crockery, toss all her possessions hither and tither. Comically, impotently, she asserts her grande dame authority by trying to shoo them away with a broom. Even though we don't witness her end, we know she is doomed by these curiously possessed creatures. It is as inevitable as my family's dream fate.

All my life I have feared the irrational, feared entrapment in its schemes. All my life I have been tempted by it too. And, in anger, succumbed to it.

FOR A SIGNIFICANT PART of the day I was left alone with the radio, and it worked on me much as my reading did. School was over by mid-afternoon. I would come home, change clothes, and, often enough, find the other kids to play a pickup game of whatever sport was in season—football, basketball, baseball.

But in winter darkness descended early, and I would be back home in time for that hour or so when whoever was in charge of these matters focused all their attention on us kids, with their Hop Harrigan–Jack Armstrong–"Terry and the Pirates"–Tom Mix–"Captain Midnight" radio programs.

They were each fifteen minutes long and basically posed the heroic and unyielding camaraderie of brave but otherwise ordinary-seeming young people (Jack Armstrong and his pals Betty and Billy) under the guidance of an older mentor (Uncle Jim) against highly conspiratorial evil, always managed by a master criminal of relentless deviousness.

There was no parental outcry against these programs. I suppose they were exploitative, in something like the way the Saturday morning cartoons are said to be for today's children. Certainly they were filled with violent action. But they did not rivet attention in quite the way television does. You could read or talk and still catch their drift.

Their sponsors were not apparently in pursuit of our souls. They only wanted our mothers to keep Wheaties or Quaker Oats in the pantry. They were occasionally after our cereal box tops and "twenty-five cents to cover the cost of postage and handling," in return for which they offered the fair exchange of a decoder ring.

Listening to these shows, I would hazily thumb through magazines. My parents did not read books. The matched sets of Dickens and Victor Hugo sat untouched on the shelves that flanked the fake fireplace in the living room. But they did read periodicals, kept in an antique brass bucket next to the easy chair. The *Saturday Evening Post, Collier's, Liberty, The American,* my mother's women's magazines jostled there with the stuff grandpa contributed. About the only magazine I did not much care for was *Boy's Life*. It was too obviously kid stuff, offering no glimpses of the adult world I craved.

It was the same at school where we were obliged to read *My Weekly Reader*, intended to keep us abreast of current affairs but simpleminded if you were already reading *Time* at home.

Because he was in advertising, my father received a free subscription to the magazine and early on, before I was seeing many movies, I discovered its Cinema section, not knowing that I was reading my sainted predecessor, James Agee, but liking the snappy authority of his unsigned reviews. I always turned first to his page when the magazine arrived, and I have to believe that it was not just the prose that attracted me. There was something about the act of criticism itself—its assertiveness, its ability to subvert the sometimes pompous, often expensive, object under review—that appealed to me. I always moved on to the other review sections—art, theater, books, music—before duly skimming (or entirely skipping) the front where the national and international news was reported. I was a Back of the Book guy long before I knew there was a Back of the Book.

THE MUTTER OF PRINT countered the more boisterous fantasies emanating from the radio, and the total effect of those wasted, invaluable afternoons was curiously calming.

This dreamy mood would evaporate when my father returned from work. Supper was served almost immediately— around six o'clock. By 6:30 on Monday, Wednesday, and Friday I was back at the radio for "The Lone Ranger." After that in the early evening there were the crime stories to listen to: Mr. Holmes and Dr. Watson, of course. But also, depending on the day of the week, "Mr. Keene, Tracer of Lost Persons," "Nero Wolfe," "Inner Sanctum," "Suspense," "Big Town." The last, about a metropolitan newspaper and its crime-fighting city editor, helped romanticize journalism for me.

Later in the evening the comedies would take over—"Fibber McGee and Molly," Bob Hope, Red Skelton. Sundays, around dinner time, there was an especially good lineup—"The Great Gildersleeve," Jack Benny, Edgar Bergen and Charlie McCarthy, Fred Allen, with brief interruptions for "The Fitch Bandstand" and "The Manhattan Merry-Go-Round." The former featured swing orchestras and was sponsored by a hair tonic with an unforgettable jingle ("Use your head, save your hair, use Fitch shampoo"). The latter imagined a night on the town in New York, where one was transported from one famous club to another, just managing to catch one of the show's regulars as he or she broke into a current hit tune.

You could get a similar taste of metropolitan high life on "Mr. First-Nighter," which imagined a devoted playgoer (always greeted by a welcoming chorus—"Good evening, Mr. First-Nighter," "Right this way, Mr. First-Nighter"—as he entered a theater and settled down to enjoy the drama, which we, of course, heard right along with him.

Radio was the most outrageously stylized of all media: Eight nightclubs in a half-hour? And what life did Mr. First-Nighter lead away from the little theater just off Times Square that he obsessively attended.

But all radio premises were unexamined. One unquestioningly accepted the fact that Jack Benny was always tightfisted, Bob Hope always the cowardly wolf. Fibber McGee and Molly's or The Great Gildersleeve's funny friends always appeared in the same order every week. So did the people (Mrs. Nussbaum, Falstaff Openshaw, and Senator Claghorn) whom Allen and his wife, Portland, called upon when they descended to Allen's Alley to sample public opinion.

These programs featured recurring gags as well as recurring characters. Benny's visits to his vault or his attempts to start his ancient Maxwell automobile have passed into legend. And there was the notoriously squeaking screen door at Mr. Peavy's drugstore, which Gildersleeve opened every week. But perhaps the most eagerly awaited moment in radio was the opening of the closet at 79 Wistful Vista Drive.

This was the address of Fibber McGee and Molly, who were played by sometime vaudevillians Jim and Marion Jordan. Fibber was the American Dreamer personified. He had no visible means of support, but he was always working on a get-rich-quick scheme (perhaps significantly, the one episode I remember in detail involved his attempt to write a best-selling novel).

His other characteristic—the source of his nickname— was his habit of regaling his friends with tales of past, entirely imaginary, glory. Molly's function was to deflate his self-aggrandizements. The essence of their relationship was defined once a week when, as she cried out a warning, he would, unthinking, open his famously overstuffed closet and everything would fall out of it, crashing, clunking, rattling, in a brilliantly constructed, constantly varied sequence of sound effects.

Sound effects were the purist expression of the medium's nature. There were newspaper features on how they were created, often by the humblest means—cellophane crumpled near a microphone was a campfire, coconut halves rhythmically applied to a sand table simulated horse's hooves—and we talked about them all the time.

Radio's small weekly variations on standard themes constituted just about the right amount of excitement for programs aimed chiefly at staid adulthood. There was, though, a difference in quality between nighttime and afternoon radio listening, in that it became a family affair in the evenings. My grandfather would usually arrive sometime during the crime melodramas, which did not interest him, then settle down with me for the lighter fare. Eventually my parents would join us, and the whole family would be grouped around the radio, not quite staring into its little dial, glowing a faint orange on the bookshelf next to the Dickens, but yet glancing over at it at particularly gripping moments.

We constituted a little audience, aware of each other's responses. There was no drifting off into fantastic reverie in this context, no privacy of the kind that surrounded me in the afternoons. This was entertainment in the more traditional meaning of the term.

ONE PROGRAM, however, had the power to transport me out of this routine. That was the "Lux Radio Theater," which on Monday night did one-hour broadcast versions of the new movies. It was hosted by Cecil B. DeMille, who was, of course, one of the few producer-directors who in those days received billing above the title.

An impression was created that DeMille was the program's auteur, though of course he was not. He merely introduced the drama and supplied such narrative links as it required. But with his humbug voice, all pomp, melodrama, and falsely heightened emotion, he did so thrillingly.

At the same time he created a spurious intimacy between his audience and haute Hollywood. For at the end of the program he would bring his stars back for a seemingly informal chat, the main function of which was to plug their new films. Then one of them would say, in effect, "But enough about us, tell us about your next program, C.B." Whereupon he would announce next week's adaptation and its stars. After the title and after each star's name, the audience, responding on cue, would let out a long "ooohh" and burst into applause. Then he would sign off: "This is Cecil B. DeMille saying, Good night to you from Hollywood." Except he pronounced the word with pauses between each syllable, a rising inflection on the "ly" and a drawn out "wooood."

It was silly and marvelous. I wanted to be with him in paradise.

THAT WAS IMPOSSIBLE, of course. But a simulacrum was within range. In those days you could buy toy microphones, which you could plug into your radio and "broadcast" over it, hearing your voice over the instrument's speaker. I wore out the on-off button on one of these microphones and had to get a new one.

I spent many happy hours perfecting the special rhythms of the radio announcers, using magazine ads and newspaper stories as my copy. I got rather good at dramatic pauses and rising emphases. Even today, when I make one of my television shows, I like doing the scratch track narration, which you have to do before shipping the rough cut off for the network's approval. My nasal whine embarrasses me. But I like my style.

CLAUDIA ROTH PIERPONT says—indisputably, I think—that at this time "all popular culture aspired to the condition of the movies." As the "Lux Radio Theater" clearly proved, one could be effectively at the movies even when one was not at the movies.

Radio, for example, employed audio versions of such visual techniques as the montage, the cross-fade, and the dissolve—and emphasized suspense, conflict, and comic high points with movielike musical scores.

The comic books accomplished something similar visually. Their panels used an alternation of close, medium, and long shots just as the movies did. Indeed, they used radical angles— up and down—more freely than anyone in the movies—Orson Welles being for me, at the time, the unseen exception. For a comic book artist, deep focus was a trick far easier to bring off than it was for Gregg Toland. They even enjoyed an advantage the movies could not match: their artists could change their frame sizes at will, in effect exploding it to wide screen when it suited their purposes.

This was not obvious to me at the time. But the migration of favorite characters from one medium to another was. Don Winslow, Superman, The Green Hornet, Flash Gordon, Batman, and most of the famous detectives became true multi-media stars—available eventually in books, movies, comics, radio, you name it.

Leslie Fiedler holds that the defining quality of popular art is the ability of the art object to slip effortlessly from medium to medium "without loss of intensity or alteration of meaning." As Pierpont puts it, they are free of "the tug and traction of words as they move thoughts into place in the mind."

All these fictions shared generic and narrative conventions, many of which could be traced back to nineteenth-century theatrical melodrama, Dickensian novels, pulp stories of all kinds. I was, needless to say, unaware of that cultural history then.

Nor did I notice that it was only types, arche- and stereo-, who could apply for admission to this narrative company. Among them were enigmatic spies, hot pilots, brave pioneers, bad-tempered and big-hearted top sergeants, black mammies and their shiftless mates, sly and cruel Oriental master criminals, lazy

Hispanics, organ-grinder Italians, pip-pip Englishmen—that whole, literally mind-bending panoply of dehumanized others.

These were the unhesitatingly accepted familiars of popular fiction in those days. Yet they were not yet overfamiliar—not to me. Interesting, but comfortably so, is more like it. They are still interesting now, but uncomfortably so.

It seems to me something of a miracle that I grew up to be a relatively humane and liberal-minded adult. Maybe it was the artesian water.

4

"Pack Up Your Troubles . . ."

SO IT WAS with me—a kid avoiding reality, living largely in other people's fantasies—when the bombs suddenly rained down on Pearl Harbor. I was listening to a football game that Sunday afternoon. It was an eastern conference NFL game, involving, I believe, the Washington Redskins and someone or other. It was of no consequence to me. I was listening because that's what little boys with nothing much on their minds did on Sunday afternoons.

I had no idea where this Pearl Harbor was, though between them the radio announcers and my parents quickly placed it for me. My mother noted that one of her friends had recently returned from a vacation in Hawaii where she had had a good time. She also observed that the grandmother of another friend had all her life warned of the "yellow peril." Thus, simply, did she define the edges of her response.

One of the irritations of my childhood was the familial desire to protect me from the untoward, which because of its obvious melodramatic potential I always wanted to know more about. But in this instance there was no way for them entirely to evade this shocking news. Which, naturally, excited me.

For grown-ups the war was many things: an adventure, an opportunity, an inconvenience. For some, of course, it was a tragedy. But I was eight years old when Pearl Harbor was attacked, and twelve years old when Hiroshima was bombed, and for me the war was the most wondrous alternative reality ever invented.

I WAS, I think, more stirred by the news from Pearl Harbor than my schoolmates. "Isn't it terrible—about the war?" I kept asking them on the Monday morning after Pearl Harbor, my voice dripping with a vague sanctimony. But no one would engage in that conversation—perhaps sensibly.

Later that day President Roosevelt's "date that will live in infamy" address was piped into all our classrooms via the school's public address system. We listened to it, puzzled and silent.

Later we discussed Representative Jeanette Rankin's refusal to vote for the declaration of war against Japan—Congress's lone holdout. We didn't think it traitorous, merely incomprehensible. A couple of days later she did vote for the war against Germany.

In the first months of the war everyone was stunned and stirred in ways that I had not previously observed. People dwelled on the sneak nature of the Pearl Harbor attack—so unsportsmanlike, so profoundly un-American. It seemed to make grown-ups feel angry and determined in a manner uncharacteristic of them.

But the rhetorical conventions and romantic fictions by which we came to understand and respond to the war took time to develop—roughly as long as it took for the tanks and planes to begin rolling off the production lines in useful numbers.

We had to make do for a few months with what could be quickly run up—mainly by Tin Pan Alley, whose turnaround time was shorter than Hollywood's. We were almost immediately enjoined to "Remember Pearl Harbor" (as we did the Alamo). It is, I think, the first popular song whose words I memorized. But not the last. "Praise the Lord and Pass the Ammunition" ("and we'll all stay free"), soon followed. It was based (it was said) on the fighting words of a navy chaplain, pressed into service loading a big ship's battery when much of its crew was killed.

I bawled right along with the singer whenever I heard these songs on the radio. They offered the first inkling of the war's power to transform routine. It was if someone decided to make a vast epic film, incomprehensibly complex, yet rich in quite comprehensible dramatic situations, and invited me to attend it from the safety of my living room or neighborhood theater.

Grimness was at first heavily in the air, a feeling that the "American Patrol," to quote another patriotic air, had been less than "vigilant." Many adults were apparently not quite as certain of a victorious outcome as they pretended to be. Including my grandfather.

On the first Christmas of the war, three weeks after Pearl Harbor, he saw to it that I received every gift on my Christmas list, including the vague make-weights of puzzles, games, and books far down from the Lionel Electric Train that headed it.

His largesse puzzled me. That night, as I climbed into bed, I asked my mother about it. "Well," she said, "grandpa thought that next year we might not all be together."

It was a troubling response, since we all deferred to him on geopolitical matters. I wondered what he imagined. My father drafted; my mother and me following him from one dismal army camp to another? Or perhaps a devastating enemy invasion?

A vivid picture of our little family fleeing, like European

refugees on roads choked with traffic, entered my mind. My mother in a babushka. A cart drawn by a frightened horse. Stukas screaming down out of the sky, their strafing machine guns chattering.

It is absurd. Where did that horse come from? Or, for that matter, the babushka? It is a newsreel image, of course. Or possibly an adaptation of something out of *Life* magazine. Yet there it is, as strong and distinct in memory as any reality I can recall from that time.

DID THIS constitute "defeatism?" I don't know. I do know that the press, in those early days of the war, constantly urged us to shun that emotion. Just after Pearl Harbor this was not easy, for the news remained alarming for many months. Bataan, Corregidor, the Battle of the Atlantic, the Germans rolling across Russia toward Stalingrad. A national guard company of tankers, from Janesville, in Rock County, where our summer place was located, had been mobilized in 1940 and was decimated on Bataan, the survivors enduring Japanese prison camps for the rest of the war. Their martyrdom was much in the papers and on our minds.

There was a great civic bustle in Wauwatosa in the war's first months. I'm sure that was true of every American community. It was, if you stop to think of it, the only possible response to the war. You could not, for example, heroically throw yourself on an occupying soldier, knife in hand. Or join the underground. You could only do what you could to avoid such desperate contingencies ever arising.

So we dealt with rationing. And joined bond and blood and scrap drives. And planted victory gardens as soon as the ground thawed in the spring of 1942.

And nodded approvingly when the American Tobacco Company announced that "Lucky Strike Green Has Gone to War," meaning that the green ink used to color the brand's cigarette packs had some more pressing—if never explained—use in the emergency. Later the rumor went around that they had been trying to dump the color for years and used the war as an excuse.

I think this sense of crisis, of a faraway danger that might yet strike close to home, was good for us. It gave us something outside ourselves and our petty priorities to think about.

CIVILIAN DEFENSE was our first thought—imposed on us from above. It was absurd. What danger from enemy attack could we possibly be in, deep as we were in the Midwest? Yet it was perhaps a measure of everyone's earnestness that we took it seriously, especially in our house.

For my father was elected air-raid warden for our block. He ran against Art Will, who lived in the big house on the corner—a double lot—and had two sons, Johnny and Jimmy, who were part of our neighborhood gang. I don't know who nominated the candidates, and there was no campaigning for the job because nothing was really at stake; the loser would be designated assistant warden.

Immediately after the election, Ed and Art were issued equipment—armbands bearing a red, white, and blue Civil Defense insignia, a World War I vintage helmet painted white and also bearing an insignia, and a stirrup pump to extinguish small fires. Long before the war was over, the pump was found to be useful for spraying the weeds in our driveway.

But we did have two or three air-raid drills. At nine o'clock in the evening the firehouse siren sounded, the street lights went off, and my father set forth on his rounds, a red-lensed flashlight in hand, since we were told the glare of an ordinary light could be used by enemy bombers to guide them to their target.

Everyone doused their lights and pulled their shades. I remember peeking out from under one in the living room to watch my father solemnly attending his civic duties. They did not seem entirely ridiculous at that moment. We had heard the Murrow broadcasts from London. We had seen pictures of the raids there.

It was rather thrilling to imagine similar scenes of havoc on North Sixty-eighth Street. It was both possible and not quite possible to imagine my father racing into a half-gutted building to extinguish a fire or prize a fallen beam off a child.

Possible, that is, in the sudden dark and silence of the drill; less so the next morning with the sun up and the newspaper on the doorstep and my father stepping out of the bathroom just down the hall to toss—with exasperated playfulness—a wet, cold washrag from the bathroom into my face to shock me out of bed. He had a good arm; he never missed.

I RECENTLY READ an interview with Michael Frayn, the English playwright, who is about my age. In it he mentioned the "transformations" of his family's house by German bombs falling near it during the Blitz—broken windows and skylights, shattered crockery. He said it disturbed his parents but excited him.

Later on, when the V-2s hit, the fun understandably went out of it—the sudden cutting of the rocket's engine, its silent, unpredictable fall. But until then—oh, lucky boy! How desperately we—or was it perhaps only I?—desired transformation, some experience that would shake us from our routines, give our lives a dramatic turn. Elsewhere that seemed to be happening, or have a lively potential for happening. We felt left out of the excitements that early in the war gripped the East and West Coasts, where there was some not entirely misplaced anxiety about enemy incursions. For a while these seemed to impart an enviable edge of risk to daily life there.

On the West Coast there were rumors of submarine sightings and even a documented enemy aircraft raid against a forest in Washington state. Beaches were festooned with barbed wire. And, of course, all the Japanese-American citizens were interned. On the East Coast the German U-boats crept close to the shore; at least one landed spies or saboteurs on an isolated Long Island beach. The newspapers reported their arrest and, later, the fact that one of the spies was executed.

Even after these threats diminished, the shipyards and aircraft factories remained, drawing workers from all over the country. Eventually, of course, the port cities of both coasts thundered with the passage of millions of servicemen bound for battle overseas.

The war could not be ignored in these places; it was an inescapable presence in the daily lives of their residents. That, manifestly, was not true where we lived. And in some way that left us with hurt feelings.

I remember my father coming home from a meeting of one of his civic organizations—he was a faithful member of the Cooperative Club and the Milwaukee Advertising Club—pleased by the speaker's insistence that, contrary to popular opinion, Milwaukee had a sufficient concentration of heavy industry to make it a prime target for Axis bombers or saboteurs. The metropolitan area's apparent absence from the enemy's strategic calculations—and Washington's, of course—had left its civic leadership feeling neglected, not entirely first class. The implication was that if everyone else were going to be bombed, they wanted to be too.

Against this eventuality many of us were armed with a little booklet containing silhouettes of the world's fighting planes, to help us identify them if any should appear in the sky. All we ever saw were Piper Cubs and the occasional commercial DC-3 making its approach to the county airport on the south side of town. Later, it would be renamed Mitchell Field, after the martyred airpower visionary Billy Mitchell, who was a native of Milwaukee and much revered locally.

He had been a rich kid, the son of a U.S. senator. The Mitchell mansion, spaciously situated on Milwaukee's main street, had been converted into the Wisconsin Club, our most prestigious social club. My parents had met there, at a dance, on a blind date.

How Billy Mitchell had become such a passionate advocate of airpower I do not know. But his court martial for the overenthusiastic advocacy of his ideas was the stuff of local legend, which was secured when the B-25, beloved workhorse of medium bombers, was named after him by a government making belated amends.

One suspects he was not an entirely nice guy. People with a burning faith in a single idea so rarely are. Yet the airpower fanatics dominated much of the strategic debate during the war. *Victory Through Air Power*, based on a best-selling book by one Alexander de Seversky, became a strangely beautiful Disney film. Its animated sequence of massed bombers filling the screen remains for me one of the thrilling images of the war, its implication of a warfare that might be surgical and antiseptic one of its most disturbing notions as one looks back.

That vision of mine, of our family inserted into the pictures of terror-bombed refugees, drew its reality, I think, from the talk about airpower. We know now that it was something of a sham; despite the millions of tons of explosives we poured down on Europe, war production was only temporarily distressed, the morale of its workers if anything heightened by the bombings. What we mainly achieved were the deaths of a million innocents.

At home, however, we innocents wondered just how the clever and ruthless enemy might reach us, as far inland as we were, and so justify the expense of my father's helmet and stirrup pump. A Civil Defense pamphlet carried the answer to that question. It contained a map showing how Milwaukee could be struck by the enemy. All it required was an Axis aircraft carrier taking up a position in Hudson Bay, from which its planes could be launched. This was a grand, improbable enterprise my friends and I eagerly discussed.

And Warner Bros. eventually fed. In *Northern Pursuit*, Nazi airmen, led by handsome Helmut Dantine, are landed by submarine in Hudson Bay and mush their way through the snows to an abandoned mine. There a small bomber, shipped into the country in crates labeled as mining equipment, awaits assembly and a bombing mission over the Soo locks on the Great Lakes. Errol Flynn is the Canadian Mountie who foils the scheme, which at the time continued to seem quite plausible to us, despite the tacky special effects in the concluding bombing run.

In any event, the Doolittle raid on Japan in April 1942, launched from "Shangri-la" (as President Roosevelt mysteriously had it) and carried out by Mitchell bombers, lent a certain credence to this plot. If we could do it to them, why couldn't they do it to us?

SPIES, TOO, were an improbability we enthusiastically embraced and worried about: "Loose Lips Sink Ships."

Even my grandmother, of all unlikely people, joined in the alert against them. One day, glancing out her window, mild-mannered, timorous Mildred Hendricks observed that a neigh-

bor had run an antenna out of his window and affixed it to a telephone pole a few feet away. Doubtless he was a shortwave radio
enthusiast—it was a common hobby at the time. Grandma, however, was convinced he was a spy—especially when, peering more
closely, she thought she discerned maps of some kind on the
walls of his room.

Agitated family conversations followed. Should she or
should she not notify the FBI? We decided that this was no time
for nice hesitation. Better safe than sorry. No one observed that
the Underwood Hotel in Wauwatosa, Wisconsin, was not necessarily an ideal vantage point for espionage.

Besides, my father and I had by then seen *Joe Smith, American*, in which an ordinary factory worker, played by Robert
Young, is seized by enemy agents and tortured to reveal the secrets of the bombsight he is working on. He manages to escape
without betraying vital information. He also has a very gratifying
revenge. Though blindfolded when he was abducted, he picked
up auditory clues about his routing and memorized them. Using
these, he leads the FBI to the enemy's lair.

Joe Smith proved the need to stay more than usually alert
during wartime, also that appearances could be deceiving. For
the spy ring's mastermind was played by Jonathan Hale, who also
played the harmlessly, humorously choleric Mr. Dithers in the
Blondie series. The casting was ingenious. Who would have
thought Mr. Dithers could be an enemy agent?

ONE MORNING early in the war we turned out—my mother,
my father, and I—at seven in the morning to see the first contingent of draftees from our town off to basic training. A boy who
lived on our block, Bob Hanel, was among them.

The high school auditorium was filled with well-wishers.

There must have been prayers and patriotic speeches, but what I remember was the draftees filing onto the stage to receive shaving kits, gifts from the town, or perhaps from the Chamber of Commerce. A small, determinedly cheerful man, who according to my father often acted as toastmaster at functions around town, and was regarded as "quite a character," led us in singing "Pack Up Your Troubles in Your Old Kit Bag," his arms pumping enthusiastically.

I don't believe I'd heard the song before, but it has a rather plaintive tune, and I started sniffling as the adults bawled it out. Some of them had tears in their eyes too. But there was something defiant in their tone as well.

Afterward we went outside, where buses were waiting to take the new soldiers off to basic training at Camp Grant in Illinois. There was a great milling about as the young men shook hands with friends and embraced their mothers and fathers. I remember Bob saying something cheerful to me as, shyly, I tried to think of something useful to say to him.

As the buses drove off I remember Mr. Hanel crying and my father patting his shoulder and saying to him, "This thing will be over sooner than you think." "This thing" was a phrase people often used as a euphemism for the war. It was like the euphemisms they used for death.

THAT EARLY MORNING RALLY was, I think, public patriotism's high-water mark in our town. There were no further send-offs on that scale.

But a little later Bud Halliwell, a cousin on my mother's side, was stationed at Great Lakes Naval Training Station outside Chicago, and he came to see us once or twice. Milwaukee was a place a lot of the guys from Great Lakes liked to visit when they had a pass—probably because it was less daunting than Chicago, more manageable for kids from small-town and rural America.

I had never met Bud, but I remember waiting eagerly for him, and I remember my first sight of him—brisk, slender, and tall (he had played basketball in college) in his ensign's uniform, striding up our block. He too was a nice fellow, easy to talk with and attentive to me. My mother, who did not like cooking, nevertheless put on a festive dinner, served in the dining room where we usually ate only at Thanksgiving and Christmas. Bud excused himself early, claiming a "rendezvous" with some of his buddies downtown.

"Rendezvous." I had heard the word on the radio, I think, or read it somewhere, but I had never heard it used in real life. It had a smoky, romantic ring to it. I conjured up an image, probably borrowed from the movies, of a bar, all mirrors and chrome, and Bud and his shipmates in brave, rueful, conversation there, maybe flirting with a mysterious, glamorous woman—though where you would find such a bar or such a woman in Milwaukee in those days I can't imagine now.

Bud was assigned to a baby flattop and saw action in the Pacific. We sent him one or two packages. They contained the usual nonperishable snacks, probably some warm socks, and some music fan magazines, which I helped pick out. Bud was interested in big-band swing; it was one of the points of reference he had found with me.

In return he sent me a grey navy garrison cap adorned with a handsome insignia. When I wore it to school one day, Larry Morgan, a few years older, the neighborhood bully, and the first true asshole I ever encountered, enviously informed me that you could be arrested for wearing part of a uniform if you weren't actually a serviceman. I didn't believe him. But I didn't fully disbelieve him, either. After that I wore the cap only around the house.

AT SOME POINT fairly early in the war, when the always anxious boosterism of our town was appeased, the war was in effect domesticated. It became another worthwhile civic project, like the annual Community Chest or Red Cross drive, only larger, more a part of our day-to-day lives, instead of a mere annual occurence.

It seems to me that there was always a signboard in the shape of a thermometer on display in front of the band shell in The Village. It showed the goal of the latest bond or blood drive, and, by the rising level of the fluid in the tube (always red), how close we were to achieving it. What pride when droplets splashed over the top, showing it had been exceeded.

But the war's intrusions into our daily lives did not prove exigent. Sometimes they were fun. Everyone, for instance, had a big ball of salvaged tinfoil in the kitchen, to be turned in for reuse when it attained a certain heft. In our house I was in charge of it. We also soaked the labels off tin cans and flattened them under foot (another job I liked); when we had a carton or two of them, they were recycled too.

Every now and then there was a major scrap drive. Trucks manned by Boy Scouts would appear on our streets of a Saturday morning and everyone would load their bundled newspapers, whatever heavy metal reposed in their attics, whatever bald tires they found in their garages, onto the trucks and send them off to some unnamed Arsenal of Democracy.

Once a week war stamps were sold at school, and my grandfather always gave me $2 to purchase them. They were placed in a little book, and when the book was filled it could be exchanged for an $18.75 bond, worth $25 if held to maturity ten years later. War bonds were also a standard birthday and Christmas gift from him. They were intended to help finance my college education; by the time they matured I had well over a thousand dollars in savings.

Our mothers now handled ration stamps along with their household budgets, and everyone schemed for B and C cards, permitting them to buy more gasoline than the standard A card allowed. These more generous allotments were, in theory, only for those whose travel was deemed essential to the war effort, so a certain prestige attached to them.

Activities like these may or may not have brought the war home to everyone, but they certainly reduced its threatening aspects. Searching my day-to-day life during the war, I am surprised how little it intruded on our activities. Possibly we played soldiers more than we might have in peacetime, but we continued to devote more of our time to sports. Nor did the war intrude heavily on our lessons at school, except during geography period when it became a sort of teaching aid.

Perhaps this is only a child's-eye view of it. Perhaps, as the war wore on, the grown-ups remained as excited and anxious as they had been in its early months. Perhaps by presenting a calm face they were doing what they could to allay the fears they imagined their children might be harboring. That would have been like them. It was—it is—the Way of the WASP.

But looking back now on the war's ideological artifacts, particularly the movies, I see something more than a natural emotional reticence in their response to the crisis. Simply: the official agenda for the war was a liberal one, and our town's citizens were, in the most profound sense, conservatives.

The movies—in fact all popular fiction and journalism—

tended to stress the leveling aspects of the great struggle. That most famous of wartime movie clichés, the platoon where Jew and Gentile, cowboy and cabby, green kid and grizzled old-timer lay down together in foxholes and discover they are not so very different after all, was not something that greatly appealed to a suburbanite who had invested much of his life's effort in achieving exclusivity.

These movies also stressed the universality of the struggle for liberal, democratic ideals. This too was a notion the typical Wauwatosan looked upon suspiciously. Forget our historic Midwestern isolationism; the very idea of laying down one's life for a Russkie or a Chink (or a Jew), despite official insistence that under our disparate skins we were brothers, went against the grain. Went against common sense, for that matter. They were different, those folks. Anybody could see that.

SO WE MARCHED along, secure in our prejudices, secure in our good natures, never quite seeing the contradictions between the two. I suspect that if the war had not happened, we would have continued forever that way.

But we needed it. This great, overarching, perilous drama shook us out of our complacencies and forced us to consider other ways of thinking and being—especially if, like me, you were unformed, wondering what you might become and how to become it.

For example, I'm sure I would have "liked" the movies if the war had not happened. But I think I would have liked them in the same way other people do, as a diversion they can pretty much take or leave. I do not think they would have gotten into my head as they did if they had not had the war as their great subject, not enjoyed the unique reciprocity between this overwhelming reality and its heroic, deadly, inspiring representations in this powerful and omnipresent medium.

Even in those comparatively few cases where the war was not a film's primary subject, it was nearly always present in some metaphorical sense that was not especially difficult to discern—particularly if the movie's characters were in some way obliged to deal with pain or loss. Mainly, however, the movies gained from the war—from their great topic—a resonance, an intensity that I think they had never quite enjoyed before and never have since.

I am not saying the movies became "better" as a result of this. They were probably, from a purely aesthetic standpoint, a little worse—too many obligations to the demands of the relentlessly propagandizing state. But given their domineering position in the media mix, they compelled if not a complex response, a consequential one.

For the war lent a certain urgency, a certain uplifting sobriety, a certain idealistic glow to the movies. They reinforced my sense that people like us—ordinary middle-class folk—were up and doing elsewhere, proving that suburban constraints were not necessarily ironclad. And, of course, they always insisted on putting heroism within reach of ordinariness. Over and over again, in every possible context, they insisted that there was nothing special about the amazing grace their protagonists found within themselves under wartime pressures, that indeed that grace was one of the inherent gifts bestowed on us by democratic citizenship.

This was, of course, nonsense. It may even have been—in the long run, for me and my generation—dangerous nonsense. Dangerous in the sense that it created false anticipations of adulthood, falsely idealized expectations—at least in me, trying so hard to decipher the mysteries of the universe.

NATURALLY I did not see any of this at the time. But I can identify the moment at which I perceived that the movies were—or could be—something more than one among several ways of agreeably passing the time, when they reached out and enfolded me in some kind of magic that, despite an adult lifetime spent trying, I cannot fully analyze.

My mother was uncommonly insistent: we must all see *Yankee Doodle Dandy*. So off we trooped, one weekend night in 1942—Ed and Helen and I—to the nearest theater, which was called the Tosa (the common, newspaper headline contraction for our town's name). Mom, I'm sure, was expecting a nostalgic treat—reprises of the good old songs ("45 Minutes from Broadway," "Mary, Mary")—and she was not disappointed.

I didn't know what to expect. I had never seen a James Cagney movie. I had never seen a traditional backstage musical. What I got was my first lesson in the transformative power of the movies.

The film is, of course, a biopic, how deeply fictionalized I have never had the slightest desire to find out. As it opens, Cagney's George M. Cohan is playing in *I'd Rather Be Right*, a Rodgers and Hart musical comedy that mildly satirizes Franklin Roosevelt. Cohan receives a telegram backstage, summoning him to a meeting with the president. He is alarmed. Perhaps he has given offense.

But no, FDR wants to give him a medal for writing his many patriotic songs. He asks Cohan to tell him a little bit about his life. The movie illustrates the tale Cohan recounts. Beginning with George's birth (on the Fourth of July) to a family of vaudeville troupers, it traces his rise to fame as a songwriter-playwright-star, a premature retirement, and his return to the stage. He tells Roosevelt—who is seen only from the back, a treatment the movies in those days reserved for Jesus—that his is a typical American story. Everything he has achieved is attributable to America's being the land of opportunity. Roosevelt heartily endorses those sentiments.

But we're talking magic, not plot. In fact I think the movie works so well in part because its story line operates from such a banal base to achieve its transcendencies. It also works because it is in black and white—the tonalities of realism, as opposed to Technicolor, which always promised something epic, scenic, or fantastic when it was deployed. It also helped that it was directed by Michael Curtiz, he of *The Adventures of Robin Hood* and *Casablanca* among dozens of movies of insanely varied qualities. Curtiz was a great, dark European stylist, apparently without an abstract idea in his head. But he had a capacity to give himself with equal enthusiasm to the good, the bad, and the stupid, and he gave himself to this movie in the same heedless spirit his star did.

Cagney's was a career composed of transformations. He was such an unhandsome, unstarish sort of guy—short, a little thick, his accent still hinting of his native New York streets. But there was precision and a raging energy in the way he attacked a role (and attacked is exactly the right word), and he had—as I would discover when he became an idol of mine—a unique capacity to move from the impish to the tragic in a single twinkling moment. I think he, more than Bogart, was the movies' great existential hero, defining himself circumstantially as he went along.

Much later, when he was making his last movie, *Ragtime*, I came to know Cagney. I made a television program and wrote a book about him. He had long been in retirement and had apparently suffered some minor strokes, which left him slightly depressed and a little vague. But for some reason he took a shine to me and tried hard to summon up his memories when I interviewed him.

He felt that Jack Warner had exploited him, forcing him into too many cheap quickies, not realizing that those sharp, half-forgotten little pictures were his great glory, the films in which his quicksilver nature—those sudden shifts from toughness to tenderness—shone most clearly.

His rebellious nature had brought Cagney close to communism in the 1930s, but that was all behind him now. He had embraced the politics of his old pal, Ronald Reagan, a choice that had isolated him from many of his old show-folk friends (excepting the genial Pat O'Brien). When I showed him my film about him I think he was seeing some of his work for the very first time—and seeing some of his old pals for the first time in years. He laughed at the tragic parts and cried at the funny bits, particularly those that involved people like his buddy Frank McHugh.

Be that as it may, in our conversations about *Yankee Doodle Dandy* he was always unambiguous. It was the first-class production he had always wanted from Warner, and he loved it in an almost childlike way. One of his favorite directors, Raoul Walsh, once told me that Cagney was the one actor you could kill off at the end of a movie without outraging his fans. These endings often depended on whether the square people in the film had the time to civilize his deviltry before it brought him to doom.

But *Yankee Doodle Dandy* contains nothing of that. It is a foursquare celebration of American virtue, with Cohan's character uncomplicatedly embodying everything Cagney believed in.

The moment—I don't think I'm exaggerating here—that forever captured me for the movies occurs in a reconstruction of one of Cohan's early musical successes, *Little Johnnie Jones*, in which he plays an American jockey who goes to England to win the Derby. It provides Cagney with a great solo dance, in the course of which he hurls himself at the side of the proscenium, is briefly almost parallel to the stage floor, then bounces back into his tap routine—legs stiff, ass outthrust.

Okay, it's an old hoofer's trick, but I had never seen it before, and its defiance of gravity—something we didn't see much of in Wauwatosa—wowed me.

But then Johnnie Jones is robbed of his victory. He's accused of fixing the Derby, and he sings a downbeat chorus of "Yankee Doodle Dandy." Evidence of his innocence, however, is to be found on an ocean liner heading to America. Confederates aboard it will send up a rocket, visible to Johnnie, anxiously waiting on shore, should they find it.

Finally, the rocket goes up . . . and the look on Cagney's face is maniacal. He turns into a dervish, hurling himself into a wild dance of joy, relief, vindication. Talk about transformations! From gloom to triumph in a matter of seconds. But the joys of this movie—its capacity to shake you out of your spectator's reserve, to pull you into its emotional scheme—are not over.

It soon proceeds to its biggest production number, "You're a Grand Old Flag." It begins conventionally, as a show-stopping theatrical routine. But as it develops, the stage seems to grow larger and larger as curtains are opened, until it accommodates hundreds of chorus boys and girls, representatives of all of America's fighting forces, both contemporary and historical, as well as farmers, factory hands, workers, Boy Scouts, nurses—the entire panoply of brave, good-hearted American life.

Behind them are projected patriotic views—the Capitol prominent among them, seen against a spacious American sky. Cagney at some point does a jaunty, saluting tap dance, then he joins hands with the actors playing the rest of the Cohan family

(Walter Huston, Rosemary de Camp, Jeanne Cagney, the actor's sister) and they march forward, hand in hand, through opening scrims to the conclusion in which hundreds of people are singing: "Should old acquaintance be forgot, keep your eye on that grand old flag."

Even to me it was obvious that no stage in America—not even Radio City Music Hall, about which we read so much in those days—could accommodate this vast vision. It was, I would later learn, another fairly standard movie trope. Especially at Warner Bros., where Busby Berkeley was long accustomed to breaking free of the realistic proscenium so as to accommodate his hundreds of chorines in their half-surreal, half-militaristic routines.

But this was my introduction to the convention. Ordinarily such breaks with reality would have caused me to pull back from the spectacle. Kids are such determined realists. But not this time. The sequence, with its steadily building patriotic fervor, simply overwhelmed me.

At the movie's climax Cohan gets his medal and says his final farewells to Roosevelt as we hear the strains of "Yankee Doodle Dandy" softly on the sound track. Now he is making his way downstairs from what is supposedly the president's second-floor study in the White House. The staircase is almost an abstraction. No White House, no mansion anywhere, could realistically accommodate it.

The music becomes louder, more insistent now, and Cagney, full of irrepressible joy, starts doing bucks and wings on the stairs. I've still not seen a more infectious movie moment. And damned if I don't start to mist up—no matter how many times I reencounter it.

Cagney emerges from the White House into a parade. The picture was completed before Pearl Harbor, and the troops are wearing World War I uniforms. They are, naturally, singing "Over There." Cohan swings in beside them. He does not sing until a soldier asks, "What's the matter, old-timer? Don't you remember this song?" "Seems to me I do," says Cohan. "Well, I don't hear anything," replies the soldier. The old song-and-dance man joins the chorus, his fame subsumed in the mass as he joyfully swings into democracy's irresistible march toward final victory.

5

Know Your Enemy

AS JAPANESE PLANES streaked toward Pearl Harbor, perfidious Japanese diplomats were talking peace with Secretary of State Cordell Hull. So the papers said the next day. There were pictures of the Japanese leaving the old State Department building, looking distinctly sneaky. These images are permanently entered in the photographic record of that high historical moment.

Typical, we immediately thought. It occurred to none of us that the diplomats probably did not know of the attack either. For their reputation for cruelty and duplicity, forged in Korea and China and everywhere else in their "Greater East Asian Co-Prosperity Sphere," had long since preceded the Japanese. They were already what they would remain throughout the war—the Others, capriciously beyond the rational understanding of civilized humanity, therefore beyond redemption.

There was truth in this representation. If you talk to veterans of the Pacific war, most of them will mention how few prisoners we took, because the Japanese, on the whole, preferred death to surrender. The banzai charges, the kamikaze attacks that frightened even Bull Halsey—all this enhanced their strangeness in Western eyes.

Which continues. When they discuss the enemy's motives, the histories mention that in the late nineteenth century, when they were looking for Western political models to emulate, the Japanese chose the wrong one—Prussia instead of the United States. The continuing influence of the Samurai tradition, and the influence of Bushido, the code holding that the highest honor was dying for the emperor, are also mentioned.

Iris Chang, in *The Rape of Nanking*, makes a powerful case for the routine sadism of day-to-day Japanese military life, which enforced discipline by habitual cruelty. She speculates that the lowliest members of this caste system found it easy to torture and kill people still lowlier in their eyes—civilians.

But none of that quite explains Japanese rapaciousness. The world knew about Nanking. Pictures and eyewitness accounts were widely circulated at the time, even though it became—at least until Chang wrote—a forgotten holocaust. We did not understand the frenzy and extent of the crime—some 250,000 deaths, between 20,000 and 80,000 rapes. Nor were we aware of the mindless cruelty with which these crimes were conducted. Chang's account is so horrific that it is at times unreadable.

The death toll at Nanking was larger than that of Hiroshima and Nagasaki combined. The civilian deaths at Manila, which, late in the war, the Japanese torched rather than surrender, are estimated at 100,000. And in recent years the stories of the "comfort women," thousands of females from captured territory forced to serve in brothels for Japanese soldiers, have been thoroughly documented. In other words, Nanking cannot be regarded as an isolated instance.

It remained vividly on people's minds during the war. Even I knew about it, though for quite a while I didn't understand

what the word "rape," either specifically or as metaphorically applied to Nanking, meant. All I knew was that it was a subject that
arose in movies like *Dragon Seed* and *China*, though the details of
the crime were always, of course, elided.

Even so, one of the moments many people vividly remember from their wartime moviegoing occurs in *So Proudly We Hail*,
which is about American nurses ensnared by the debacle in the
Philippines. One of them, played by Veronica Lake in her typical
no-nonsense way, is trapped by a leering Japanese soldier. She
gives him the come-on. He advances eagerly upon her. He does
not see the grenade she has slipped into her bra, but we have.
There is something weirdly satisfying about his violent destruction at this moment, when his sexual anticipation is at its height.
Never was the idea of death before dishonor more satisfactorily
played out in cheap fiction.

It is far more vivid than the conclusion of *Cry Havoc*, which
is also about nurses on Bataan. They are caught in a bunker with
no hope of rescue. We hear the Japanese at the top of the stairs.
We know and they know that their fate must be rape and degra-
dation. We are left, of course, to imagine the details of their martyrdom. We wish for some hand grenades. None are available.

IN HIS evenhanded book *War Without Mercy*, about the racial
nature of the Pacific war, John W. Dower balances crimes of this
sort against the wholesale slaughter of Japanese civilians by aerial
bombardment—which, besides Hiroshima and Nagasaki, includes the 1945 incendiary raid on Tokyo, which resulted in a
firestorm that killed close to 84,000 people. He also mentions
battlefield atrocities against Japanese soldiers. He does not mention, because they are beyond his book's purview, the horrific Allied bombing raids in Europe against targets like Hamburg and

Dresden, which resulted in largely civilian casualties of 45,000 and an astonishing 135,000, respectively.

These statistics are sobering. But possibly irrelevant to the present argument. I don't think it's possible to compare the systematic horrors of the Bataan Death March or the forced labor of POWs on the Burma-Siam "railroad of death" to unsystematic American atrocities in the Pacific war. A simple statistic tells much: only one in twenty-five Allied soldiers died in German prison camps; one in three died in the Japanese camps.

The apparently mindless brutality of the Japanese as they advanced (and retreated) through Asia and the South Pacific, together with their suicidal determination to fight to the last man, costing untold thousands of casualties on both sides, remains a story told mainly in anecdotes. There is, to my knowledge, no serious, systematic history of their wartime conduct.

If that story is ever written, I suspect it should not be mingled with the differently ambiguous history of strategic bombing. After the bombing of Guernica during the Spanish Civil War, and of Rotterdam and Coventry early in World War II, the democratic nations indulged in much moral posturing about the extension of the war to innocent civilian populations. But by soon-to-be-established standards, casualties in these raids were paltry, and, in any case, the rules of warfare simply (and brutally) changed.

For, all pieties aside, it quickly became clear that bombing, ostensibly aimed at war factories and transportation centers, must inevitably kill civilians, that indeed the people manning these installations were civilians. To put the matter simply, strategic bombing became, at some point in World War II, an ineradicable part of warfare.

We may deplore it and satirize its Strangelovian emphasis on dehumanizing statistics, we may question its military effectiveness, and we are surely free to believe that racism—the very Otherness of the Japanese that was so heavily stressed in the popular culture of the time—was a factor in the decision to employ the atomic bomb against them. But we must also argue that the Holocaust, which was, after all, aimed entirely at the most innocent of civilians, has to be weighed in the balance when we consider the Hamburg and Dresden raids.

So it goes, on into the ever-darkening night of endless moral arguments, might-have-beens and should-have-beens. But the crucial point is this: during World War II strategic bombing became one of the unquestioned routines of war, massively utilized by all combatants. Finally Hiroshima and Nagasaki must be regarded as the logical extension of that probably unavoidable mode of thought.

WHICH DOESN'T necessarily exclude some of its more absurd vagaries from our quizzical regard. For instance, the movie *Bombardier*. In training, one of the bombardiers receives a letter from his mother in which she raises the thought that he may be learning to become a mass murderer. A chaplain addresses her fears and her son's:

> I believe in peace as much as your mother and those organizations she belongs to. But peace isn't as cheap a bargain as those people put on it. Those people lock themselves up in a dream world. See, there are millions of other mothers looking to you, to boys like you, to destroy the forces of murder your mother mistakenly attributes to you. The enemy's targets are everywhere. But yours are clear and confined—not women and children, but their arsenals for spreading death. That's why American bombardiers are trained to hit the target. There's a

little prayer for that, Paul: "God give me not the spirit of fear, but the power and love for the oppressed, a sound mind and a clear eye. God make me a good bombardier that I may destroy the poison in his cup and quench the violence of fire and over-come the false gods who make war with the lamb. For he is the Lord of Lords and King of Kings, and they who are with Him are called and chosen and faithful."

Set aside the loony invocation of the Deity and concentrate on the implication that bombing could be surgically accurate. We tended to believe that, not so much because we believed par-ticularly in the sound mind and clear eye of our bombardiers—though the movies constantly showed them to be uncannily accurate—but because we had the Norden bombsight. It was, as far as the movies were concerned, the icon of American techno-logical (and, by implication, moral) superiority.

It was also the war's most fiercely guarded secret. In the movies airmen were always risking their lives to destroy it so it would not fall into enemy hands. That it worked effectively only when the weather over the target was clear, was not a point often made.

THE PREFERRED TOPIC remained Japanese inhumanity. I was unaware of it at the time, but there was sober discussion, by re-sponsible officials, about utterly destroying the Japanese as a na-tion and a people, on the grounds that it would always be impossible to bring them into the company of civilized nations. Hiroshima and Nagasaki were the end product of that argument.

Had I heard it, I would have accepted it. In war movies—in life as well—someone was always justifying this or that harsh military act with some variation on the idea that "You started this war, now you're going to pay the price."

Japanese atrocities were so melodramatic, so dramatizable. We more or less saw them yank the fingernails of a female American war correspondent in *Behind the Rising Sun* (the editing was artful), heard the screams of a tortured American aviator, captured after the Doolittle raid, in *The Purple Heart*. These were, indeed, his last sounds, since whatever they did to him rendered him mute. In this war without mercy, as Hollywood conducted it, this was business—with its ineluctable racist overtones—as usual.

By late 1942 I was attending the movies virtually every week, and I have to say that their obsession with the cruelty, duplicity, and implacability of the Japanese enemy permanently affected me. One constantly saw, among movie Germans, evidence of civility. That was never true of the Japanese. Many were shown to have been educated in the United States, but they were, if anything, more merciless than their less well-traveled countrymen.

I was not alone in my fear of them. When we talked about going to war (should it last long enough for us to grow to draft age), what scared all of us kids the most was having to fight the Japanese. I am not alone, I think, in my continuing, unspoken (until now) mistrust of them. I fight it. But I have never entirely defeated the prejudices the movies—our propaganda in general—instilled in me.

Conversely, ironically, the Japanese may never have entirely shaken off the way they were viewed by General MacArthur's occupying army, which saw them as wayward but educable children.

The Germans, the general would pontificate, were "quite as mature" culturally as the "Anglo-Saxon" victors. But "Measured by the standards of modern civilization [the Japanese] would be like a boy of twelve compared with our development of forty-five years." Few disputed this portrait of the former enemy as pre-moral.

Yet MacArthur's occupation did not enthusiastically pursue war criminals. Especially it did not pursue the emperor, whom recent scholarship shows to have been far from the isolated figurehead that MacArthur's people insisted he was. Rather, he was active in the councils of war, especially in urging his high command to fight on after they knew they were beaten. But the occupation was eager to rehabilitate the Japanese as allies in the cold war, and the emperor was crucial to that effort.

As a result, the Japanese themselves have remained, by all accounts, in massive denial about their war crimes. The processes of guilt and atonement that have preoccupied Germany for more than a half-century have not been embraced by the Japanese.

Or pursued by many Western historians. In the United States we remain deeply concerned with the wartime internment of Japanese-Americans—such a vivid failure of American democracy. We are not wrong in this. But we remain largely unconscious of Japan's war crimes, mostly because the vast majority of its victims were Asians in their anonymous millions. They have few Western voices to speak for them—no Elie Weisel, no Primo Levi, no Shoah Foundation.

THIS SILENCE represents a reversal of former conditions, at least as far as movies are concerned. The great majority of combat movies made during the war—the films that most of us automatically think of first when we recall our moviegoing in this period—involved Americans fighting the Japanese rather than the Germans.

That's because we were engaged with them face-to-face,

hand-to-hand, well before we were similarly involved with the Germans, which did not occur until our landings in North Africa almost a year after Pearl Harbor. Aside from two or three films about the war in North Africa, there were no important American films about land combat between Americans and Germans until after the war was over, when *The Story of G.I. Joe* and *A Walk in the Sun* were released. What we had, instead, were stories of the Resistance (*Edge of Darkness, Commandos Strike at Dawn, The Moon Is Down, Uncertain Glory*), espionage (*Desperate Journey, Above Suspicion, 13 Rue Madeleine*), the battle of the North Atlantic (*The Navy Comes Through, Corvette K225, Action in the North Atlantic*).

In the convoy pictures the enemy was pretty much an abstraction. In the spy and resistance movies he was there—cruel and sneering—but his victims tended to be conquered Europeans. As far as the movies were concerned, the war against Hitler was largely fought by these surrogates.

There weren't as many films about combat with Japan as you may think—perhaps twenty-five or thirty of them, using the broadest possible definition—and most of them were rather uninteresting. You never heard so many minor-key and rhythmic variations on "Anchors Aweigh" or the Marine Corps or Air Corps hymns, never saw so many idiotic romances, typically between a girl and some wise guy who was disapproved of by a brother or father serving in the same unit.

Whatever his romantic arrangements, or lack of same, this character was always politically unconscious. He might be someone whose enlistment is due to end shortly and he can't wait to get out (William Bendix in *Wake Island*, John Garfield in *Air Force*), or maybe a hot pilot, like John Carroll in *Flying Tigers*, who's out for himself and has to be painfully educated in the value of team play. Very often he is an urban American and, one now sees, he is playing a variation on the character Cagney played in his prewar service comedies—a basically good-hearted but childlike figure who must be taught discipline, possibly even achieve heroic martyrdom, before the picture is over.

I can't remember now if I liked these movies. I suppose I must have, since I saw so many of them. Lots of men my age continue to think well of them, ironizing their clichés but responding to their triumphalism. Taken together, though, they became one big, rather unparticularized war movie, imposing itself on memory because its tropes, drawn from many sources, were so repetitive, so "universal."

What we see in these movies is a genial, good-natured America, trying to retain those qualities against a relentless enemy. It is in fact amazing how much bad, predictable comedy these movies contained. The guys—isolated on some godforsaken island, eating cold K rations or worse—were always dreaming of a big steak. Or, alternatively, of a busty blonde, either real or the pinup variety. Sometimes they picked up a stray dog on which they lavished comically intense affection. At least one of them would be equally besotted by the Brooklyn Dodgers.

They were usually discovered in a somewhat befuddled condition. Pearl Harbor or not, they were not yet on full fighting alert. They were fractious with one another and also rather hoping they could do the job inattentively, with time off for bad—that is, prankish—behavior.

What these guys—representing the full range of American types, from college boys to farm boys, but always including an old-timer who is often seen to be plagued by some minor physical disability like sore feet—need are two things: a hard-assed commander who can whip them into fighting trim, and a mission that will test his values against their lazier civilian ones.

He appears at training camp—Pat O'Brien, say, the long-time superego to Cagney's raging id, or some actor who had previously played gangsters and was thus a known tough guy. He is usually at first disliked by his men—the notable exception being Randolph Scott's impersonation of Lt. Col. Evans F. Carlson, in *Gung-Ho*. That film purports to be a semi-documentary record of a special force that, early in the war, made a daring raid on the Japanese stronghold on Makin Island. The attack was of dubious strategic value, but, like the Doolittle bombing raid on Tokyo, it did wonders for American morale.

Carlson is accurately represented as someone who had studied Communist tactics in China, had utter faith in them, and commanded his "raider" battalion in what he understood to be Maoist style—gently, informatively, democratically (at least by Marine Corps standards). Interestingly, the movie was never criticized for endorsing communism, possibly because it was not written or directed by a Communist. Its lasting interest lies in the fact that, via its title, it permanently introduced a phrase to our language and was, as Jeanine Basinger says in her fine-grained study of *The World War II Combat Film*, the first "dirty dozen" movie—most of these guys are misfits in civilian life, some of them close to psychopathically so.

That aside, *Gung-Ho* plays by genre rules, right down to the inevitable Dodger fan. And this group, arduously trained to kill as heedlessly as the enemy, eventually achieves that goal. Which implies, of course, that the nation will achieve its larger victory. And learn its lesson. Which is never to let anyone sneak up on it again.

Movies like this one, for all the discomforts and losses their characters suffer, are finally comfortable, reassuring movies. The issue is never in doubt. Democracy will prevail.

Going back to these films now, on the far side of *The Greatest Generation* and *Saving Private Ryan* and Stephen Ambrose's books about World War II, we can dimly discern a similar celebration of American dutifulness. We put this point more grimly now, without the lame humor, without the girls, without the martial music and the frequent improbabilities of plot. Above all, we add to them now an awareness of war's inevitable waste and tragedy.

ONLY A FEW FILMS made during the war can be even distantly compared with *Saving Private Ryan*. *Air Force* is one of them. It was directed by Howard Hawks from an epic-length script by the militantly liberal but non-Communist Dudley Nichols. It offered a simple, linear story of the crew of a B-17 called the *Mary Ann*, which takes off with a flight of eight other bombers from San Francisco on December 6, 1941, heading for Pearl Harbor. Historically there *was* such a flight. Precisely because it was anticipated to arrive at about the time the Japanese launched their attack, it added to the confusion of radar posts on Oahu, which mistook the incoming enemy for the Americans they were expecting.

The film makes more than it should of the notion that sabotage played a role in the devastation of Hickam Field, where most of our planes were destroyed on the ground. In fact there were Japanese spies operating in Hawaii at the time, but no effective saboteurs. It also makes something of the dubious notion that the Japanese are good fliers when the odds are heavily in their favor but tend to run when the fight is a fair one.

But these debatable points—and the *Mary Ann*'s improbably heroic concluding involvement in what must be the Battle of the Coral Sea—aside, the film is matter-of-fact and low-keyed in a manner typical of Hawks. The *Mary Ann*'s crew is looking for some corner of the war where they can be useful. To that end they keep moving westward across the Pacific—to Wake Island where they refuel just before the island falls, to the Philippines where the ship is almost destroyed and its pilot is killed, to the Coral Sea, before reaching safety in Australia. Some reviewers drew an analogy between the B-17 and a covered wagon heading into Indian country.

But this odyssey—stirring as it sometimes is, particularly in the crew's suspenseful effort to repair the plane in the Philippines before the Japanese overrun them—is not *Air Force's* true subject. It is really about welding the ethnically and emotionally disparate crew together into a group that will serve the plane and its mission.

In this sense it was a typical Hawks film. There has always been a certain irony in the director's preferred subject—he was himself a great, reserved loner—as well as in his factual, anti-heroic manner, since he was given to occasional self-aggrandizements rendered the more plausible by the soft murmur in which he delivered them.

But its refusals set *Air Force* apart. To begin with, the Japanese are not particularly excoriated. The sneakiness of the Pearl Harbor attack is, at worst, treated with taciturn contempt. Mostly the Americans keep vowing to have their innings later.

The plane's aged crew chief (Harry Carey, in a marvelously restrained performance) is concerned with his son, a young officer stationed at Manila airfield where they are heading. He's too proud of the boy—in war movies a sure signal of impending doom. The *Mary Ann's* pilot (John Ridgely) learns from the commander of the Philippine airfield that the boy was killed on the ground in the first raid; he never got his plane into the air. He hands over the kid's belongings, which in turn are delivered to Carey wrapped in a white handkerchief—his wings, a cigarette lighter, his lieutenant's bars. The chief looks at them sadly and reprises a similar moment from Hawks's earlier aviation picture, *Only Angels Have Wings*: "Not much to show for twenty years."

So it goes in *Air Force*. Ridgely's character is mortally wounded. His crew gathers around his hospital bed and, as he nears death, the *Mary Ann*'s captain begins going through a take-off procedure, to which each crewman responds as he would if this were a real flight. The captain dies when his imaginary plane is airborne, heading into the rising sun. The scene was written as a favor to Hawks, who was his great Hollywood champion, by William Faulkner, and it is curiously moving. When the captain dies, a doctor simply says, "That's it, boys," and Carey gruffly orders them back to work on their crippled plane.

A little later, when the youngest member of the crew, temporarily detached to serve as a gunner on a navy fighter, is machine-gunned in his parachute as his plane goes down, there is no vengeful hysteria at this fairly common atrocity. Carey and John Garfield, by now a full-fledged member of the group, simply wrap the dead soldier in his parachute. "Better get him out of here," one of them says.

In short, there are no speeches and no hate-mongering in *Air Force*. It is not necessary. It has its implausibilities—most notoriously, Carey and Garfield picking up the plane's heavy machine guns and firing them from their hips, which is impossible to do in reality—but that's a minor bow to Hollywood heroics. Its business is to show how a peaceable American microcosm mobilizes itself, not for some great crusade but for a risky, dirty job. These guys are not fighting for a better world. They are fighting to preserve a much smaller world—the airplane that depends on them, as they do on it.

I suppose *Air Force* took such a firm hold on me because little-boy gangs are all embryo Hawksian groups, and this film taught us much about their functioning. *Thirty Seconds Over*

Tokyo, which recounts Jimmy Doolittle's raid on the Japanese capital as well as several other enemy cities, does the same thing on a somewhat larger scale. It goes into persuasive detail about the special training—emphasis on the teamwork required—that preceded the bombings.

As everyone knows, the planes were launched from the aircraft carrier *Hornet*, whose flight deck offered only about one-third the takeoff length the bombers usually needed. Also, since the *Hornet* and its task force were spotted by Japanese picket boats, the pilots had to take off eight hundred miles east of Tokyo instead of the planned four hundred miles, which is why most of them fell short of the Chinese airfields where they intended to land.

Nonetheless the raid was a great success. This was not because of damage inflicted—the planes each carried only three five-hundred-pound bombs and a few incendiaries, not enough to do much harm—but because of its effect on morale, both in the United States and Japan.

At the time, a little more than four months after Pearl Harbor, when all the news was bad, the fact that the war had been carried to the enemy homeland had a wonderfully stirring effect on Americans. Also, as a *Hornet* crew member recently told me, "it put the fear of God" in the Japanese. Most important, it caused them to move up their attack on Midway, obliging them to leave two aircraft carriers behind and greatly improving the odds for the Americans in this greatest of the Pacific war's turning points.

The story of the Tokyo raid is told through the eyes of Capt. Ted Lawson, who with Robert Considine wrote a best-selling book about the raid, and the film, written by Dalton Trumbo and directed by Mervyn LeRoy, is very workmanlike and anti-heroic in tone. Perhaps there is more than we care to know about the new marriage of Lawson (nicely underplayed by Van Johnson) to Ellen (Phyllis Thaxter), who announces her pregnancy the day he signs on with the Doolittle mission. "How come you're so cute?" he keeps asking her. "I had to be to get such a good-looking fella," she keeps replying.

On the other hand, she is rather bravely resigned to fate. If her husband should die, she remarks, quite dry-eyed, a little bit of him will live on in their child. There is, as well, a good little passage on the *Hornet* a night or two before the raid, when Johnson and Robert Mitchum, playing another pilot, discuss their dream of jointly owning a ranch after the war. In the course of this exchange, no mention is made of Japanese cruelty or sneakiness. Both men instead state their lack of hatred for the enemy.

Finally, there is a moment of unique and refreshing frankness when Doolittle—brusquely played by Spencer Tracy—informs his men that inevitably civilians will be killed in this raid. If that bothers any of them, he says, they are free to leave, no questions asked. None do, of course. We were already past such niceties.

The raid itself is a swiftly handled special-effects sequence— Lawson's plane, *The Ruptured Duck,* isn't over Tokyo for much more than thirty seconds of screen time. Far more time is spent on the ground in China, where Lawson, one of whose legs was shattered in landing on a rocky beach, must eventually deal with its amputation. This he does with a realistic amount of fear and with a certain acceptance once the operation is performed.

A good deal of praise is lavished on the airmen's Chinese rescuers, but it is not misplaced. In postraid reprisals the Japanese likely executed thousands of Chinese in the areas where the planes landed. I have seen one estimate that placed the total at an astonishing 200,000.

Even so, all but one of the Doolittle crews escaped capture (three of the men who fell into Japanese hands were executed for "war crimes"). And Ted Lawson finally returns to his Ellen. Their reunion, with him reluctant to be seen by her until he has mastered an artificial leg, but with Doolittle arranging for them to meet before that happens, is also managed with minimal sentiment. This movie has no compulsion to hate.

WHY THIS STRATEGY did not commend itself to other filmmakers is unclear. Routine Hollywood hackery cannot be discounted. Neither can government pressures. The fact that so many major war films were written by leftists, both Stalinist and non-Stalinist, cannot be ignored either. They had a taste for a particular kind of overheated common-man rhetoric that Trumbo, their coreligionist, largely avoided in *Thirty Seconds Over Tokyo.*

But no one at the time cared about these rhetorical flourishes—not the critics, not the audience. Three examples should suffice to make my point.

Bataan, released in 1943, was the first significant land-combat film of the Pacific war, and it set the tone for much that followed. It starred Robert Taylor, Thomas Mitchell, George Murphy, and a very young Desi Arnaz among thirteen men of disparate ethnicity and social class who are assigned to defend a bridgehead on the eponymous peninsula. Their job is to "buy time," not just for American forces retreating toward the last stand on Corregidor but, by implication, for the entire American war effort.

Eventually all these soldiers will die here, generally illustrating, as Basinger observes, the basic tropes that applied throughout the war to small-unit combat films: don't stand up in your foxhole, don't climb a tree to get a better view of the action, don't make crazed charges at the clever enemy, don't leave your position on a scouting mission, even if you strip off your uniform to improve your mobility. Above all, trust the enemy to be anything but "no-tail baboons." They are, rather (to borrow another common movie description), "yellow-skinned, slanty-eyed devils." After they capture one of the patrol, his tortured screams, from out of the mist, are an unforgettable lesson in the enemy's sadism.

At the time the "realism" of *Bataan* was praised by critics, though looking at it now you can see that it was shot almost entirely on an MGM sound stage. In fact the film worked on us primarily as a horror film. Most of its action is shrouded in heavy fog, and the Japanese—who seem to multiply like aliens in a sci-fi movie—are presented as unparticularized, ghostly creatures creeping eerily about under this cover, always cleverly countering whatever ploys the Americans attempt.

Bataan is not as spooky as it seemed to us kids in 1943. Still, we are talking about war without mercy here, in which characters and situations borrowed from earlier genre efforts—the film is an unacknowledged remake of *The Lost Patrol*—are pushed to the edge of hysteria.

In the end only the grizzled sergeant (well enough played by that glum pretty boy Robert Taylor) is still alive, manning a machine gun as the Japanese, in their multitude, emerge from cover to overrun his position. "You didn't think we'd be here," he screams. "We'll always be here." An inspirational voice-over speaks over the gun's chatter: "So fought the men of Bataan. Their sacrifices made possible our own victories at the Coral and Bismarck Seas, blah blah blah. . . ."

Okay. But what was really always there in the movies was the unremitting cruelty of the Japanese. In *Destination Tokyo*,

Cary Grant, as a submarine commander, has to explain why Mike the torpedoman had to die. The sub has shot down a Japanese Zero in surface action, but its pilot has survived. A small boat, including Mike, is sent to rescue him. But the Jap kills Mike with a hidden knife.

Grant tells his sailors that Mike's last gift to his son was a pair of roller skates, "the best that money could buy." But when the Zero pilot was that age, "his father put a knife in his hands." Grant traces this contrast through the teens, then concludes: "I figure that's what Mike died for—more roller skates in the world, including for the next generation of Japanese kids." A nice, balancing touch of tolerance—from Albert Maltz, also soon to be a member of the Hollywood Ten.

The sub accomplishes its mission—sneaking into Tokyo harbor to gather reconnaissance information for the Doolittle raid while incidentally (and suspensefully) providing an appendectomy for one of the crew, conducted with improvised instruments by the ship's pharmacist's mate. In its last sequence the sub sails into San Francisco Bay with its crew on deck discussing their coming liberty. The conversation is, naturally, of food and girls, but one guy is heading for a "platter shop" where, he says, he intends to "get drunk" on Dinah Shore records. Another sailor reflects philosophically on their life: When you're out there, all you want to be is back here, but when you're home all you think about is being back out there—in combat. That struck me at the time—as it still does—as a curiously truthful line, stated in a nicely offhand way.

Objective Burma, which starred Errol Flynn, is notable for a particularly vicious verbal passage, the co-creation of another Communist, Lester Cole (with Ranald MacDougall), adapting a screen story by Alvah Bessie, yet another member of the Hollywood Ten. Overall, under Raoul Walsh's direction, the movie is slightly better than the customary combat picture. But eventually the main body of Flynn's patrol comes upon the bodies of a small group that had been detached for scouting purposes. They have been tortured to death. Henry Hull, playing a sort of father-figure war correspondent, has this speech, delivered at the near edge of hysteria:

> I've been a newspaperman for thirty years. I thought I'd seen or read about everything one man can do to another, from the torture chambers of the middle ages to gang wars and lynch-ings of today. But this. . . . This is different. This was done in cold blood by a people who claim to be civilized. Civilized? They're degenerate moral idiots, stinking little savages. Wipe 'em out I say. Wipe 'em out. Wipe 'em off the face of the earth.

Who by that time (1945) would dare to argue with him? Indeed, I think we have to concede this point: the movies' representation of the war with Japan was, the odd hysterical speech aside, more truthful, in its insistence on this war's merciless and brutal nature, than their presentations of the war against Germany ever were.

6

Tortured Europe

WE WERE GIVEN to understand—in the movies, elsewhere too—that the Germans were gripped by a kind of temporary insanity, from which they might eventually be salvaged. This was the official Office of War Information line. It preferred them not to be monsters. It liked movies that showed there were a few good, liberal-minded Germans working underground to redeem the Fatherland from the Nazi aberration.

This portrait of Germany insisted that, the underground aside, its citizens were–what else should one expect of a totalitarian regime?—rigid, programmed. It was important to them that their trains ran on time. But this was a weakness exploitable by the more flexible and imaginative Americans. One thinks of what was—honestly—one of Ronald Reagan's finest screen moments, when he befuddles Raymond Massey's hopelessly square Nazi interrogator, curious about how the new superchargers in our planes work, by talking jive talk to him in *Desperate Journey*.

The fact that the Germans were occasionally portrayed in film as comic menaces (*The Great Dictator*, *To Be or Not to Be*,

The Devil with Hitler) while the Japanese never were is perhaps a sign of their redemptive potential. To laugh at an enemy is to keep him within the realm of the human.

There was, to be sure, no lack of smirking sadists in Nazi regalia. But they often seemed to regret it when torture was called for. And Hollywood tended to avert its eyes when the rough stuff began. I can recall only two instances where we were obliged— very briefly—to look: Joan Crawford's face being burned in *Above Suspicion* (an uneasy blend of espionage melodrama and romantic comedy) and *13 Rue Madeleine*, in which Cagney, as a captured OSS agent, is glimpsed under the lash.

The convention in these films was for the well-spoken, even rather intellectual commandant of the local garrison to turn the interrogation regretfully over to his sausagelike underlings. Walter Slezak was especially good in roles of this kind. One thinks of his attractively competent and seemingly civilized U-boat commander taking over Hitchcock's *Lifeboat* and very nearly steering its survivors into German hands. Or of the spymaster, pretending to be an anti-Nazi refugee but running his espionage ring in wartime New York, in *The Fallen Sparrow*. His particular target is John Garfield's Spanish Civil War veteran, whose torture, almost to death, he oversaw in Europe.

Best of all, perhaps, was the same actor's smooth, amused "protector" of the small French town in which, eventually, Charles Laughton's timorous schoolteacher achieves heroic martyrdom in *This Land Is Mine*. Major von Keller comes perilously close to talking Laughton's character out of his heroic self-sacrifice.

This would have deprived us of one the actor's best moments, a long courtroom speech in which, reluctantly, he claims a manhood almost henpecked into oblivion by his overprotective mother. The movie was much criticized at the time, and when it was released in France after the war it outraged audiences and had to be withdrawn. But I was strangely moved by it. I liked the nobility of its utterances, and the whole notion of self-conscious self-sacrifice, in which you not only lay down your life for a cause but get to make a formal speech explaining your action, was new and curiously thrilling to me.

Something similar happens in *The Moon Is Down*, in which another cautious character, the mayor of a Norwegian town, played by mild-mannered Henry Travers, quoting from Greek tragedy no less, joins the hostages doomed to a firing squad rather than submit to the blandishments of Cedric Hardwicke's weary Nazi commandant. How patiently he tries to win its occupants over to National Socialism, with what subtextual *weltschmerz* does he finally apply—after the local mine has been blown up by the underground—sterner measures to his charges.

Perhaps the strangest aspect of this movie is a lonely young German junior officer who is romantically drawn to the widow of a resistance martyr and is murdered by her at the moment when he thinks he is being invited into her bed. It's a variation on the *So Proudly We Hail* trope, but this time our sympathy is not entirely with her. This self-conscious humanization of the enemy by John Steinbeck, on whose novel the movie was based, was heavily criticized at the time.

As many of these rather ambiguous Nazis suggest, there was almost no discussion in the movies about the fact that the Germans were truly the Others—masters of a vast, rationally organized, fully industrialized killing machine without precedent in human history.

THE MOVIES' most vivid example of Nazi penology was not a concentration camp at all. It was rather the prisonlike breeding ground for the master race portrayed in *Hitler's Children*. It produced what may be the most famous movie still of the war—Bonita Granville kneeling, trussed to a flagpole, awaiting a flogging.

Granville was playing Anna Miller, an American exchange student of German extraction who in the prewar years falls in love with Karl Bruner (Tim Holt), an ardent Hitler youth. She is selected to join the German eugenics program but refuses to produce little blond *herrenvolk* for the state. She is scheduled for sterilization. But first she must endure more public humiliation and pain. In the film, after she is tied to the pole, her blouse is ripped down the back (though we see no exposed flesh) and we hear one or two offstage whip cracks (but no screams) before Holt steps out of the line of neatly regimented witnesses to halt the punishment. This eventually assures their joint martyrdom, which owed as much to romanticism (no sex without love) as it did to totalitarianism.

Hitler's Children was a sensation at the time. Never mind that its portrayal of state-sponsored sex and sterilization was both coldly regimental and, yes, sterile. Never mind that its topic was enough to send Joseph Breen and his censors into a tizzy of Catholic prudery. In an uncrowded field it was one of the more vivid Hollywood representations of totalitarian excess. We went to it hoping for the best—that is to say, the worst—and came away feeling that its melodramatic energy more or less compensated for the cool dispassion with which it presented its hot ostensible subject.

I SUPPOSE you could argue that, by stressing the Nazi desire to breed an Aryan master race, *Hitler's Children* implied that something ugly might be happening to the other "lesser" breeds contained within the Third Reich. But basically moviedom diminished or ignored the vast tragedy of European Jewry.

A prime example was *Mr. Skeffington,* in which Claude Rains plays an upwardly mobile American Jew (complete with English accent) who has made a Wall Street fortune. He enters into a loveless marriage with a social butterfly played by Bette Davis, who is obsessed with retaining her youth and a gaggle of yearning swains. When the marriage becomes unendurable, Skeffington and his beloved daughter decamp for Hitler's Germany to tend his "interests" there. When she returns to New York without him, it is rumored—truthfully, it turns out—that he has been placed in a concentration camp.

This is rather mysterious. Skeffington, after all, is an American citizen—a *prominent* American citizen. One would imagine that the Nazis might more logically have ignored him or quietly deported him. The possibility that they might have caused him to disappear without an embarrassing trace cannot be ignored. But no, he somehow reappears in New York, old before his time—doddering, broke, blinded by his oppressors.

But the movie is not about the concentration camps. Of their full extent and true genocidal function, nothing is said. They are merely a plot device, preparing the way for an O. Henryish ending. By now his former wife has lost her looks to illness, but he, of course, cannot see what has become of her. Happily, she has run her long-ago divorce settlement into a tidy fortune. They are free at last to love unencumbered—except, of course, by neatly instructive irony.

All one can say for *Mr. Skeffington* is that it at least implied that its protagonist suffered for his Jewishness. That was generally not true of those few movies that alluded to the death camps.

When they were liberated in the European war's last days, and the first pictures from them appeared on the front pages and in the newsreels, everyone was shocked.

For until then the camps had been represented in the movies, in the press generally, as particularly strict maximum-security prisons (*The Mortal Storm, Escape*), a little bit like those in chain-gang pictures. Their victims were always portrayed as heroic dissidents, enduring their torments for political principle, not because of the accident of birth. The camps always appeared to be survivable, even occasionally escapable.

The Seventh Cross, for instance, is set in 1936, when, it is historically true, the concentration camps mainly housed political opponents of the Nazi regime. It opens with seven men more or less waltzing out of a camp. One of them is quickly killed, which does not prevent him from serving as the film's ghostly narrator—a favorite device of wartime movies. The rest, save one, are quickly rounded up, including a "little Jew" (this hasty, patronizing phrase is one of the film's two brief allusions to Nazi anti-Semitism).

The movie's best sequence finds one of the seven, a famous circus acrobat, scrambling for his life across the rooftops of Mainz, pursued by the usual Nazi stumblebums. He gives them a good run, but finally the Nazis corner him. He poises himself on the edge of a roof and then reverts to what was once the climax of his act—a sort of death dive. Except this time there is no net to catch him.

It is a superbly defiant public moment, especially since the director, Fred Zinnemann, presented it with near-casual realism. Yes, we thought, one might choose this alternative—spectacular and in some sense inspirational, since a large crowd has gathered to watch the chase—over torture and death on one of the crosses erected by the prison camp commandant for the recaptured escapees.

The seventh of these, intended for Spencer Tracy's George Heisler, remains empty. For George, who is presented as a man embittered by the failure of the German people to oppose Nazism, must live and learn. We don't know why George was imprisoned, but seeing the picture now, one has to believe that he was a Communist, though that identification is never made. Nevertheless it is the little people—most notably a frightened, apolitical, but fundamentally decent couple played by Hume Cronyn and Jessica Tandy, and a barmaid played by Signe Hasso—who bind up his wounded hand, hide him, secure him false papers, and send him on his way to Holland. Others who help out include a nice assortment of class types—a Jewish doctor, a rich architect, a football player, a rather mysterious intellectual.

George at least gets to sleep with the barmaid, who offers to accompany him to Holland. Naturally he must reject her. She would interfere with "his work."

But *The Seventh Cross* is very muted emotionally, all vague generalities when it comes to politics. It refuses, as almost every wartime movie about tormented Europe did, to concretize the issues. It refuses to allow anyone a firmly stated ideological motivation for action; it is as silent about the passionate leftism of Nazism's most dedicated European opponents as it is about the Nazis' genocidal agenda.

A couple of months after the war ended, Dwight Macdonald wrote the following in his magazine *Politics*:

"We were a little nervous when she was taken," the girl's mother said afterwards. "You never know what will happen when they start to use the electric needle. But we should not have worried. She never gave the Germans a single name or address. And no one was arrested."

The girl was a member of the French underground; she was caught by the Gestapo; she was tortured, while her mother was held in a nearby cell so she could hear her daughter's screams; and she died. This was Europe under the Nazis: the matter-of-fact reference to torture; the technological modernity of the instrument; the mother's politicized attitude— "we should not have worried" since "she never gave a single name."

Many questions, obviously, are raised by this chilling anecdote. I want to consider only one of them. It seems to me that one could resist torture only if one were passionately committed to an ideology. And as a practical matter in wartime Europe, that ideology would have to have been Communism. I don't believe one died for the kind of liberal sentiments the Laughton and Travers figures proposed. Surely one could not long endure the kind of pain the Gestapo meted out in its cellars without being armored in a belief system equal in force to that of the Nazis.

But such subtleties were not available to Hollywood. The notion of Communist heroism was as anathema to the Office of War Information as Jewish victimhood was. As kids, of course, we did not have the slightest understanding of the deadly politics of Europe. Good Guys versus Bad Guys was fine with us—was, in fact, all we could encompass imaginatively.

IT IS FAIR to say, I think, that when we contemplated the Nazi enemy in movies, anywhere in popular culture, we were dealing with what one eventually learned to call motiveless malignity.

These people were simply mean for meanness's sake. Or occasionally for perversity's sake.

Consider the best scene in *Hangmen Also Die*, which is about the assassination of Reinhardt Heydrich, the notoriously sadistic SS officer who organized Kristallnacht, presided over the Wannsee Conference at which the "Final Solution" became official policy, and oversaw the extermination of Polish Jewry. In it Heydrich (played by Hans von Twardowski) is presented as an effeminate homosexual. He enters a staff conference powdered and rouged, strolls coquettishly among the officers, pauses before some rough trade, drops a glove, and then waits as his apparent sexual victim very reluctantly picks it up.

This is Fritz Lang's little joke. Or possibly it was Bertold Brecht's, who worked with him on the screenplay. Or maybe the drollery was invented by the Communist John Wexley, who eventually more or less stole Brecht's writing credit from him. Whatever the case, it is historical nonsense, since Heydrich was a famous womanizer.

The rest of the picture carries a very Brechtian subtext (apparently greatly reduced in its final version) that equates Nazism with American gangsterism, a theme he returned to in *Arturo Ui*. But the film doesn't even get the details of Heydrich's demise or the reprisal for it right. It has him murdered on a street in Prague, and it offers some hostages being shot as a result.

Hitler's Madman—directed by Douglas Sirk, whose lush (not to say overripe) manner was better suited to the fifties weepies where he made his name—offers John Carradine (in a rather effective performance) as Heydrich. It was not as well received critically as *Hangmen*, which benefited from Lang's and Brecht's repute, but it was more nearly correct about Heydrich's nasty (hetero)sexuality, the manner of his death (on a country road at the hands of British-trained partisans), and the terrible reprisal for his death—the extermination of Lidice. A choral recitation of Edna St. Vincent Millay's poem on that subject provides the film's rather powerful coda.

That doesn't make it any less flamboyant (there's a particularly vivid confrontation between Heydrich and Catholics trying to go about their rituals, ending in a priest's death) or any more forthcoming about his role in the Final Solution. Mainly the business of *Hitler's Madman* is living up to its ripsnorting title.

IF IT HELPED to be armored in ideology when you confronted the Gestapo's sadism, it may be that it helped screenwriters to be similarly armored as they confronted their typewriters. Leftist screenwriters—and there were at the time virtually no other kind, both Communist and non-Communist—more than anyone else set the intellectual agenda—if that phrase is not too grand—for American movies during the war.

The victims of Hollywood's blacklist—who were, indeed, Communists—have in the last decade or two been converted into innocent victims of McCarthyism, heroes of the American resistance to political oppression. It is now frequently said that they wrote nothing that could be construed as Stalinist propaganda. The argument is that such material could not possibly worm its way past the reactionary moguls.

But that is not entirely true. Hollywood's Communists wrote a surprisingly large number of important movies during the war. They did not particularly hide their political sentiments. Sometimes, indeed, they were brought to the fore as the Office of War Information encouraged them to place a human face on Stalin's Russia.

Mostly the Hollywood left contented itself with celebrating the dutifulness, the uncomplaining heroism of ordinary citizens.

You can't really tell the difference between those written by Communists and those written by liberals. All you can say of this lot is that if their political sins were minimal, their rhetorical ones were heinous.

But there are three portraits of Russian life—*Mission to Moscow*, *The North Star*, and *Song of Russia*—all of which manifestly follow the party line and are particularly vivid examples of awful screenwriting.

Mission to Moscow is the most notorious of them. It was adapted from Ambassador Joseph E. Davies's memoir of his years as American envoy to the USSR, and he was actively involved in the preparation of the script (by Howard Koch, an unadmitted Communist). In it, the Purge Trials, the Hitler-Stalin pact, and the Soviet attack on Finland are vociferously defended by Davies, who is played as a sophisticated rube by Walter Huston. It also, naturally, attacks British appeasement and American isolationism, casually insists that the Soviet Union is a democracy, presents an avuncular, pipe-smoking portrayal of Stalin, and has a particularly goofy passage in which Mrs. Davies (Ann Harding) and Mrs. Molotov, wife of the Soviet foreign minister, share makeup tips while touring a cosmetics factory. (In fact Molotov's wife had once worked in the cosmetics industry—which proves, I suppose, that truth is ever stranger than fiction.)

What I remember best about the movie is another of those weirdly effective moments from Michael Curtiz. Davies and his family are passing through Berlin on their way to Moscow, and during a layover at the train station Curtiz does a linked series of tracking shots—a time-consuming specialty of his that was always driving cost-conscious Warner Bros. executives crazy—which vividly summarized the evils of Nazism: a bookstall selling nothing but *Mein Kampf*, Hitler Youth marching through the station singing a militant anthem, prisoners huddled pathetically in a corner, awaiting transport to a concentration camp. The symbolism is blunt, but it is the best of Curtiz's continuing efforts—raked camera angles, brisk montages—to pep up a movie that insists on talking itself to death.

What I was doing at *Mission to Moscow* at age ten is a mystery. Maybe its title suggested it was some kind of spy picture. More likely, my grandfather encouraged me. He had been at law school with Davies, whose career as a corporation lawyer had vastly enriched him. Grandpa wrote the ambassador a fan letter after he read his book and proudly showed me the note Davies sent back.

Curiously, I didn't dislike the movie. In those days I enjoyed movie presentations of famous living people. It seemed to me bold, even rather cheeky, to imagine their private lives. Besides, what did I know about Purge Trials? And Davies, I was led to believe, was virtually a family friend.

No other movie remotely approached the ideological fervor of *Mission to Moscow*. Mostly the movies about the Russians wanted to show them as "people who think and act as do Americans," which is the way Samuel Goldwyn put it as he was placing *The North Star* in release. It is about an all-singing, all-dancing Ukrainian village, populated by such all-American types as Dana Andrews, Farley Granger, and Anne Baxter, whose idyll is interrupted by the Nazi blitzkrieg. By the time it was released, even its writer, Lillian Hellman, devoted though she was to the Soviet cause, was disgusted with the changes imposed on it by Goldwyn and the director, Lewis Milestone. She had intended, she said, to write a semi-documentary.

What she found her name attached to was an idiotically idealized resistance drama. It is very neat and clean in the Goldwyn manner—he was a fastidious man, notorious for tidying up his sets so the audience would not be offended by reality's detritus—

and it featured Huston and Harding again, this time as the local doctor and his wife. She is tortured (off-screen, of course) to reveal the hiding place of the partisans, which include all the town's healthy males; she is seen crawling pathetically through the streets after the Germans have done their worst.

Huston's big moment comes in a confrontation with Erich von Stroheim, yet another brainy, "civilized" Nazi. He wearily deplores the ideology he claims reluctantly to serve (also as a doctor) but nevertheless drains the blood from the village's screaming children in order to make plasma for wounded German soldiers. Before killing him, Huston tells him that he hates him more than the committed Nazis because he goes along with them even though he knows better.

Again, I rather liked the movie. I could see that it was too sunny and scrubbed up. But I adored movies about tormented Europe—filled with skulky double-crosses, double-dealings, and double lives. The notion that ordinary citizens—not excluding women, children, and old folks—could go about their innocent business by day and turn into terrorists by night appealed to me. I could project myself into similar scenarios. Goldwyn, though, was so ashamed of the movie that after the war he permitted its reediting. All the ideology went, and it played on television for years, under the title *Armored Attack*, as a straightforward action piece.

Song of Russia was the most ludicrous of the Stalinist fantasias. It was written by two Communists, Paul Jarrico and Richard Collins (and directed by Gregory Ratoff), and finds Richard Meredith (Robert Taylor) as an American symphony conductor visiting Russia as the war begins. "All hail the cultural achievements of free people everywhere," says the leader of his welcoming committee, which is a not entirely unfair representation of the movie's dialogue and point of view.

The movie's best hoot is a vast Moscow nightclub, done up in MGM's grandest art deco manner. While its band plays a version of "The Music Goes 'Round and 'Round," Taylor remarks, his voice full of wonder, "I can't get over it, everyone seems to be having such a good time. I always thought Russians were sad and melancholy people—you know, sitting around and brooding about their souls." Shortly thereafter he pays the pianist (Susan Peters) he has fallen in love with his highest compliment: "If I didn't know I met you in Moscow, you might be an American girl."

The movie got Ayn Rand's cork at the House Un-American Activities Committee hearings after the war. The reactionary novelist (who was of Russian birth) remembered a dissolve from the American flag to the Russian accompanied by a music cross from our national anthem to theirs. This suggested to her that the movie equated Americanism and Stalinism. But she remembered the imagery incorrectly. The passage was just innocent movie shorthand, not an ideological statement.

On the other hand, the movie certainly did represent the Soviet Union as a fully free society with Taylor finding analogy after analogy between Soviet and American life. Somehow he misses the Gulag, the mass murder of twenty million citizens killed by Stalin. The picture now looks more naive than menacing. Even at the time one was aware of how desperate a concoction it was, straining to put a face both good-natured and ideologically instructive on its improbable narrative.

DO I THINK, upon mature consideration, that these three films and a few others (*Sahara*, *Action in the North Atlantic*, *The Master Race*) that managed a phrase or two of party-line rhetoric, a situation or two that might have pleased a Communist ideologue, presented any danger to American democracy? Hardly. None were hugely successful at the box office, and the dutifulness with which Americans took up the cold war just a few years later indicates that wartime pro-Soviet propaganda had no lasting influence.

The value of its Hollywood members to the Communist party lay elsewhere: they were an enthusiastically milked cash cow, and they offered a not entirely unreasonable hope that they might take control of the Screen Writers Guild. It would have been no small matter for the Communists to dominate a union capable of shutting down an industry that was both a major economic force and one that glamorously touched so many Americans.

That the Hollywood Communists, like their brethren elsewhere, somehow maintained their loyalty to Stalin's Soviet Union despite the very crimes *Mission to Moscow* rationalized is one of the great mysteries of twentieth-century American culture, too large to address here. There are, however, two aspects of the war, as Hollywood saw it, in which the Communists were complicit; one was a style of address, the other a matter of silence.

Wartime rhetoric is the easier of the two topics, because it became the prevailing tone of all popular culture at the time. It is present in the clipped brusqueness of Edward R. Murrow's radio reports from London under the Blitz. It is there at the conclusion of *Casablanca* ("It doesn't take much to see that the problems of three little people don't amount to a hill of beans in this crazy world"). And in the famous ad for a railroad about the kid in "Upper Four" thinking about "a dog named Shucks or Spot or Barnacle Bill" as the troop train bears him away to a premature confrontation with his own mortality: "There's a lump in his throat and maybe a tear fills his eye. It doesn't matter, Kid. Nobody will see . . . it's too dark." It is what we remember from Norman Corwin's end-of-the-European-war panegyric, *On a Note of Triumph*:

> So they've given up
> They're finally done in, and the rat is dead
>   in an alley back of the Wilhelmstrasse.
> Take a bow, G.I.,
> Take a bow, little guy.
> The superman of tomorrow lies at the feet
>   of you common men of this afternoon.

And so on. It's tough and tender—choked sentiment. It owes something to Hemingway and to the less aspiring sorts of popular fiction that imitated him. Its artfulness lies in its hints of the ineffable, which the speaker is too manly—too busy with more urgent, practical, and worldly concerns—to fully articulate, but which we know he knows about.

Maybe he'll get around to all that is left unspoken when the war is over. Maybe he won't. It's not important. What's important is that this language taught us how to accept and sustain loss without entirely succumbing to it and thus rendering us useless for the great struggle. As Philip Roth observes in *I Married a Communist*, it is a (vulgar) style that every serious writer of our generation absorbed and eventually had to purge from his—perhaps not her—sensibility, since it was pretty much a guy thing.

A good example of this manner occurs at the conclusion of *For Whom the Bell Tolls*, the timid adaptation of Hemingway's novel about the Spanish Civil War. The screenwriter was the ubiquitous Dudley Nichols, who was always, as Richard Corliss observes, rallying the masses to some sort of transfiguration. The director was Sam Wood, an anti-Communist so virulent that his will specified that his heirs take a loyalty oath before being allowed to collect money from his estate. And the project attracted the anxious attention of Joe Breen's Catholic censors, whose co-religionists had largely been on Franco's side. As far as I can remember, neither side in the Spanish Civil War is openly identified by name in the film. You have to guess at the ideology of the movie's good guys.

It stars Gary Cooper as Robert Jordan, the American college professor who, under the impress of war, has become an unlikely demolitions expert, working with partisans behind the lines. Ingrid Bergman is Maria, the innocent Spanish girl whose father, the Republican mayor of her little village, was killed by the Falangists when they occupied the town. She was herself gang-raped by them and had her head shaved. In the movie her hair is growing out in a fetching, tousled boyish way that was heavily publicized at the time.

Maria has been rescued by the partisans, and she and "Roberto" have fallen in love, consummated in the once-infamous sleeping-bag sequence—during which, in the novel at least, the earth was alleged to move when they attained climax.

At the end of this tale Jordan must supervise the dynamiting of a bridge that Franco's forces must cross in order to sustain an offensive. He succeeds, but in the course of the action he suffers what appears to be a broken leg, so that he cannot retreat into the mountains with his guerrilla band.

This strikes one as a not very good excuse for martyrdom. Surely he could endure the pain of riding a horse for a couple of hours with a fracture, given the lugubrious alternative.

But no matter. He will stay behind, armed with a machine gun, fighting a rearguard action while the others make their escape. Maria, of course, wants to share his fate. She is also naturally hysterical. Equally naturally Roberto—hey, this is Gary Cooper—is calm and resolute.

"Maria, listen. Don't . . . don't say anything. We won't be going to America this time," he says, referring to a dream they have shared. "But always I go with you, wherever you go. Understand?"

She does not. What is this desperately improvised hint at mortality's transcendence to her? But Roberto overrides her protests. "No, Maria. What I do now, I do alone. I couldn't do it if you were here. Stand up, Maria. Remember you're me, too. You're all there will ever be of me now."

More caterwauling ensues. But he persists. "There's no goodbye, Maria. Because we're not apart." He calls for Pilar (Katina Paxinou), earth mother to the guerrillas, to lead her away, then addresses his lover one last time. "No, don't turn 'round. Go now. Be strong. Take care of our life."

The girl is thrust onto a horse and is galloped off, blubbering. Roberto settles down with his gun. The last we see of him he is firing at the steadily advancing Falangists. He cries out: "They can't stop us. Ever. She's going on with me." Sound effects and music rise, obscuring his final words.

All right, all right—death is somehow transcended, each will somehow be with the other, presumably through all eternity. It sufficed to get us out the theater, blinking sadly, but not inconsolably so, in the afternoon sunshine.

But Maria is right. Live is live, dead is dead, and loss is final, not to be consoled by martyrdom, however gallant. Or by supposedly indissoluble mystic connections. Robert Jordan is about to become a crumpled heap, an anonymous body left behind on a nameless road in a half-forgotten war. She will doubtless not forget him entirely. But equally doubtless her life, imagining she outlives the war, will proceed apace. Eventually there will be another Roberto.

Yet one developed in those days an ineradicable taste for this sort of thing. It is not too much to call it the official attitude toward the war as it was transmitted to us by every aspect of popular culture. Adults might or might not take it with a grain of salt. But if you were a kid, the rhetoric was as plausible and persuasive as it was ubiquitous.

Walter Benjamin said that the aim of fascist rhetoric is to make us acquiesce in our own demise. This was democracy's literary device, aimed at achieving a similar end.

But what did I—or anyone I knew, including grown-ups—know of literary devices? I merely counted it against the adult world that no one I knew in it talked about the war in the way people did on the radio or in the movies.

WE COME NOW to a more difficult matter: Hollywood's continuing silence about the fate of the Jews in Hitler's Europe. Only a couple of times did it improve on *Mr. Skeffington* or *The Seventh Cross*—even when it earnestly tried. Take, for example, *The Hitler Gang*. It was the personal project of Paramount's production chief, Buddy DeSilva, and aimed to trace the rise of Nazism from Hitler's service in World War I through the Night of the Long Knives in 1934, when he fully consolidated his power.

Written by Frances Goodrich and Albert Hackett, the husband-wife team who would later adapt *The Diary of Anne Frank* for Broadway, and soberly directed by the usually action-oriented John Farrow, it makes extensive use of captured German footage and historically accurate reconstructions of events like the failed beer-hall *putsch*, the writing of *Mein Kampf*, even a slightly sensational presentation of Hitler's supposed infatuation with his niece, Geli Raubal. The Breen office obliged the studio to elide the fact that Hitler and the girl were blood kin as well as the generally accepted fact that she died by suicide. The script's original hints of homosexuality among some Nazi leaders were also omitted in the release version, replaced by the curious—not to say ludicrous—idea that the girl was murdered by Hitler's cohorts because she was a distraction from his great destiny.

But even so this was, by Hollywood standards, quite well-documented history. Except in one respect. It very briefly presents anti-Semitism as something Hitler rather opportunistically embraced, not the profound conviction it was. This was a place this movie simply didn't want to go.

Few did. In movie after movie, virtually every victim of the Nazis was shown to be someone who had dared to "speak out" against them, and what they spoke for was always something an American could get behind—for example, the right not to be pushed off the pavement by a storm trooper. As late as 1945, in *Hotel Berlin*, we saw a Jewish woman, wearing her yellow star, brutalized because she had strayed without permission from her "quarter" in Berlin. As if, by then, there were any Jews living openly, even in a ghetto, in the German capital.

That film was co-written by a Communist, Alvah Bessie, who recounts, in his entertaining memoir, that in discussions with the producer he had raised the point that the underground leader who takes refuge in the eponymous hostelry really ought to be identified as a Communist, since that's what such figures tended to be in reality. If he was sophisticated enough to understand that, what else, we may fairly wonder, did this veteran of the Abraham Lincoln Brigade know about life and death in wartime Europe?

Another Communist, Lester Cole, did a little better on this subject. He wrote one of the two movies I know of that alluded significantly to the fate of the Jews under Nazism. That was *None Shall Escape*, a low-budget Columbia release of 1944. It consists of a series of flashbacks from a postwar war crimes trial—a pre-

scient touch, that—which rather intelligently traces the embittered embrace of Nazism by a seemingly civilized schoolmaster:
World War I wounds, an inability to find work appropriate to a
man of his bourgeois status in postwar Germany, the drift toward
Nazism, finally, once World War II has begun, the return to the
little Polish town where he once taught and almost found happiness. He comes, of course, as a sneering conqueror—commandant of its occupying forces and a rapist besides.

This figure is well played by Alexander Knox, and the picture is well directed by Andre De Toth, a Hungarian emigré who
had lost an eye to fascist thugs in a student riot in the interwar
years. For our purposes, its crucial scene takes place in a railroad
station where Jews, awaiting transport to a concentration camp,
are urged to rebellion by their rabbi's die-on-your-feet-don't-
live-on-your-knees speech. These sentiments were proudly, self-
consciously borrowed for the occasion from La Pasionaria by
Cole, who had some trouble getting Harry Cohn to approve the
scene. Their rising is quickly, brutally put down by the Nazis.
But at least the rebels' Jewishness and its tragic consequences are
openly stated.

In that same year the same studio made another modestly
budgeted film that actually revolved around the theme of Jewish
identity and its consequences. *Address Unknown* was based on a
well-known novella of the time and was strongly directed, in a
richly expressionistic manner—it doesn't look like any other
American movie of the time—by the great production designer
William Cameron Menzies. It is about two families, one Jewish,
one not, as the Nazis rise to power. The fathers are an Aryan,
Martin Schulz (Paul Lukas), and a Jew, Max Eisenstein (Morris
Carnovsky), who are best friends and partners in a San Francisco
art gallery. The former returns to Germany to buy art for their establishment, leaving the latter to manage the store. Martin's son,

Heinrich (Peter Van Eyck), and Max's daughter, Griselle (K.T. Stevens, who was the daughter of Sam Wood), are in love, but she wishes to become an actress in the old country and returns with "uncle" Martin.

He is soon seduced by Nazism, personified by a nobleman, whose allure is seen at first to be more social than political. Under his patronage, Martin rises to a substantial position in the new Germany's cultural bureaucracy.

Griselle, though, is National Socialism's victim. She finds work as an actress, but at a rehearsal of a stage production that owes much to Max Reinhardt's *The Miracle*, the famous Weimar Era success, a censor orders her to cut portions of a religious speech consisting of quotations from the Beatitudes. In performance that night she plays the scene as written. The censor rises from the audience to denounce her as a Jew. The crowd turns riotous, and Griselle must run for her life, the SS and their dogs at her heels. She appears at Martin's home, but he refuses to take her in, and we hear shots and a scream off-screen, signifying her end.

To be sure, she is, like Mr. Skeffington, an American citizen. She might better have run for the American embassy than to Uncle Max. But the film, in this passage, is pitched at a persuasively panicked level. We believe her outraged American courage as she confronts the censor in the theater, and we believe her astonished fear as the crowd turns into a mob.

Eventually her fate—which, admittedly, only hints at the larger tragedy of European Jewry—is learned by her father and her lover in the United States. The younger man—remember he is the new-minted Nazi's son—begins sending Martin letters in what appears to be code. They are, in fact, nonsense. But they catch the censor's eye, and Martin cannot explain them. Eventually he succumbs to the police state's terror—and his son's revenge. It is a wonderfully neat, curiously satisfying ending, with Heinrich's last letter returned to him stamped with the movie's title—*Address Unknown.*

Like *None Shall Escape*, this movie was meant to play as a second feature and is less than ninety minutes long. If it does not portray the death camps, it—alone of Hollywood's wartime products—at least offers a brief vision of Kristallnacht and leaves no doubt as to the eventual fate of the Jews.

SO WHAT WE HAVE, when we come to "The Jewish Question," as Hollywood elucidated it, are two low-budget movies that garnered only minor publicity—the comedies *The Great Dictator* and *To Be or Not To Be*, which in the midst of their merriment at least hinted strongly at Nazism's most deadly agenda—and a handful of major productions that only vaguely, ambiguously suggested the vast tragedy proceeding in Europe.

Dare we condemn Hollywood on this matter? Its silence mirrored that of America's highest officialdom, which we cannot now doubt knew by the middle of the war that the concentration camps were in fact death camps. We know, too, that the Office of War Information did not think publicizing the tragedy of the European Jews was effective propaganda. It remembered the anti-Semitism of the America First movement, and it had polls showing that fully 40 percent of Americans thought the Jews had "too much power" in the United States. Like everyone else, Hollywood preferred this war to be seen as a people's war—little guys versus the bully boys. Nothing compelled it to attempt to imagine the unimaginable. Rather the opposite.

But let's, for now, not be too easy on Hollywood. Its writers in particular, but also some of its directors, stars, and producers, were not all ignoramuses—whatever fun the Eastern literary establishment made of them. If anyone in America had access to, say, the left-wing political journals where the likes of Varian Fry were publishing their warnings about the Holocaust, it was they. There was, as well, a large German-Jewish emigré community in wartime Los Angeles, and it too would have had access to the most terrifying news out of Europe. Indeed, by the middle of the war the *New York Times* (albeit in its back pages) was publishing stories that left little doubt about the Final Solution.

But set all that aside. By March 1943 Ben Hecht, at that point one of the most highly regarded of all screenwriters, had written and mounted a pageant called *We Will Never Die*. It was "Dedicated to the Two Million Jewish Dead of Europe" (a fair estimate of the lives the Nazis had at that point taken). This work, with music by Kurt Weill, was directed by Moss Hart. It played Madison Square Garden and the Hollywood Bowl among other huge venues. Its cast included at various times stars as major as Edward G. Robinson, John Garfield, and Frank Sinatra. But officially it was marginalized. Even some members of the Jewish establishment, like Rabbi Steven Wise, condemned it. Hecht—on his way to the violent Zionism that preoccupied his later years— came to feel, in retrospect, that the piece preached only to the radically converted.

But still. . . . Thanks to his and other efforts sophisticated people knew very well what was happening in Europe. It is just that, frightened of anti-Semitism, persuaded not to question our "official" war aims, only a few took up this cause. But Lester Cole could imagine the unimaginable. So could such almost anonymous Hollywood hands as Kressman Taylor and Herbert Dalmass, the writers of *Address Unknown*. And vulgar Harry Cohn, head of Columbia, had the gumption to put both films into production. The question of why other similarly themed movies neither preceded nor succeeded them has to haunt Hollywood. The question of why this silence was surrounded by a deeper, more controlling nationwide silence, has to haunt us all.

EVEN ME. Certainly no one ever spoke of the Jewish tragedy in my hearing. That silence was not meant to protect my delicate sensibilities. I truly do not believe that my parents or any of their friends knew what was going on.

But still, I think now: Suppose we had not lived where we did. Suppose we had lived in one of the several Milwaukee neighborhoods that had a substantial Jewish population. Or even in its "Jewish" suburb, Shorewood. There I imagine we would have had hints of what was happening: the relatives in Europe who suddenly fell silent; the emigrés needing help to escape and resettle; the terror, early in the war, at the apparent irresistibility of Hitler's legions; and, yes, the disgusted awareness of the casual anti-Semitism of American life.

My father interrupted my enthusiastic babble about Dorothy Lamour and her sarong one night by asking if I knew she was Jewish. I didn't, of course. He went on to say that the movies were pretty much run by Jews—the radio networks too.

My grandfather occasionally spoke of this or that legal colleague as "a good little Jew."

And places like Shorewood were, in those days, all over America, known as "Kike's Peak."

No one ever explained what difference this should make to me. I think they assumed that would become clear to me later. "You've got to be carefully taught," the song says. But often enough we were—thank God—carelessly taught.

7

Cinemaddicts

IT IS TUESDAY, July 21, 1998. I am standing in the driveway of the Pflanz funeral home in Portage, Wisconsin, with my two daughters, Erika and Jessica, and my second grandchild, Georgia Mae. She is seven weeks old and more or less permanently attached to Erika's breast.

My mother has died, less than a month short of her ninety-fifth birthday. Her friends—many of them strangers to me, except as names mentioned in mom's account of her adventures in our weekly phone calls—are gathering for the service. Some of them stop to introduce themselves, offer condolences.

In their midst a vaguely familiar figure appears, hesitates, then approaches me. He introduces himself as Danny Seyfert. He wonders if I remember him. I don't tell him that, thinking about writing this book, not a week has gone by lately without my thinking about him, wondering what has become of him, how life has treated him.

Well enough it turns out. He has worked in middle management for the Miller Brewing Company in Milwaukee most of his life and has recently retired. He shows me his employee pass, pictures of his wife and children.

He has followed my career with mild interest. He asks me if I ever actually met Walt Disney, about whom I once wrote a book. He seems reassured that I did.

Danny could not stay for the funeral. He was merely in the neighborhood, had read the obituary, and dropped by to pay his respects and, I guess, to see if I was still alive and senescent. Satisfied, he took his leave. "I've got a heart problem and my prostate's been giving me trouble, but I'm still here," he said cheerfully as he melted back into the American vastness.

DANNY! I'm pretty certain I would not have turned out to be what I am if I had not known him fifty and more years ago. My passion for the movies derives, in significant measure, from his.

He lived next door to us during the war and for a few years thereafter. He was a skinny, pale boy, perhaps three years older than I was. He always wore glasses and suffered from asthma acute enough to prevent him from playing games. Once or twice I tried to play catch with him, and he always backed away from the ball, his long, thin fingers splayed and stiff, fighting instead of embracing the object flying toward him.

He worked hard for his good grades. But he was also awkward with people, alternately shy and intense, not amusing, not easily lovable to adults. He was a loner, without any friends, so far as I could tell, except me.

I can see now that the Seyferts didn't quite fit into the Wauwatosa scheme of things. Danny's father worked, sometimes on the night shift, at one of the factories on Milwaukee's South Side. You would sometimes see him, a gentle, kindly soul, carrying his lunch pail, setting off for work at dinner time when all the other fathers were coming home. Danny's mom was, like mine, more intense than her mate and worked as a clerk at the notions counter at Schuster's department store.

The Seyferts didn't have a car, didn't take vacations, and lived in an attic apartment in the house immediately to our north. This was a blunt advertisement of their lack of local status and a particular irritant to my mother. She did not blame the Seyferts for living as best they could afford. She blamed Mr. Koch, who owned the house, for creating the situation in the first place.

She had been led to believe that our street was zoned for single-family dwellings. But Mr. Koch, who managed the high school's elaborately equipped stage, was handy with tools. And he had observed a minor variant in the zoning ordinance which permitted him to create rental units in his home. Since there was a housing shortage—all those war plants booming in Milwaukee—he decided to take advantage of it.

My mother, who did not relish diversity, ethnic or economic, in close proximity to her, sensed "an eyesore" in the making. She investigated at city hall and brought home a zoning map that seemed to show that Mr. Koch was within his rights.

She thought it might be a misprint. She consulted my grandfather, the real estate lawyer. He doubtless looked into the matter. He doubtless reported that nothing was to be done about it.

That did not deter her disapproval. Surely a moral law was being flouted here. And flouted again. For as soon as he had created the Seyferts' attic dwelling, Mr. Koch began carving a smaller apartment out of his ground floor, which he rented to a young married couple.

His handiwork offered few amenities. The attic, for example, was uninsulated, breathlessly hot in the summers, freezing in the winter. Plywood walls and ceilings had simply been laid over unfinished studs. Windows were few and small. Danny slept in what was more an alcove than a room, dark and narrow.

Downstairs Mr. Koch's teenage son, Billy, was often found lurking at night in the side yard that separated their house from ours. Mom thought he was trying to peep into her bedroom. This was not the case. Billy later confessed to me that the young marrieds led an active sex life and could sometimes be observed at their revels because they did not always fully lower their shade. "Hot Springs" was his memorably descriptive phrase.

My mother was volubly convinced that Billy was "a ne'er-do-well." She was more tolerant of Danny. Not entirely welcoming, but tolerant. My father took the same tack. "An odd duck," he would sometimes say of Danny. "Why do you want to be inside on a nice day like this?" he would not unreasonably inquire as we headed off for a Sunday matinee.

GOOD QUESTION. But I needed a movie pal, for I needed not just to be seeing movies. I needed someone to talk to about them, gossip and speculate about them. We spoke to one another's inner nerd. We shared this curious lust, this guilty pleasure. It answered the predictability of our lives.

Danny was not my only moviegoing friend. I had another regular cinematic companion, Kenny Siegesmund, who lived down the block—a quiet, intelligent boy who went on, I've been told, to an academic career in physics. But Kenny was just a nice, agreeable kid who absorbed movies as equably and dispassionately as he did everything else.

Danny, though, was certifiably movie crazy. And, given our age difference, had the power to crank me up to his obsessional level.

We usually went to the Tosa, four long blocks north, or to the Times, eight shorter blocks east. They played the same bills— double feature, newsreel, short subject, cartoon, the occasional serial (we got hooked on *Batman* in 1943). The Tosa had recently been remodeled in the moderne style and featured "love seats," chairs in which a boy and girl could sit without an armrest inter- vening. But for no particular reason we preferred the Times. It was a long, low structure, which obliged it to use rear projection. You knew the picture was about to start when the projectionist, a large, cheerful-seeming man, strolled down the aisle and headed backstage. He was always greeted with cheers from the kids who dominated the audiences on Friday nights and Sunday after- noons, when we usually went. He always carried a newspaper to read between changeovers. This was a source of some conversa- tion between Danny and me. Imagine being so blasé about the movies!

His audience was not. Admission to these theaters was eight cents when I started going to the movies, eventually rising to twelve cents by the time the war ended. Anyone could afford that.

Adults, unless they were shepherding little kids, knew to avoid these Friday and Sunday shows and their mass of squirm- ing, preadolescent energy. We rarely talked back to the screen, but there was a constant murmuring among ourselves.

We weren't critical or hostile, the way college audiences are, just restless and bouncy. We gave everything a fair chance— comedies, musicals, romances, combat movies, spy stories—and disappointments were expressed with the odd groan, maybe a whistle or two, only occasionally with a generally audible wise- crack.

The point was to surrender to a movie's thrall, be unable to shake it off on the walk home. You could imagine that the shadows might hide a Japanese sniper. Or, conversely, that you could sing and dance like Gene Kelly—though never like the more elegant Fred Astaire. We worked hard to bury our doubts, suspend our often sorely taxed disbelief.

This was a largely private drama, playing inside your own head. You didn't talk about it with your companion—especially silent Kenny. But Danny was different. He was a discusser, a chatterer. We would speculate about what we had seen—plot points, gags, how a dramatic moment or a special effect had been achieved. Or sometimes how it had failed to work persuasively. We often talked about the stars, sharing what we knew about their lives off screen.

About most of these matters we were misinformed. But this is where Danny was different from the other kids; he was determined to know more.

THE PROBLEM WAS that there was almost no reliable information easily available to us. The *Milwaukee Sentinel*, a Hearst paper, carried no movie reviews at all—only the columns of Winchell and Louella Parsons. The former was more interesting to me than to Danny, who was immune to New York glamour. Winchell's punchy, neologistic prose seemed to catch (or possibly help set) the rhythms of the city. It made me yearn to be a part of it.

Parsons's column read like a small-town weekly's social notes. Mysterious figures like Hollywood's "most eligible bachelor," attorney Greg Bautzer, flitted through her column as he fucked his way through the A-list of female stars—though, of course, Parsons never hinted at an agenda so base. Mostly she reported the dating news from such glamour spots as Ciro's or Mocambo. Approval of new alliances was often breathlessly voiced; disapproval of separations and divorces was often broadly hinted.

Rebellious stars, taking suspensions from their contracts rather than roles they disapproved, were often cluckingly scolded by Louella.

The *Milwaukee Journal* then a distinguished but culturally conservative newspaper, was even less useful. It offered brief, un-informative reviews, signed by initials, of the new pictures when they opened in Milwaukee. It also ran a "Screen and Radio" Sunday supplement, featuring off-register color pictures of actors and actresses accompanied by wire-service interviews with them. It tended to emphasize Milwaukeeans who had gone on to movie fame—Spencer Tracy, Pat O'Brien, Jack Carson, Dennis Morgan were inordinately well covered in its pages.

But still it was not enough. In this case youth was *desperate* to know more, and resourceful Danny filled the information gap. He had discovered movie magazines—*Photoplay, Modern Screen*, and the rest. He bought each new issue as soon as it appeared and shared it with me.

They had an insiderish tone. But that was just a trick of style, hiding the fact that these publications were completely controlled by the studios. In return for access to their stars, they saw to it that almost nothing untoward about them ever appeared in these pages.

The exceptions, of course, were stars who were on suspension for refusing a role. Or who insisted on having an affair with someone inappropriate. Then the fan magazines, like Louella Parsons, would express the hope that they would soon return to their senses.

In general these magazines stressed the notion that the stars—the odd yacht or polo pony aside—were regular guys and gals, leading ordinary middle-class lives. Hollywood itself was portrayed as a hardworking, early-to-bed, early-to-rise town— Milwaukee with palm trees and drive-ins.

Emphasis was placed on the fact that movie stars had to report to the studio as early as 6 a.m. in order that their hair and makeup be in place for the day's first shot three hours later. You couldn't be out partying at all hours and be ready to face the early-morning cameras.

THE PICTURE that most perfectly captured the fan-magazine vision of the industry was *Hollywood Canteen*. Ostensibly it was a celebration of the institution that famously provided doughnuts and dancing to GIs passing through Los Angeles during the war.

The movie delivered on its implied promise of showing us glimpses of the stars off-guard, being splendidly, casually human. They are observed at the canteen waiting on tables, doing the dishes, trading rather forced banter with the servicemen.

There's an amusing passage in which Dane Clark, playing the more cynical of its two protagonists, is dancing with a woman whom he keeps telling looks just like Joan Crawford. She remains coy on the subject of her identity, though of course we in the audience know who she is. When the Clark character finally discovers that she really is Crawford, he faints. We chortled hugely at this display of an innocence he had, throughout the rest of the picture, been at such pains to hide.

One gathers that a few above-the-title names were faithful canteen functionaries, but that for most of the stars it was a photo-op. They would sing a song, tell some jokes, then disappear. KP was not a regular obligation.

The day-in, day-out work of the place was done by more anonymous figures—starlets, day players, crafts people. In its way the movie was faithful to that aspect of canteen life.

For its essence lies with Robert Hutton, whose career in

those days consisted of playing good-natured naiveté. He had a prominent Adam's apple, which bobbed visibly when he gulped in amazement, which was often. At one point in the film he gets to go backstage at Warner Bros., where he is given a ride on one of Busby Berkeley's cranes. He reacts as if he's on a roller coaster. On the other hand, he has met and fallen for one of the canteen hostesses. This was Joan Leslie, who played in the picture under her own name. She had been working in the movies since 1937, first as a child actress, then as an ingenue—she had been Cooper's girlfriend-wife in *Sergeant York*, Cagney's wife in *Yankee Doodle Dandy*. She was perhaps a little too prominent to be a canteen regular. On the other hand, possibly not. She was scarcely a great star, just an agreeable one.

It was against canteen rules for hostesses and servicemen to see each other off the premises. But "Slim," as Hutton's character was known, and Leslie evade that prohibition. She takes him home. It is a little white bungalow with a picket fence around it—more small-townish than suburban. She has a mom and dad who are the souls of Midwestern sweetness. There is a porch with a glider. The soldier and the starlet kiss there. The promise of permanence is implied—should he survive the war.

Here the movie's confusion of realms nears the exquisite, for Joan Leslie was actually named Joan Brodel, and her parents and sister—who was played in the film by her real-life sister—are called by that name in the film, though her parents are played by professional actors (the ubiquitous Jonathan Hale was her dad).

Leslie had first appeared on a stage when she was three, had begun working as a full-time professional at nine (appearing in a sister act). One does not imagine that picket fences were a large part of her experience.

But I'm certain Danny and I thought the Warner Bros. crew

came over to the Leslie home to shoot the courtship sequence. It was logical; they had obviously shot Hutton's vertiginous crane ride on a real studio soundstage, and it looked as if the canteen set was the real deal too.

Hollywood Canteen is the perfect example of our prevailing muddle. We have real movie stars playing democratically idealized versions of themselves—aware of the effect they are having on the starstruck servicemen they are dancing and joshing with, yet also trying to overcome that effect, set them at their ease. We have the lesser star, Leslie, playing a somewhat fictionalized version of herself while her male peers, Hutton and Clark, play fully fictionalized everyman characters, thrust into a casually glamorous world yet treated reassuringly by it. No swells, no snobs, no high hats here in dreamland.

What was one to think? Mainly, I suppose, that democracy—the thing we were fighting for—was wondrous in its workings. And that it had attained a state of near perfection in Hollywood, where celebrities and commoners might plausibly dream of lying down together. Fame—that great awkward bundling board separating the known from the unknown—was allowed in this picture only as a joke we could all get over.

DANNY AND I bought into that fantasy. It was a way of gaining a purchase on the Hollywood mystery. It was also a way of evading it.

Hollywood's power to impose this bland vision of its life on the country is, when you look back on it, astonishing. It derived, of course, from inherent economic strength. In this period the studios annually produced more than four hundred movies per year, at least twice the number they now make. The majors

(MGM, Warner, Fox) and even some of the minors (RKO, United Artists) were also vertically integrated economic entities, controlling exhibition through their theater chains.

Isolated in far-off Los Angeles, with almost all the major talent bound to them by long-term contracts, the studios also had virtually full command of what the other media reported about their doings. This power was enhanced during the war years by the fact that Hollywood had little competition for our attention. Everything from the draft (which affected sports) to travel restrictions (which limited vacation choices) diminished the quality of, or access to, other forms of amusement. Between eighty and ninety million movie tickets were sold every week.

Danny and I were privy to any number of interesting facts: we knew that Louis B. Mayer was the highest-paid executive in the United States, that Betty Grable's legs had been insured for a million dollars with Lloyds of London, that Esther Williams had been a champion swimmer as a teenager before the movies found her.

Now and then a scandal could not be contained—the statutory rape case against Errol Flynn, Chaplin's paternity suit—and would make it to the front page of the raffish *Sentinel*. Also, surprisingly, a rumor would sometimes make its way out of Hollywood and into the heartland—the Spencer Tracy–Katharine Hepburn affair was one such item.

Still, we were kept in the dark about the way things really worked in the industry. We didn't know anything about its society or sociology. We knew nothing about the processes by which movies were actually made. We didn't quite believe the phrase of the falsely knowing: "It's all done with mirrors." But we didn't know what the alternatives were.

Here is a discussion we once had. It was about one of the

many scenes of hand-to-hand combat we witnessed at the movies between 1942 and 1945. In this one the deaths by bayonet were particularly realistic. We wondered how those could be so persuasively managed. We speculated on the possibility that the all-powerful studios might be able to recruit on death row for victims. Better to be run through on a movie set, we thought, than die in San Quentin's gas chamber.

This seemed to us not at all far-fetched. We had read about prisoners aiding the war effort by volunteering for dangerous medical tests. Why not put yourself forward for scarcely less important morale-building activities?

All right, we were dopey kids. But I don't think we were that much dopier than adult "cinemaddicts." Maybe our speculations about how those things worked in the movies were more fantastic than those of the grown-ups, but the only alternative to the industry's domineering publicity machinery was the dismissive cynicism with which the literary-political-intellectual community viewed Hollywood.

Faint whiffs of that attitude occasionally reached us. But it was based on suppositions about motives that were not much less fantastic than those pumped out by Hollywood's kept press.

Looking back from today's perspective, when what were once Hollywood's deepest secrets—a movie's gross, the sexual and addictive preferences of its stars—are everyone's business, I'm not sure we were dreadfully disadvantaged.

IN ONE RESPECT I, at least, was advantaged. For all the crazy suppositions we embraced to fill our gaping ignorance, for all the idiocy of our childish learning, somehow the notion got through to me that the movies were in one important respect just like any other subject. They presented a body of knowledge that was capable of being studied—and perhaps useful in some way that was imperceptible to me at the time.

In other words, I recognized a hunger that ultimately I would learn to feed on, a hunger for something other than junk food. I do not think I would have developed that appetite without someone like Danny to sharpen it.

There was, though, a difference between Danny's tastes and mine. Remember the age difference between us. To borrow a faintly risible term, I was in "latency" when we started going to the movies together. He was entering puberty.

This meant that my interest in movies was more practical and down to earth. Little boys like to know how things work, how people earn their livings. For example, I began noticing names in the credits—Howard Hawks, Raoul Walsh, Vincente Minnelli, Alfred Hitchcock. I began to wonder what, exactly, a "director" did. It was obviously important, since these names usually appeared alone on the last card of the main titles.

I don't want to make a claim for myself as a premature auteurist. But I did check out the two or three books the library had on moviemaking. They turned out to be out of date.

One, for instance, showed the camera immobilized in a little soundproof booth, as it was in the early talkie days. But that didn't square with the production stills we saw in the magazines, where the blimped camera was mounted on a dolly. Another volume explained the business about mirrors—it was the Shuftan process, which used them to make composite shots in the camera.

Danny was mildly interested in such matters. But I don't think his heart was really in it. His concerns were much dreamier.

He tried to take possession of the stars. Literally. When he was finished with a movie magazine he would painstakingly cut out the portraits of his favorite stars and paste them in scrapbooks. He had many of them, and they were, as I recall, cross-indexed by some method of his own devising.

He was, in short, caught up in the pinup craze. It was a fad unique to the war years: horny GIs, far from home, far from their sweethearts, tacked up pictures of scantily clad movie stars and starlets on barracks walls and bulkheads and sighed wistfully over their charms.

This habit was widely winked at. Bob Hope made jokes about it. In *Star-Spangled Rhythm* a nameless dancer (played by Vera Zorina, in a sequence choreographed by George Balanchine, who was then her husband) hops off the page a GI is mooning over and dances in his dreams. At the end of the sequence she is seen to be doll-sized in relation to him.

This carried a curious erotic charge. Imagine! A gorgeous, completely silent yet otherwise fully animate woman doing a dance of desire, who was yet small enough to tuck into your pocket. The possibilities! Some lonely night in your foxhole, you could take her out and toy with her, strip her perhaps. What protest could she offer in her silence? What defense could she mount in her tinyness?

Here, not in Rita Hayworth on the rumpled bed, not in Betty Grable peering coquettishly over her shoulder, did the pinup craze reach its apotheosis, as a form of safe sex for guys far from home.

Before 1942 one did not see many pinups. But the growth of tributary media like the newspaper Sunday supplements and the movie magazines would have created a growing demand for them, war or no war. Also, they were a handy way of "developing" pretty young contract players. The studios could write off the modest keep of their term contracts by busying them in the stills department between bit parts.

The war, of course, shone an altruistic light on this activity. For example, GI's far from home might be imagined to be nostalgic about the national holidays. So if Christmas was coming, the girls would pose in abbreviated Santa Claus outfits. If it was soon to be the Fourth of July, they'd be caught holding a sparkler or rocket or mounting a penislike rocket or oversized firecracker. As for Valentine's Day—forget it. The number of lacy hearts that surrounded these pretty faces and forms is incalculable.

The war added immeasurably to the photo opportunities. The girls could be photographed amidst red, white, and blue trimmings. Or wearing shorts as they planted their victory gardens. They might be seen in a WAVE uniform with its skirt fetchingly raised by an imaginary breeze. These objects of our boys' yearning affections were often quoted about how happy they were to do their bit for morale.

Some of them continued to pose for pinups even after they attained name recognition. Hayworth and Grable were authentic stars when they posed for their immortal shots. But generally speaking, actresses who specialized in more serious roles did not have to submit to this kind of exposure. They could draw the line at head-and-shoulder portraits.

When Greer Garson donned an abbreviated kilty outfit for her role as a music hall performer in *Random Harvest*, stills of that scene were widely printed. Captions made something of the fact that the recent Academy Award winner, usually a rather chilly screen presence, had shapely legs. Danny and I earnestly discussed that point and agreed that it was so.

It seems to me that Danny's scrapbooks concentrated on the best-known women—celebrity skin. On the other hand, skimming through his magazines we did not make fine distinctions when a good pair of gams was on display. I recall Danny saying one day, "Legs wouldn't mean anything unless they led somewhere." I chortled knowingly to hide my unknowingness.

We came close to gorgeousness only once. The Andrews Sisters made a personal appearance at Schuster's one Saturday afternoon, and we were there, each armed with seventy-nine cents to purchase a record the ads promised they would autograph. Of the three—Patti, Maxine, and Laverne—we thought Patti was the dishiest. She had a curvaceous, cheerleaderish figure and a perky manner. When they had told a couple of jokes and sang the song they were promoting—"Don't Sit Under the Apple Tree (with anyone else but me)"—we pushed into Patti's line for our autographs. The sisters were using white ink in their pens so the signature would show up boldly on the dark center of the disc. We had never seen anything like that before. But Patti signed the record impersonally—"The Andrews Sisters." We were both disappointed; it was an autograph that wasn't quite an autograph. But we put the best face we could on the day. After all, we each had in our possession an object that had been demonstrably and literally touched by fame.

I suspect Danny's picture collection had uses unimaginable to me at nine or ten years old, not yet the after-school whack-off artist I would soon become. Yet I was not incurious sexually. I was beginning to wonder what lay beneath women's clothes. I was studying the underwear ads in my mother's magazines. What I was not doing was remembering my only authentic sexual encounter.

THIS HAD OCCURRED before we moved to Wauwatosa, when we lived on the ground floor of a duplex on Prospect Avenue near Milwaukee's lakefront. I must have been three or four years old. Next door there lived a little girl of my age, with whom I often played. Even my mother's capacious memory could not summon up her name when decades later I asked her to try to remember it. She thought perhaps that the child's mother came from a family that owned a restaurant, that her father was a local bandleader.

Sometimes in the afternoon the two young mothers would pool their resources and hire a sitter to watch over the two of us while they went shopping. She was a young woman of high school or possibly college age (I was too young to make a distinction), dark-haired and soft-voiced. I can recall no other details about her.

One day, as she read a newspaper, we sat at her feet playing with blocks or some other set of small toys. Accidentally (or so I think) my hand brushed her ankle. The warmth of her flesh under the silk of her stocking. I slid my hand upward along her calf. She did not pull away or object.

My hand slid further up, under her skirt. I grasped her more firmly. I attained the bare flesh above her stocking top. I began a nervous monologue. I was a doctor. I would "fix her up." She adjusted herself slightly to accommodate my explorations. I'm not certain, but I think by now my little playmate had joined me in this fine new game.

I reached her underwear. I slid a sly finger or two into the leg of her panties. Another small adjustment in her position. I found something furry and warm and wet. I lingered there for a time. Then—gently, no words spoken—she pushed my hand away.

She never lowered her newspaper. The pretense was that she was so absorbed in it that she did not notice what I—we?—were doing.

The incident was repeated perhaps two or three times. I asked myself no questions about these occurrences. They were purely pleasurable. I felt no guilt about them, though I knew, somehow, that they must be kept secret.

My thoughts now are more of her than of me. I understand the possibility of mild perversity cannot be dismissed entirely. On the other hand, neither can a sort of innocence.

The world was less instructing in those days, before the talk shows and tabloids. The newspaper with which she shielded herself from herself would have offered no counsel about this situation; if she was indeed lovelorn, she was doubtless so in ways beyond the reach of the columnists then specializing in that condition. Nor would she have found anything like it in any book or movie she might have encountered.

Was this a peculiar, passive form of child molestation? Possibly, though obviously I was the aggressor. Anyway, that's a topic that doesn't much interest me.

I'm more interested in making up a plausible story for her. I imagine her as a young woman still living at home, unable to find the privacy in which to indulge her sexual impulses. Or maybe she was just afraid to succumb to her boyfriend's rough importunings and preferred this soft, safe outlet.

Maybe, like me, she enjoyed having a dirty little secret. Maybe, giggling shyly, she shared a version of it—sanitized or melodramatized—with her girlfriend over cherry cokes at the drugstore soda fountain, a version touched with surprise and dismay but with a moral and exculpatory coda attached.

As for me, the recollection is vivid—how could it be otherwise?—but not formative and, I know, far from singular. To judge by the anecdotes of male contemporaries, the maids and baby-sitters of America were, in that vanished age, almost solely responsible for gently absorbing the curious energies we could not name, sweetly satisfying the yearnings for which we had no words.

Now we make too much of such memories, just as we used to make too little of them—especially those that can be shaped into a retailable anecdote that seems to offer some conventional psychological resonance.

We all have our child's garden of Rosebuds, but they don't usually explain us any more satisfactorily than his lost sled explained the subsequent career of Charles Foster Kane. It's just that they work—or can be made to work—for some narrative purpose.

But as Welles himself said, upon mature reflection, that's all "dollar-book Freud." What instructs most of us—the majority who achieve adulthood without shattering trauma—most profoundly are not childhood's occasional blinding moments but its dim, long days which must be filled with some kind of imagining.

A VEIL OF INNOCENCE covers this era in American life. The official prudery of the period continues to rule our memories of it.

There was, for instance, something sanitized about most pinups. They were unnaturally contrasty, hard-edged. The women were more often than not photographed upright—peppy and cheerleaderish, not more seductively prone.

Practically speaking, these images had to be keen enough to knife through the murky processes by which most publications reproduced them. But the effect was somewhat to objectify the subjects. You were rarely seduced by them. Rather, you debated style points. Everyone was a judge in a never-ending beauty pageant where you were encouraged to look but not touch.

What was true in Danny's attic was true outside it. Wolf whistles, the occasional "woo-woo," were this contest's highest accolades. If a woman offered a serious come-on to, say, Bob Hope's movie character, he could be counted on to retreat in comic consternation. By and large, wartime popular culture drained women of their seductiveness, men of their predatory qualities.

I didn't know it at the time, because I had not seen many such films, but the war killed romantic comedy. Its purring promise—that intelligent men and women must have been to bed and must return there as soon as they worked out whatever problem briefly vexed them—was dismissed. Comedy was now more raucous, less sexually consequential.

Something similar occurred in serious drama. The high romantic style, generally historical in setting, virtually disappeared, replaced by contemporary melodramas in which losses were sustained but were bravely (and quickly) transcended by *Mrs. Miniver* or the Hilton family of *Since You Went Away*. The idea was not to let people mope, to get them up and doing as quickly as possible. Which meant being up and serving freedom's cause. To which romance was irrelevant, if not a downright hindrance.

Chances were that if a boy and girl really, truly loved each other, one of them would die. That was true in both *Mrs. Miniver* and *Since You Went Away*. Intense romantic distraction was punished. "Don't you know there's a war on?"

so, in every possible way, the official culture shyly, secretively, but authoritatively spoke. And it was an official culture. We were unaware that film, with its silver nitrate base, was classified as war materiel, which could not be frivolously wasted. We didn't know anything about the Office of War Information's censorious activities.

But there is always, of course, an unofficial culture, telling dirty jokes, spreading subversive rumor. Inevitably it touched Danny and me.

There was, for example, a remarkable Tru-Vue film of Danny's. Tru-Vues were a Bakelite variation on the stereopticon. You fed little reels of 35 mm film into a slot on the side of the viewer, then pulled a lever that placed behind the eyepieces two identical shots of the same subject, which in turn created the illusion of three-dimensionality. These films, neatly packaged in tiny red and silver boxes, contained perhaps a dozen such pictures and were sold three for a dollar at most camera counters.

Danny had a large collection of them, neatly filed in boxes also obtainable from the manufacturer. Mostly the company dealt in the same sort of material the stereopticon people had— scenic views of faraway places. They also had a line of comic strips featuring the likes of Dagwood and Blondie. But among these innocuous titles there lurked "Backstage at Earl Carroll's Vanities."

Carroll was a sort of minor-league Flo Ziegfeld, who mounted elaborate variety shows featuring comics, vaudeville acts, and statuesque showgirls. He had moved to Los Angeles from New York, where his theater was adorned with a momentarily famous slogan: "Through These Portals Pass the Most Beautiful Girls in the World."

This Tru-Vue offered glimpses of them changing costumes, painting on makeup, waiting to go on stage. Two of them were snapped bra-less. These were the first naked nipples I had ever seen. I could not get enough of them.

At Danny's I would pretend an interest in the Grand

Canyon or Yosemite. Indeed, broad-gauged scholars that we were, we shared an authentic curiosity about the world's natural wonders. Trapped in wonderless Wisconsin, we longed to experience them firsthand. I suppose the impulse was quite similar to the desire to see a woman naked. Inevitably I would get around to the Earl Carroll film.

We would discuss whether the girls had been taken unawares or had cooperated with the lensman. The idea that women might be comfortable in their bodies, easy about exposing them to the staring world, was a concept foreign to our giggly-smirky innocence.

Looking back now at that world, where all movies were oppressed by the Catholic censorship imposed by the Breen office; where David O. Selznick's struggle to use the word "damn" in *Gone with the Wind* was a legend to us; where for six years we impatiently awaited *The Outlaw* while Howard Hughes battled the censors to promulgate his wet dreams of Jane Russell; where sex was the most inaccessible of life's many mysteries, the daring of the Tru-Vue folks seemed remarkable.

Or, who knows, maybe it just slipped through—product of some carelessness or subversion in the lower Tru-Vue ranks.

SO IT WENT. Rumors abounded of a stag reel starring the very young Joan Crawford. Eight-pagers were in general, furtive circulation. They were cheesily printed comic books in which Mickey Mouse and Minnie Mouse, Dick Tracy and Tess Trueheart could be observed in merry sexual congress.

Occasionally there was erotic sustenance to be found in more openly available forms. Imagine my delight when I came across the scene in *The Maltese Falcon*—the book, not the otherwise excellent film—where Sam Spade takes Bridget O'Shaughnessy into the bathroom and makes her strip to see if she had purloined one of Gutman's hundred-dollar bills.

On the day we gathered in the junior high school auditorium to mourn FDR's death, the girls were passing around a paperback copy of Vina Delmar's *Bad Girl.* Giggling, they let us guys borrow it. The "good part" was a scene where the heroine is obliged to visit a back-alley abortionist, strip in front of him, and submit not merely to his examination but to other kinds of groping as well.

On Third Street downtown, the Empress burlesque theater flourished, and the high school guys were often there. They would sometimes repeat the raunchy jokes they picked up on those occasions—when, that is, they deigned to speak to us at all.

It was beyond their powers, though, to describe the female flesh they saw unveiled in that stale and smoky atmosphere. For that we had to wait our turn.

There was also—most important to Danny and me—the legend of *Ecstasy,* which carried this well-worn story:

In 1932 a nineteen-year-old Hedy Lamarr, then known as Hedwig Kiesler, had run naked before the camera. Through the sun-dappled Czechoslovakian woods she gamboled before plunging into a sparkling pool where she paddled about on her back, nipples poking above the water's surface. Murky stills of this sequence were occasionally to be seen.

Later she married a Nazi munitions baron named Fritz Mandl, who disapproved of this exposure. He was known to have attempted to buy up every print of *Ecstasy.* This naturally added to its titillating reputation.

Of course he failed. The movie regularly played the White House, next door to the Empress, the one local theater that dared to run exploitation films produced outside the membership of the Motion Picture Producers Association.

In the meantime, Louis B. Mayer, on one of his talent-scouting trips to Europe (both Greta Garbo and Greer Garson were netted by him on such voyages), signed Lamarr to an MGM contract.

Looking back, David Thomson finds "conscientiousness" in her sexuality, which, he adds, often wore "a worried look." It is an accurate characterization. She caught on here only briefly, mainly as an exotic conversation piece.

But that was beside the point. The point was that a famous woman—not some anonymous stripper—had appeared naked before the public. Granted she had done so before she was famous. But the evidence of her shame—or wantonness—was still available, if tantalizingly just out of our reach. *Ecstasy* drove Danny and me crazy. It was, *The Outlaw* aside, the movie we most wanted to see.

But we could never figure out a way to sneak in, however often we discussed it. I was twenty-one years old when we ran it at our college film society. It turned out, of course, to be desperately, soporifically pretentious. But such was its reputation that we made a bundle on it—enough to support our less racy presentations for a semester.

WITHOUT being able to articulate it, I think the idea that movie screens were like large, lighted windows before which everyone was a voyeur was clear to Danny and me.

Around twenty-thousand movie screens glowed and beckoned in the United States during World War II—plenty of lighted windows. One went and peered in hopefully. They made a lot of movies in Hollywood. They couldn't police all of them. Surely some carelessness must sometimes slip through.

It never did. For we reckoned without the compulsive suspiciousness of Joseph Breen and his censors. We might laugh at the notion that all of married America slept in twin beds. But we never saw otherwise at the movies.

Only a few movies of this time hinted at an alternative reality. *Double Indemnity* was one of them. We read about it, heard about it, but knew enough not to ask our generally tolerant parents if we could see it. We accepted the judgment that we would not "understand" it.

I did see *Going My Way*, the movie that beat out *Double Indemnity* for the Academy Award that year. My grandfather took me, and we chuckled and misted up at the warm-hearted doings of its fractious and celibate priests. I was not at the time dismayed that this agreeable (and fatuous) picture won the Oscar.

I understood, albeit dimly, that movies were obliged to sublimations larger than any the Bing Crosby and Barry Fitzgerald characters endured. I understood that movies needed to encourage us to concentrate on the mission, on winning the immediate victories on which the ultimate victory would be built.

Yet there was a famous, carefully posed still that illustrated most of what the production code forbade. In it a blonde, brazen and sullen, posed with her foot on a dead man. She was pointing a revolver at the stiff. A tommy gun was to be observed propped on the floor next him. Lacy underwear peeped from beneath the woman's gown. Low cut and slit-skirted, it displayed her almost naked bosom as well as the inside of her thigh. Narcotics and booze were laid out on the table next to her. The lifeless body, a caption informed us, was that of a cop, representing "the law defeated."

Everything in that still was prohibited on the screen.
We studied that picture and wondered why.
We dreamed not just of the better postwar world so many movies promised. We dreamed of one entirely different in certain largely unspoken respects.

8

The Usable Past

UNACKNOWLEDGED by Danny and me—unrecognized by us, really—our parents already had access to a better world. It lay for them in the past, not in the future. The historian Michael Kammen observes in *Mystic Chords of Memory* that the period between 1915 and 1945 witnessed a great nostalgia for the past in the United States. John D. Rockefeller, Jr., began recreating Colonial Williamsburg, Henry Ford started work on Deerfield Village. All over the country smaller roadside attractions housed collections of our historical detritus. At the same time, Kammen tells us, membership in historical-patriotic organizations, which required proof that an ancestor had endured the hardships of founding the American empire, swelled inordinately.

By European standards (and high cultural standards) it was a relatively brief (and thin) history. During the war our British allies made short, inspirational films like *Listen to Britain* and *A Diary for Timothy*, both of which featured Dame Myra Hess giving her famous morale-building lunchtime concerts at London's National Gallery. The latter contained excerpts from John Gielgud's *Hamlet,* too. Those were cultural traditions centuries old yet still vital, worth fighting for. We had nothing comparable.

But still. . . . Our history was, at last, lengthy enough to celebrate. And it contained at least some sustaining values for difficult times. I don't know how much this mattered to my mother and my grandfather, but they certainly toyed happily with their souvenirs of the past.

My mother began collecting antiques as soon as we moved into our new house. She particularly loved pieces from the late nineteenth century—sentimental Currier and Ives prints, an Empire table, a finger-carved lady's chair, and her particular love, milk glass from the Victorian era. The piece to which she gave pride of place was a dish, on whose cover a graceful girlish hand, wearing a ring with a blue stone, gently grasped a dove. Later a high school girlfriend of mine claimed to be spooked by the piece: it looked to her as if the bird was being throttled.

My mother's baby grand piano, her wedding gift from her father, dominated our living room. On it she accompanied herself as she sang "Love's Old Sweet Song," "In the Good Old Summertime," "A Bicycle Built for Two," even "Woodman, Spare that Tree." On Christmas Eve we would all gather around the piano as she led us in carols, always ending with "Silent Night."

The organizations to which mom was most devoted were the Daughters of the American Revolution and the Mayflower Society. My grandfather, an amateur but passionate genealogist, had supplied her with the ancestral credentials required for membership, and both took great pride in their lineage. He also supplied me—by dint of who knows what genealogical sophistry—with ancestral links to Ulysses S. Grant, Douglas MacArthur and, indeed, Franklin D. Roosevelt.

This heritage somehow reassured my mother. She eventually outgrew it, but in those days she was socially rather tense, ever alert to slights, ever concerned with the good opinion of her peers. But our heroic breeding was unassailable. In her mind, I think, it guaranteed our status—perhaps our future—no matter how it might be challenged.

I, the family's sole contribution to that future, am named Richard Warren, after one of our several putative Mayflower ancestors. "The only nobleman on the voyage," my mother would say rather smugly. She insisted he had sailed with the Pilgrims as a matter of principle, not out of necessity.

When I was challenged or put down by some other kid—or just screwed up—she would remind me that I came from "good people." This was of far less inspirational or practical value than she and my grandfather imagined. Yet I liked being woven into a historical skein, and I developed a taste for the confluences and coincidences of history. Perhaps that's why I was drawn to historical novels. Maybe that's why a lot of the books and television shows I've made are attempts to recreate or preserve the past, link it with the present. It is one of the ways that I have most truly remained my mother's son, and my grandfather's grandson.

ITS EASY TO FORGET that the 1940s were historically closer to the turn of the nineteenth century than they were to the end of the twentieth. My parents grew up in the parlor culture of the years preceding World War I, and their appreciation of its apparent lack of complexity was woven, ever unquestioned, into their ways of being.

They were not alone. All my friends' parents, obviously, were of their generation. So too were most of the people making movies; it was natural for them to revert to a lost and seemingly more innocent time for subject matter. *Yankee Doodle Dandy* contains a sequence that perfectly exemplifies this attitude.

It offers the fiction that Cohan retired prematurely from the theater (he was actually never long absent from Broadway) and, rusticating, began to feel old and out of it. One day some jive-talking teenagers, driving a flivver painted with comic slogans, pull into his retirement retreat, looking for directions. They treat him as a moldy fig. They've never heard of him or his songs. It is his need to reassert his relevance that propels him into his comeback. We understand, even if Cohan doesn't, that his music, his values, will never go out of style—not as long as America remains freedom's last, best bastion.

Not that the flag always had to be waved. Sometimes it was not patriotism *per se* that was challenged, just good old-fashioned personal values. For instance, *Strawberry Blonde*, another splendid Cagney vehicle. His character, Biff Grimes, is, like Cagney himself, the ambitious son of Irish immigrants, who hooks up with slick, crooked Hugo Barnstable (the estimable Jack Carson) to pursue get-rich-quick business ventures and a pair of attractive women named Virginia (Rita Hayworth, never lovelier as the film's title figure) and Amy (Olivia de Havilland), who is slightly plainer, infinitely more sensible. Biff, naturally, lusts after Virginia but loses her to Hugo and marries Amy on the rebound.

Hugo, rising fast in business and politics—he's very moderne in his wise-guy corruptibility—employs Biff and allows him to go to jail in his place when a workman is killed on one of Hugo's shoddy construction sites. Biff serves his term and returns sadder, wiser, and, thanks to a correspondence course, a dentist. He has a chance to wreak mild revenge on Hugo when he appears with a toothache. But Biff sees that his sometime "confrere" and the sometime light of his life are miserable in their marriage. The gift of his own contentment is a painless extraction of the offending tooth. The gift to us—aside from a sunny comedy with just the right amount of dark shadings—is a moral lesson.

For slick Hugo Barnstable is a good talker with big ideas—it's tempting to call him a sort of embryo Bill Clinton, since there's no moral core to the man. If he does not get his comeuppance from Biff, we at least get the right idea. Happiness is, above all, honor's derivative. And honor is always a threatened, old-fashioned thing.

TAKE, FOR EXAMPLE, the kind of character Errol Flynn tended to play. Next to Cagney, he was my favorite star. I loved his air of not giving a hoot about everything the movie seemed to be taking seriously—until at the last, redeeming moment he signed on to whatever its agenda was.

I saw him first in yet another Walsh film, *They Died with their Boots On*, a deliciously mythic account of George Armstrong Custer's tragic career. He played Custer's hell-for-leather cavalryman with perfect boyish charm, in a movie that is at pains to propose that America's manifest destiny is threatened by internal betrayal. The Indians are being riled up by the usual corrupt gunrunners and firewater dealers, and it is easy to make the analogy between them and the people who sold scrap metal to the Japanese, which came back to us—according to a particularly rife wartime rumor—in the form of shrapnel stamped with American trademarks.

But if that dramaturgy strikes one now as stale and conventional, there is, near the end of the film, a scene of heartbreaking and, to me, immortal romantic power. Custer must leave his wife for his fated end at the Little Big Horn. The bugler is sounding "Boots and Saddles," and they both sense he will not return. He insists she keep his prized watch for him. She knows it is his lucky talisman and refuses. But he breaks its chain while she's not looking and presses it on her. Then he discovers her diary, full of gloomy forbodings. She dismisses them; they're just womanly vaporings.

And now, at last, he catches her in a final embrace, offering what is, I think, one of the loveliest romantic lines in all of movie history: "Walking through life with you, Ma'am, has been a very gracious thing." He exits briskly. She swoons. And I still swoon when I reencounter that scene—not least because Flynn underplays it with such graceful sobriety.

Flynn strikes a similar note at the end of *Gentleman Jim*, which is yet another of Raoul Walsh's vastly underrated movies of this period. Its Irishry is more raucous than *Strawberry Blonde*'s, but its windmilling energy was well taken here, since the film recounts the (heavily fictionalized) rise to the heavyweight championship of the world of James J. Corbett.

Flynn's Corbett comes from a numerous, brawling Irish family in San Francisco. He is comically determined to rise in class—to become a member of the snooty Olympic Club and win the hand of a cool, bemused, constantly rejecting banker's daughter (Alexis Smith). To that end he becomes a boxer in what we might call the postmodernist manner—quick on his feet, dancing, jabbing, taunting his way through the traditionalists who are slow-witted, flat-footed, aiming always for the single knockout blow.

If you see the movie now, you can't help but see something of Muhammad Ali in Flynn. All along we know he must challenge John L. Sullivan (Ward Bond) for the world's championship. All along we know Corbett's new style must befuddle the older man. Inevitably he wins the big fight.

At a victory party, Sullivan appears to hand over his championship belt. The party goes silent. Corbett says he's glad he didn't have to fight the John L. of a decade earlier. Sullivan says he doesn't know how they might have come out back then. But no matter. "I don't know about this gentleman stuff they're handing out about you. Maybe you're bringing something new to the fight game, something it needs, something it never got from fellows like me. I don't know. But I do know this: though it's tough to be a good loser, it's a lot tougher to be a good winner."

It is a moment that represents not just the reconciliation of two proud men who have baited each other throughout the picture, but the moment where what each of them represents—old-fashioned gracelessness honorably asserted and newfangled artfulness cheekily proposed—must also be reconciled.

Flynn's Corbett is up to that moment. He thanks John L. and says: "I hope when my time comes I can go out with my head held just as high as yours." We don't doubt that he will manage that; we see beneath the jokey, egocentric flash of the man to his decent core.

So it nearly always went in these evocations of the not-so-distant past. In *Johnny Come Lately*, for instance, Cagney plays a vagabond newspaperman of wistfully philosophical temperament who is recruited by a nice little old lady (played by Grace George, a famous stage actress in her only movie role) to lead the paper in the fight against vulgar modernism—specifically a corrupt municipal government. Cagney puts aside his vagabondish ways to win this struggle.

In *For Me and My Gal*, Gene Kelly is a dancer, all flash and ego, who shirks the World War I draft because he has a chance to play the Palace. He redeems himself (and wins back the disgusted Judy Garland) by disappearing into the army and reappearing as a battlefield hero with a (curable) limp and a chastened spirit.

Even Rita Hayworth's *Cover Girl* was significantly touched by the past. She owes her modeling career to the fact that she reminds Otto Kreuger's yearning magazine publisher of a woman he loved and lost in the dear, dead days of not so long ago. Old men, contrary to Shakespeare, never forget.

Neither did Hollywood. There was a whole subcategory of musicals (*Shine on Harvest Moon*; *Hello, Frisco, Hello*; *Greenwich Village*) that strummed the old songs, plucked rather idly at the heartstrings in the old genteel way. That is to say, they played to people's nostalgia, their sense that better times had once existed, but without particularly drawing moral lessons from the past. This was a genre that persisted well into the 1950s (*On Moonlight Bay, By the Light of the Silvery Moon*).

It's interesting that in our wartime movies we did not often retreat to a past much more distant than the "Gay" Nineties (and the first decade of the twentieth century), and that that period was always shown to be socially stable. There was no mention of the class conflicts which reached their historical heights in the Progressive Era before World War I. Looking at these movies you might easily think that what we were mainly fighting for was the right to unlimited ice cream socials.

A COMPARISON with Britain may be apt. Its wartime films, widely released here, tended to be very tossed-away in their heroism. Noel Coward was good at this manner—*In Which We Serve, This Happy Breed*—ordinary chaps muddling through. A favorite English movie for me was *One of Our Aircraft Is Missing*, which recounts the adventures of a downed plane's crew as it tries to make it back home through occupied Holland. It has its heroic speeches, notably one by a member of the Dutch resistance who records his pleasure at seeing members of the master race diving under the tables when the British bombers are overhead. But

under Michael Powell's direction these moments are radically underplayed. The Germans are pretty much off-screen menaces in
the film, and the members of the resistance, passing the crew
from hand to hand, place to place, are rather like the English
themselves—phlegmatic, taciturn, homey. This is the most comforting of all the movies about underground life in wartime Europe. Yet it also remains one of the most watchable of them, one
of those old movies for which you don't have to make a lot of ex-
cuses when you come upon it now.

The same, of course, must be said for England's major
movie effort of the war years, Laurence Olivier's *Henry V*. It too
remains what it was at the time—an elegant package evoking
both that country's great poetic tradition and its great warrior
tradition in a single epic. Against all the odds, I liked this movie.
Maybe I couldn't understand all the nuances of the verse, but the
sheer elevation of the language moved me in obscure but palpable ways. I could see, too, that it was a real movie, full of bustling
action, realistic performances, and clever touches. I particularly
liked Olivier's neat trick of opening with a performance of the
play on the Globe Theater stage, then dissolving through to a
representation of Henry's real world.

And, of course, the great St. Crispin's Day speech is one of
the most powerful and moving moments in movie history. Even
in my innocence I could penetrate this metaphor, could see that
Olivier was speaking to us, rallying us to the present cause—in
words that were, of course, beyond the powers of any screenwriter to imagine.

In the midst of this pomp and glory I am ashamed to admit
that I noticed, with my kid's gimlet eye for inauthenticity, the
anachronistic power lines visible in a couple of shots of charging
knights and held that carelessness against the movie.

But so what? *Henry V* is, quite literally, an incomparable

movie, not least because of its boldness as an enterprise. To mount such a production in the desperately straitened circumstances of wartime England remains a great moviemaking feat. It is possibly the showbiz equivalent of Dunkirk or winning the battle of the Blitz—an assertion of England's unconquerability.

It is also, of course, the feat that started Olivier on the road to becoming what he soon was—actor-manager to a whole country, possibly even the world. He would later say that in his career he was happiest when he was directing movies, dealing with the logistics of vast productions, which may give us a clue as to what his best self was—an actor most comfortable with the practical and the anti-heroic. This attitude deeply informs his characterization of Henry V, who is much more a constitutional monarch (at least in his relationship to his constituents) than he is an absolute monarch. I am certain that's why, without quite seeing that actor's choice, I responded as I did to this wonderfully approachable film. It was sort of a Myra Hess concert on an epic scale.

THERE IS NO comparable American epic. Except possibly—don't anyone laugh—*Wilson*.

The comparison is not as far-fetched as it may seem. Both Prince Hal and President Woody are hard-pressed, idealistic, and heroic wartime leaders with a gift for inspirational rhetoric. More important, they are the central figures in political epics—long, intricate studies of statecraft in which each seeks to avoid conflict before finally embracing it. And *Wilson*, in its sober yet gaga way, was not without idealistic instructional aspiration.

The personal project of an impassioned Darryl F. Zanuck, chief of production at Twentieth Century–Fox, it was at the time reported to be the most expensive movie ever made. In his ambiguously supportive review, James Agee noted the "almost

Shakespearian complexity and grandeur" inherent in Wilson's story.

The trouble is that Wilson's nature was unheroic—in comparison to Prince Hal, in comparison to any movie figure you could name. He was persuasively impersonated by Alexander Knox, who could never quite get around the fact that Wilson was a dry, prissy, stiff-necked character who was eventually victimized by his own rectitude.

He needed a lot of warming up. So the movie is filled with parlor songs, football games, romance both anxious (between Wilson and the woman who would become his second wife, Edith Bolling Gault) and innocent (between one of his daughters and William Gibbs McAdoo). It even offers us Wilson and Edith serving doughnuts and coffee to doughboys on their way to France.

Eventually (it is a very long movie) it shows Wilson martyring himself, suffering an incapacitating stroke in the midst of an exhausting cross-country speaking tour on behalf of his League of Nations. It also offers a warning: we must not lose this peace as we did the one following World War I.

Agee thought the movie might prove a useful tool in Roosevelt's campaign for a fourth term. The public thought it was a bore. It became one of the larger commercial failures in Hollywood history and a source of great bitterness to Zanuck, who felt unfairly punished for his good deed.

But I liked it. Wilsonian idealism, presented in the I-can-read terms of this movie, is bound to appeal to an eleven-year-old. So did the notion of Wilson as a stiff and dignified character who could yet be softened by his large, affectionate, all-female family.

Still, this is the problem with the movie. It reduces a tragically flawed protagonist to a set of familiar, family-drama tics.

Wilson is a sort of Judge Hardy (or a Claude J. Hendricks) in the White House, stern but kindly, while his (and the League's) opponents are played as elitists, impervious to the sacrifices for a better world that ordinary American soldiers have made.

Hollywood, of course, was notorious for this sort of emotional reductionism when it portrayed famous historical figures. But if you look at this movie now, you can see that what it primarily lacks is action—a few of the spectacular beats we require when moviemakers are working at epic scale and length.

Yet the movie was not inconsequential. His very sober review of the film is among the longest Agee ever wrote; he wanted it to be better than it was. I thought at the time that it *was* better than it was. This fictive Wilson lives on in some corner of my mind, the measure against which I place all the real-life politicians I always find wanting.

IN HIS agreeable, faintly bemused manner, my father went along with mom's antique collecting, grandpa's genealogical puffing, everyone's unconsidered nostalgia. But he invested nothing of himself in it. His forebears were excluded from our family chronicle. I grew up knowing virtually nothing of them, and that was no accident, as I was accidentally to discover. He sought coherence in other ways.

As an ad man, he worked at a trade that was a signature of the century's slippery newness. Not that what he did had any of the dark glamour that was beginning to accrete around his business. One of his clients actually manufactured that entertaining—and, as it turned out, carcinogenic—shoe fitter. But most of them made valves and cylinders and baling presses, and he prepared their ads for glumly named trade publications like *Iron Age*.

He was in those days an up-and-doing sort of a man. Also up and coming. Or so he made himself seem to the community's leaders—perhaps even to himself—as he busied himself with civic chores.

When I was ten or eleven the town's leadership, seeking "new blood," encouraged him to run for alderman in our ward, though he lost to the incumbent, Mr. Pollack, by a narrow margin. He never questioned the values of the men who looked favorably upon him. When I was briefly a college radical, he grew uncharacteristically angry with me when I sneered at them. The business culture provided him what nostalgia and genealogy provided my mother: a sustaining tradition, thin but sufficient to his purposes.

Or was it? He always put himself forward pleasantly, eager to please, eager for success as it was defined in that time and place. But he was not a booster, not a Sinclair Lewis character. His nature was shy and ironic, and he sometimes came close to cynicism in his "kidding."

I think now he suspected the seamlessness of the social-historical narrative everyone had embraced, understood in his inarticulate soul that the sweet songs of the past, with their implied, contradictory promises of stability and progress, were, at best, saving lies. But he was not about to interrupt anyone's dream.

BESIDES, who could be certain we were dreaming? Maybe we were involved in a narrative that included a happy ending. Certainly it was full of happy beginnings.

For immediate example, there was the case of Claude J. Hendricks. He was the first of his family to attend college, at the

University of Wisconsin in Madison, not more than forty miles from his family's farm. After graduation he read law with an older attorney, passed the bar, and sometime in this period, in the only large romantic gesture our family history records, eloped with my grandmother, Mildred Purrington.

Yes, eloped. In the middle of the night. For all I know down a ladder propped beneath her bedroom window. They made off for a justice of the peace in a rented horse and buggy. No one ever explained to me why this was necessary. "Did you and grandma really elope?" I would sometimes ask my grandfather. "So they tell me," he would always reply.

He was for a time the city attorney in Edgerton, also in Rock County. Part of his singularity was that he was a Democrat in a state where they were, until the 1940s, the third party, behind the Republicans and the LaFollette Progressives. He liked to tell how he had once campaigned for Bryan. He and a friend would drive out from town to some one-room country school and post a sign saying, "Bryan Speaks Here Tonight." They would return at the appointed hour with a phonograph and records of the "Cross of Gold" speech. He said the yokels never complained about the trick; the technological miracle satisfied them.

He soon moved on to the West Publishing Company in St. Paul, where he edited law books and where my mother was born. Then it was back to Janesville, seat of Rock County, where he entered into a law partnership with his friend Jess Earle, who was missing a couple of fingers on one hand and used to fascinate me as a child—and juries too, I imagine—by gesturing with his maimed hand to emphasize his points. You couldn't keep your eyes off those waggling stumps.

Sometime before World War I grandfather joined what was then, and under various successor names has remained, Milwaukee's leading law firm, Miller & Mack. His connection with the prestigious firm satisfied the social ambitions he and my grandmother obviously entertained.

For they were then a young professional couple on the rise. My grandfather was one of the founders of a country club. My mother was sent to a private school, the Downer Seminary, and associated there with young ladies from the best Milwaukee families. Or so she always said.

She decided against college in order to pursue a singing career. My grandfather subsidized this whim as later he would subsidize so many of mine.

She studied with a local voice coach and sang in choirs and amateur musical productions around town. Most remarkably, she journeyed once a week to Chicago, where she was coached by Mary Garden, the legendary American diva, who was then managing the opera house that her lover, Samuel Insull, had built there. My mother did not aspire to opera but thought she might make a career in musical comedy.

She retreated from that ambition, of course. I say "of course" because women of her station usually did not go on the stage in those days—unless they were escaping a desperately unhappy home or trying to repair a sudden reversal of the family's fortunes.

Instead she met my father at that Wisconsin Club dance. In my mother's retelling, their courtship had a lost-world quality about it—trolley rides to movies, strolls in the park, sodas sipped in ice cream parlors. Sometimes, if he lingered too long at her apartment after one of these outings, and the streetcars had stopped running, he would have to walk home, a journey of several miles.

There is something more Victorian than Jazz Age in these memories, yet there is a disquieting symmetry in their match too.

For they were the products of families moving in opposite directions on the social scale. Just as her father and mother were apparently rising to prominence within the city's professional class, his family was in the midst of a slow, irresistible fall from mercantile prosperity.

THE SCHICKELS were one of the solid German families that were socially dominant in turn-of-the-century Milwaukee. My paternal grandfather was named John. In Germany the family had owned a chocolate factory. Legend had it that when he immigrated to America he carried with him a $100,000 stake.

Most curious to me, he had a brother who was an intimate of Karl Marx's during the years he wandered Europe before settling down to *Das Kapital*. No one in the family knew of this history, but when my byline began appearing in *Life* in the 1960s, a Swiss scholar, studying Marx's circle, wrote to see if I had any information about this man, who had disappeared rather suddenly from the Marxian chronicle. My parents recalled him as a mysteriously prosperous figure, rather obviously a remittance man, paid to stay away from home because of his disturbing radicalism.

He may, for all I know, have found a home in the democratic socialism that for a long time dominated Milwaukee politics. When I was a boy, two of its mayors, Dan Hoan and Frank Zeidler, were indeed socialists, virtually the last of their breed holding public office anywhere in the United States. They were an affront to my grandfather, who nevertheless once took me to hear Hoan speak at a street-corner rally when he was, much later, running unsuccessfully for governor as a Democrat. Grandpa regarded that shift in party allegiance as distressingly opportunistic. He was pleased, I recall, that only a dozen or so people turned up for the occasion, most of them rather obviously idlers with nothing better to do.

Probably my paternal grandfather would have agreed with him. In Milwaukee he and a brother-in-law, a man named Herman Toser, had a wine stube where my father would recall spending the happiest moments of his boyhood, the Sundays when he sat, wide-eyed and silent, while his father and uncle—well-padded *gemutlich* men with white handlebar mustaches—entertained cronies in their bar. A photograph of them survives, great wine barrels behind them, glasses of the stuff on the table between them. Were it a genre painting, it would surely be called "The Jolly Bourgeoisie."

We must imagine Grandpa Schickel as a man for the moment, pleased to be in the company of genial and forgiving men. Later there would be less happy business ventures. And always there was his beautiful, self-centered, fiercely demanding wife. Her name was Lily. She was "French," which explained much about her to my mother.

It was said that her spendthrift ways contributed to the decline of the family's fortunes, though that surely leaves out of account my grandfather's fecklessness. Whatever happened, my father was obliged to leave college after his first year, come home, and take a job to help support his parents. He was always wistful about the student life he had briefly tasted but never fully enjoyed. When I went to college he fretted that I was not having "fun." I think he wanted me to have a coonskin coat and a ukulele, and take sorority girls canoeing on the lake.

However pressed they were, his family kept up appearances, staying on in the family home until my grandfather died sometime in the twenties. When I was a boy we sometimes drove past the house, and it seemed to me "a mansion." It was not, of course, but it was three stories tall with a turret and a gabled roof, and it caught my imagination, probably because I could not match my unassuming father with this presuming house.

When it was finally lost, there were discoveries of furs belonging to Lily that her husband could not possibly have afforded, and a safe filled with worthless mining stocks. The Remington paintings were sold at distress prices.

I heard nothing of this when I was a child, though I inquired about the elder Schickels, largely because I felt vaguely cheated by their absence. Since grandparents were clearly a source of gifts and attention, I would have liked a second set of them.

What I did not discover until I was twelve was that this silence shrouded a secret: Lily was alive. She lived on, never more than a couple of miles from us, until the late forties, in a succession of furnished rooms and, at the end, in nursing homes, supported solely by my father. At first she tried to work, but her bad temper always caused her to be fired. Later the nursing homes too tired of her imperious ways, and, I was told, new arrangements constantly had to be made for her.

Eventually she became an almost complete recluse. She had one friend who occasionally called on her. My father visited her once a week. Finally, I was told, her muscles atrophied from disuse, and she was virtually immobilized.

I assume now that she was chronically depressed. But then her refusal to "pull up her socks," as my mother was always advising me to do in adversity, was regarded as an inexplicable perversity, a source of befuddled impatience that finally settled into an abiding anger—especially on my mother's part, since Lily was the most persistent shadow on her happiness.

There had apparently been trouble between them from the start: my mother had, after all, taken Lily's boy away at a moment when she most required his undivided attention. Reconciliations had been attempted but had failed. By the time I was inquiring after my absent grandparents, it was decided—perhaps not all at once, perhaps over the course of conversations that drifted toward this conclusion without clearly stating it—to let me assume that she too had died. I am not altogether critical of that decision. Definitive death is surely easier for a child to comprehend than the murky ambiguities of this case.

I learned of Lily's existence by accident. I was home alone one summer afternoon when the phone rang. I answered and a woman asked for my mother. I said she was out. I was told to tell her that my grandmother was ready to be discharged from the hospital. I said she must have the wrong number. I had just seen my grandmother the night before. Names were spelled, phone numbers double-checked. The hospital functionary grew increasingly irritable with my stupidity. "Just tell your mother, sonny," she finally snapped, and hung up.

When I did, mild panic ensued. She angrily called the hospital. And my father. She answered my questions vaguely and irritably. No coherent explanation of the silence they had for so long maintained was offered. And I did not press for one. The truth came out over the years.

At the time I was excited to have discovered their secret, enthralled by this mystery, this touch of strangeness in our lives. I remember telling my friends about it.

Two or three years later Lily Schickel died. I was taken out of school to attend her funeral. A small, dark room. An open casket revealing a pretty, unlined face. I glanced at it briefly, then looked away, unsettled by this waxen remnant of a life I did not know, did not understand, and, perhaps by now, vaguely resented.

My father, my mother, my grandfather, and Lily's faithful friend, a woman in a cloth coat with a fur collar, were the only other mourners. Our minister spoke vaguely and briefly. What could he say about a woman who had so decisively receded from life? Did my father cry? I think so.

After the eulogy my father, grandfather, and I, along with a couple of funeral home functionaries, were pressed into service as pallbearers, hoisting the casket into the hearse for the drive to the cemetery. I did not accompany my grandmother to her grave. I do not know where she is buried.

There was something furtive about these dim obsequies. There were Schickel relatives scattered around town. Why weren't they present? If my grandmother had only one friend left to her, my mother and father had large numbers of them who would have appeared as dutiful custom dictated. Why weren't they invited?

Shame, I think. I was clearly not the only one permitted to believe that Grandma Lily had slipped away earlier. Her death now revealed my family's long, quiet lie. And, of course, its loneliness spoke of how far the Schickels had slid from prominence and prosperity. No sense broadcasting these matters any more widely than necessary.

IN THOSE pretherapeutic days many families had skeletons in their closets, cases we would nowadays address with some sort of clinical intervention. Back then they were regarded as burdens one was expected to bear as gracefully as possible. People might mention these cases, but with sympathy for the afflicted family and often enough with an approving comment about how well they were coping.

We possibly had more such cases (albeit minor ones) than most. And we were possibly more secretive about them. There was, for instance, Aunt Liz. Just whose aunt she was I am unclear about, but my mother and father, at grandpa's insistence, gave her a home for a few months before we moved to Wauwatosa. She was supposed to help care for me. That did not work out well. My chief memory of her is sitting at her sensibly black-shod feet, one of which tapped to music only she could hear. She soon disappeared, never again to enter our lives.

Then there was Uncle Oliver, who was in some vague way connected with the Progressive movement. He was, in my mother's firmly dismissive phrase, "an old reprobate." He chewed tobacco and spat indiscriminately. He was free with advice about the necessity of good bowel movements. He came and went mysteriously.

Sometimes he would appear unannounced on our doorstep. I remember the doorbell ringing early one Sunday morning, before we were out of bed, and being sent scuttling, like a scouting soldier, to peer sneakily through the living room window to see who it was. When I reported Uncle Oliver's presence, we all stayed in bed until the ringing stopped and he disappeared.

I think now that the small size of our family made us feel tense and vulnerable. We needed a raffish aunt breezing in and out with hints of mysterious sexual adventures. Or some salesman uncle full of tall tales about life on the road. Or cousins buzzing around, breaking the odd window with a carelessly tossed ball. Anything to relieve the pressure, to turn us jovially outward instead of tensely inward.

The Petermans, Bob and Alice, did the best they could in this respect—without, of course, any of us knowing that was their function in our lives. Bob was one of my father's clients, in charge of advertising, among other executive duties, at the Galland-Henning Manufacturing Company, which made valves and cylinders. He was a tall, slender, good-humored man with a receding, dimpled chin. Alice was a slow-spoken, commonsensical woman who seemed never to lose her temper and was always sweetly interested in my doings.

They eventually had three children, but Bob always had time for me. He often joined my father and me at sporting events, and sometimes he and I would go off—just the two of us—to some game or other, since his own boys were, for some time, too young to accompany him. When I was sixteen it was Bob who taught me how to drive; my mother thought my father was "too nervous" to see me properly through that rite of passage.

I think she was wrong about this; once again my father was shut out of one of fatherhood's immemorial obligations. But Bob handled the job with his customary aplomb. He had an eccentric way with words. He often referred to his wife as "Lonesome Polecat" (or just plain "Polecat"), after a character in L'il Abner. Fading athletes were, he sometimes said, "ready for the fox farm." He adored, as I did, Max Shulman's near-to-surreal account of his student days at the University of Minnesota, *Barefoot Boy with Cheek*, and worked phrases from it into our conversations.

He was, in short (and by local standards), an eccentric. But he was also a serious man. He was nuts about locomotives, and we would sometimes park by the tracks where he would identify for me the different types of engines as they steamed by—a bewildering array of letters and numbers. More important, he had a lifelong passion for American Indian culture. In Wisconsin they were a particularly downtrodden group, and he was constantly visiting them, bringing gifts, helping them address their problems with various branches of indifferent government.

One time we spent a weekend at one of their ceremonials. It was pretty awful in terms of lodging, food, and sanitation. But the songs and dancing—as opposed to what was offered at tourist spots like the Wisconsin Dells—were rigorously authentic. We were astonished to see Bob join in the dances.

Eventually he was adopted by at least one tribe. And sometimes, when they had business in Milwaukee, members of the tribe would camp out in patient Alice's guest room and den. She never complained; my appalled mother did that for her—out of her earshot, of course. This was a "nuisance" beyond her comprehension—messy Mr. Koch writ large and, worse, accepted cheerfully by people she considered her social peers.

I, of course, came to admire this side of Bob's nature. He was casual about his do-gooding but also implacable about it. It was, I saw, quite unlike the sort of charitable work with which others ostentatiously busied themselves. It was an authentic part of his singularity. Yet it did not interfere with our two-family cookouts or the casual way we dropped in and out of each other's homes for amiable, wandering conversations. He was, to put it simply, the big brother I never had, teaching me by example that it was all right to pursue your passions, especially if you did it quietly, without calling undue attention to them. That was at least as important as his and Alice's function as an extension of our family, helping us occasionally to relieve its tight littleness.

HOW PROFOUNDLY we needed to be more like the numerous, bustling Smith family of 1535 Kensington Avenue, St. Louis, Missouri, who did not have time to dwell on their own anomalies. The movie in which they appear, *Meet Me in St. Louis,* is a marvelous one. I thought so at the time, without quite knowing why. I think so now, even though in the movie histories it has yet to receive all the credit it deserves.

That's perhaps because the film is, on its surface, so sunnily nostalgic. It upholds MGM's, that is to say, studio chief Louis B. Mayer's, most basic value, which was that the American family was always to be portrayed in the most attractive imaginable light. Mischief was tolerated but it was always curable—see Judge Hardy's infallible wisdom with Andy. Loss was also all right too, if it could be turned into an occasion for inspiration—see (as we soon will) *The Human Comedy*.

Mostly, though, Mr. Mayer loved seeing pretty people singing or dancing their minor troubles away. Which is what happens with the numerous, mildly fractious Smiths—mom, dad, three daughters, a kindly, genially eccentric granddad, and a plainspoken maid—as they pass the year before the opening of the St. Louis World's Fair in 1904.

That description, however, does not quite cover the case. It makes the movie sound as weightless as a Betty Grable or Alice Faye foray into nostalgia. In fact the film did for the screen what *Oklahoma!* had done on the stage the previous year: it permitted people to burst into song as they went about their daily rounds. No longer did a musical have to be about theatrical people who could be conveniently, realistically maneuvered onto a stage to do their numbers. Perhaps more important, it allowed the hint of a darker current running beneath the bubbling surface.

This congruence was not entirely accidental. MGM had also been a major investor in *Oklahoma!*, and it hired Lemuel Ayers, who designed the show, as one of the movie's art directors. More important, *Meet Me in St. Louis* was produced by Arthur Freed, whose "unit" at MGM was filled with Broadway refugees—including the director Vincente Minnelli—who kept up with their first love, the musical stage, and were anxious to in-novate in a form that had grown as stale in the movies as it had in live theater.

The film's equivalent to *Oklahoma!*'s disturbing Jud Fry was, curiously, memorably, a six-year-old child. She was called Tootie, and she was played by the uncanny Margaret O'Brien, who was as neurotically troubled here as she had been in *Journey for Margaret,* in which, playing a war orphan adopted by Americans, she carries a live hand grenade around with her until she finally accepts her rescuers' affection.

She was one weird little kid, but not unrelievedly so. *Meet Me in St. Louis* hints that she may just be going through a difficult stage. She has, for example a charming moment when she and her older sister, Esther (Judy Garland), do a comedy song, "Under the Bamboo Tree," at a family party. As Stephen Harvey says in his fine book on Minnelli, "The child's deadpan minstrel shuffle is irresistible because she lacks the mechanical aplomb of a Shirley Temple; O'Brien captures instead the clumsy exhilaration of a kid allowed to stay up late and show off for her elders."

Mostly, though, the movie does not elide Tootie's strangeness; a lot of the time it runs on it. She has, to put it bluntly, a morbid interest in morbidity. She maintains a cemetery in which she buries her dolls when she imagines they have died. One of her pranks involves placing a lifelike (we should perhaps say deathlike) dummy in the path of an oncoming trolley car, hoping to cause a fright. When "The Boy Next Door" (to identify him by the wistful song the smitten Esther sings about him) tries to rescue Tootie from the investigating police, she hints that he may have molested her (though the movie quickly backs away from that idea).

She is also taken up with a Halloween ritual in which the neighborhood children "kill" adults they conceive to be their enemies by throwing flour in their faces when they answer their trick-or-treat doorbell ringing. Tootie volunteers to "kill" the most menacing of these figures, the Brokoffs. They are not, of course, evil—just an old couple who keep to themselves. But the child works herself into a state of truly alarming hysteria as she approaches the Brokoff home, and Minnelli's camera (and the score) draw us deeply into her fear and exhilaration. After she succeeds in her attack she chants, "I'm the most horrible, I'm the most horrible." She has to be put to bed to quiet her over-wrought nerves.

Throughout, the movie plays Tootie's strangeness perfectly. It is noted. By the Smiths. By the audience. But we all conspired not to worry too much about it, not to let it dominate our attention. It was seen as something she'd "outgrow," which was adult-hood's often-expressed hope for their children's foibles.

The film reaches its emotional high point with the "Have Yourself a Merry Little Christmas" sequence. By this time the family patriarch, the mildly choleric but otherwise indulgent fa-ther Alonzo (Leon Ames), has accepted a good new job in New York, obliging the family to abandon its well-tempered routines and jeopardizing various romantic hopes. There is a bittersweet holiday ball, from which Tootie and Esther return home dis-traught. The irony of this jolly affair being their last outing with dear friends is too much to bear.

As Garland sings a downbeat version of the song that would become a sort of wartime anthem—its about the struggle to stay cheerful far from the comforting routines of home—they are looking out on the yard where Tootie has made a family of snow men, women, and children—frozen Smiths. As the song ends, she rushes out and destroys this surrogate family with a wildly flailing broomstick.

When her father discovers what she's done, he vows to abandon his new job and remain in St. Louis. "We're going to stay here until we rot," he says grimly, abandoning his dreams for the less vaulting ones of his family. It's a disappointment the movie brushes past. A father's career never counted for much in Hollywood, not in comparison to warm family sentiments.

The picture was a huge hit—three of its songs became stan-dards—for its gently implied theme resonated powerfully with wartime America. The Smiths' stability, like that of millions of Americans, was threatened, their dear little world imperiled by forces seemingly beyond their control. Yet their ordinariness prevailed.

SOMETIMES I think about Alonzo Smith's sacrifice. I project him into a real life and wonder if he came to regret abandoning his ambition. I think perhaps he did—once the kids had grown up and his wife, Anna (Mary Astor, of all sexy people), were rattling around that big old house all by themselves.

That's because sometime during the war my father was faced with a similar decision. There was the hint of a job offer in Chicago, the details of which I never knew but which he decided to "look into."

Poor man. How could he have imagined that he could pry his wife and child away from their settled ways? Or from Claude J. Hendricks? Chicago was less than a hundred miles away. But to grandpa it might as well have been New York. Or Perth, Australia.

I don't think dad ever went for a formal interview. His opportunity blew away as quickly as it had blown up. Nothing more was said about it. Eventually, though, there were consequences.

My father was in those days a compact, vigorous, and dutiful man, with soft, questioning eyes and a sharply beaked nose, always taking me with him on his Saturday errands, which sometimes included visits to his office, where I was allowed to speak into his Dictaphone and then play back its hollow, squawky approximation of my voice. Or patiently tossing balls of all shapes and sizes back and forth with me—he loved sports and had a nice easy coordination when he played games. He had run the hurdles in high school and a favorite story was of his shorts coming down in a race, with him hobbling off the track red-faced, clutching them.

His favorite spectator sport was football. And in season he would take me to high school games around town—not just Wauwatosa High's games but those of the city schools, particularly West Division, which was his alma mater.

Once a year we would pile into the car and drive to Madison, some ninety miles west, to see a University of Wisconsin game. The Badgers had a great team in 1942, almost winning the "mythical" (as it was then called) national championship—beating Ohio State in what was billed as the title game, then, typically, being upset by lowly Iowa in the rain the following Saturday. You learned a lot about being a graceful loser following that team in those days.

Most of the time, of course, we followed them on the radio, which was hard for my grandfather, who did not believe in the forward pass. He would have agreed with Woody Hayes's dictum that only three things can happen when you throw the ball, two of which are bad.

Of all colleges, grandpa had a special hatred of Purdue. When he had been a student at Wisconsin he had gone to the train station to welcome home the Badgers after a loss to the Boilermakers at Lafayette. They had limped off the train heavily bandaged, some of them on crutches. This convinced grandpa that Purdue was a congenitally dirty team. He told that story every year before the Purdue game. It was like his prejudice against Illinois drivers. He believed they all drove recklessly and attributed this failing to the flatness of the neighboring state, where the curveless, hill-less roads did not impose a decent caution on them.

Another special treat was our yearly visit to State Fair Park to see a Green Bay Packers game. The team played half its schedule in Milwaukee at a harness racing track within the fairgrounds, and bleachers (where we always sat) were erected facing those covered stands. Pro football was not what it would become after television took up with it. It was a raffish, low-paying enterprise, highly suspect in our family.

Neither my father nor my grandfather thought it entirely proper for young men to play games for money. They felt that football should belong exclusively to their bright college days—sun-swept stadiums, cheerleaders, marching bands. After that they felt the players should be getting on with their grown-up careers.

In truth there was something slightly grim about these Packer games. In memory's eye it was always grey, with the threat of rain in the air, when we somewhat suspiciously took our seats at State Fair Park. My father often grumbled about the kind of football the pros played. The phrase "aerial circus" was sometimes muttered. That style belonged, he thought, to the Southwest Conference and similar faraway places, which probably lacked the manpower—possibly the manhood—to play the game Big Ten style—three yards and a cloud of dust.

I suppose I agreed with him in principle. On the other hand, the Packers had an authentic immortal playing for them—slender Don Hutson, an uncannily graceful pass-catching end out of Alabama, who also kicked extra points and field goals. We saw him play on the day he set a long-standing single-game NFL scoring record. To improve his mobility he wore special light pads, which the sports writers often remarked on. You could see—although I didn't at the time—football's future in his clever fleetness.

Baseball was exempt from the family strictures against professionalism; it had always been primarily a pro sport. Milwaukee had a good minor league team, the Brewers, who played in the Triple-A American Association. One of the things we dreamed of happening in the postwar world was a major league ballpark, a major league team. Both of which came to pass. In the meantime we felt bound by civic righteousness to deplore Borchart Field, where the Brewers played; it was a small old wooden park, seating no more than ten thousand fans.

But Borchart Field was wonderful in ways that impersonal County Stadium (itself now torn down) never could be. It had exactly the ambiance of the retro ballparks everyone (including Milwaukee) is now building. You were close to the action, and the lights for the night games were excellent—imparting an uncanny whiteness to the home uniforms, an unnatural green to the infield and outfield grass. Come to think of it, it was rather like a Technicolor movie—just a little brighter, a little more hard-edged than conventional reality.

For a few years the club's president was Bill Veeck, soon to become the best, the wittiest owner in major league history. He had lost a leg early in the war, but still he stood, at the end of every game, at the park's main entrance, speaking cheerfully to everyone he knew, which included my father and eventually me. He always wore an open-necked sport shirt and had a politician's gift for remembering names.

It is a gift that has generally eluded me. Yet oddly I can still recall some of the player's names from those long-ago summers. Ted Gullic, "old reliable" in center field. Heinz Becker, the hard-hitting first baseman, always being called up to the Bigs and then sent down again. Hal Peck, the fleet outfielder whose promising career was cut short by a hunting accident in which he lost some toes. Of them all only Eddie Stanky made good in the majors. But it's odd, isn't it, how these minor league names cling to memory when so much else is lost?

Perhaps one owes this recall to Mickey Heath. He was the team's broadcaster, and when the Brewers were on the road Mickey, who had once played first base for them, would do "reconstructions" of the game, creating full word pictures of a contest taking place in Louisville or Toledo, based on bare-bones telegraphic reports. His fanciful embroidery, accompanied by sound effects, was known by everyone to be a fake. But we were at least as enthralled by his technique as we were by the progress of the game, frequently speculating on the sources of his seemingly miraculous gift of gab.

I suppose he was something of a paradigm for me, transforming dull factuality into something colorful and dramatic. It was a minor skill compared to writing a novel. On the other hand, Mickey had to create his tales on the spot, in public, with no time for musing, no opportunity to reconsider the ill-chosen or inaccurate phrase. Ronald Reagan dined out for decades on tales of his misadventures in this kind of sportscasting. It was a part of his charm to which, secretly, I responded.

For it is no secret that from the time radio was invented, little boys—and big boys too—have borrowed the breathless manner of sportscasters for their interior monologues, using it to give import to their amateur athletic strivings or to provide a fictive dramatic arc to a solitary practice session around the hoop, or throwing a tennis ball against a wall and fielding the rebounds. To condition the tonalities of a generation's inner voices is no small achievement.

I think, sometimes, that I might as easily have become a sportswriter as a movie reviewer, my interest in games in those days being absolutely equal to my interest in movies. I don't know why that didn't happen. I guess we don't choose our preoccupying ephemera. Somehow it chooses us. Also, of course, there is the matter of resonance—of a relationship to the ordinary emotions and narratives of life that movies offer and that sports, which are always somewhat out of the ordinary, do not.

What they offered instead were companionable outings by which our even keel was steadily maintained. We were content. And we were prospering—even I could discern the signs of our increasing comfort. This air was maintained for years—until I finished college.

AFTER I had been working in New York for a couple of years, I was summoned home. My father had suffered a "nervous break-down." After several years of social and professional withdrawal he began to shake and itch uncontrollably. He was hospitalized and given shock therapy. But he was never his old wry and vigorous self again. He remained nearly mute and entirely passive for the last twenty years of his life.

Depression, says the cliché, is anger turned inward. The cliché applies to this case. He was, I believe, speechless with rage, but it was a rage he now deemed pointless to express. Instead he found himself towed along in my mother's ever-churning wake, parodying his former agreeableness with his silent, slow-motion assents to her plans.

Around 1970 he quit his job—he had only one faithful client left—and my mother became the curator of something called the "Surgeon's Quarters" (it was the remnant of an Indian fighting army post) in Portage, Wisconsin. There she came into her own, busily proselytizing for her roadside attraction, building attendance, making herself well known with her many interviews and appearances on its behalf. Mostly he watched television. Or held the newspaper before him, pretending to read but not turning the pages.

In those years I recalled a scene from my childhood. My father and I were in the garage beneath the house, preparing to go out on our Saturday errands. My mother shouted some instruction down the stairs—I don't recall what it was—but it irritated my father. He shouted something back. Soon they were quarreling passionately—very rare with them—yelling back and forth, unseen to each other, from the top of the back stairs and the bottom. Before long she won the argument. Whereupon my father let out a bellowing scream of frustration. And began beating his chest, like Tarzan of the Apes. It was frightening, this attack upon himself, this admission not of a single failure of assertion but, as I came to believe, hundreds of them.

There was something dad wanted—a wider stage, a larger freedom, perhaps even a touch of fame—that he did not know how to describe or achieve. I later wondered—what if he had taken that job in Chicago?

When my byline began appearing in magazines in the 1950s, I became aware that there was more resentment than pride in my father's response to what I was doing—not so much of my success, such as it was, but of my escape. He finally, obliquely, confessed to it. "I always wanted to do something like that," he said softly.

"Like what?" I asked, thinking perhaps he had wanted to work on magazines too.

But no, his ambitions were not that focused. "Oh, you know, go off to New York . . ." He paused dreamily. "The big time."

I think it's the saddest, sweetest thing he ever said to me.

For a long time my father's last years, when he was so cut off emotionally and so often embarrassing to be with, colored my memories of him with disdain. For a long time I feared his condition might be inheritable, that I might follow him into silence and suppressed rage when I reached my late fifties.

That did not happen. And I finally stopped worrying that it might. Recently—especially as I have worked on this book—my father has been restored to me as he was when I knew him first and knew him most lovingly—gently, persistently doing his best for us all, affectionate, cheerful, without pomp or artifice and above all hiding the doubts that finally overwhelmed him.

I THINK OF HIM sometimes as Johnny Nolan. Of the Brooklyn Nolans. Where the tree improbably grew.

James Dunn won a supporting actor Academy Award for playing him in Elia Kazan's adaptation of *A Tree Grows in Brooklyn*, Betty Smith's best-selling autobiographical novel. And he deserved it. His Johnny is a gentle, soft-eyed charmer, as wistful as an old Irish ballad. But he is also an alcoholic, working erratically as a singing waiter and fantasizing stardom. Some night, he dreams, a Broadway producer will hear him and hire him and make him famous.

His wife, Katie, has had quite enough of that nonsense. She has—in Dorothy McGuire's fierce and fearless performance—children to raise, a house to hold in hard-pressed circumstances. She is perpetually angry at her husband's feckless ways—hard, bitter, suspicious.

Not so her daughter Francie (Peggy Ann Garner). She adores her father, listens rapt to his tall tales. When the eponymous tree, clinging to life in their tenement's backyard, is threatened, it is he who consoles her. The tree is like the Nolans—tough, bound somehow to survive in the concrete wilderness.

Oddly enough, just such a tree—a tree of heaven—grew for a time in our front yard. It was, in reality, an annoying thing. Its buds stank and fell to the ground all at once. The same thing happened with its seeds and, in the fall, its leaves. It was like an untrained dog. You periodically had to confront the messes it made. My mother finally decreed that it be uprooted, which it was.

Possibly, in different circumstances, Francie would have been less enamored of the tree and its symbolism. For dreamer though she is, she is as much her mother's daughter as she is her father's, practical and hardworking. With her younger brother, Nealie (Ted Donaldson), she collects scrap on the street to sell for a few much-needed pennies, drives hard bargains with the neighborhood shopkeepers, and in one of the movie's best sequences gets the family a free Christmas tree.

She embodies the movie's message, which is that you must dream and aspire, but you must also work ceaselessly to attain success. In other words, you must combine both Johnny and Katie's best qualities, without succumbing to their worst ones.

Francie knows the odds are stacked against her, against all the Nolans. But she is still willing to read every book in the library—starting with the As and ending with the Zs—because she intuitively understands that for her the words they contain hold the power to change her life.

The movie reaches its turning point one night when Johnny, promising reform, evoking the sweetness of their early days, works his magic on his wife one last time. The result is a pregnancy—and harsh self-condemnation on Katie's part. The Nolans move to a cheaper apartment. And on Christmas Eve Francie is told she will have to leave school and get a job to help the family survive. Her father disappears, determined to find steady work. He dies (of exposure to the winter elements) in the attempt. He is richly mourned at his funeral by everyone who had been touched by his unfailing good nature.

It must be said that Johnny Nolan ends up in the right place in *A Tree Grows in Brooklyn*—in the country of myth. It is a place from which he can inspire without being the exasperating inconvenience he was in life, a place where his remembered charm can remain forever unsullied by hard reality.

Except, perhaps, by the woman who is carrying his child. When Katie goes into labor only Francie is present, and McGuire—always an underrated actress—pours out her panic and bitterness to the child in a great scene. She did not wish to be what she has become, a harsh, isolated woman, alienated from her children and the rest of her family (which includes Joan Blondell's cheerfully bigamous Aunt Cissie). She asks Francie to read her one of her school compositions—it is a tribute to her father—and she sees that Francie has it within her someday soon to be the woman she wished to be, her practicality tempered by an undaunted aspiration.

Reconciliation is now at hand. Cissie, who has been banished for her waywardness, bustles back into the fold to assist in the birth of the child. Later, Lloyd Nolan's stable, yearning neighborhood cop makes his romantic attraction to Katie known. Francie graduates from grade school. At the ceremony a bouquet of flowers, bought by her father before he died, is delivered. Hope—the immigrant and first-generation American hope for their children's future—is, if not entirely fulfilled, firmly promised.

It is, I think, a near-to-great movie. Partly that's due to Elia Kazan's direction. It was his debut film, and he was obliged to shoot it entirely on the Fox backlot. Even so, he achieved a locationlike realism that is entirely persuasive. He also got performances out of his cast that matched his *mise en scène*'s grittiness.

In later years Kazan would say that every movie needs some luck to succeed, and that this movie's luck was Peggy Ann Garner. Doubtless he is right. She is luminous in her openness with all her emotions. But you can't discount McGuire's remarkable ferocity or, for that matter, Dunn's doomed charm. Together they give the movie an authentic poignancy, a blend of anger and forgiveness that is unique in American movies of its time.

Certainly I took it to heart. This is somewhat surprising. A lower-class Irish Brooklyn family was far more distant from me than, say, the Waspy, middle-class Smiths of St. Louis—a city not unlike Milwaukee—were. I must have identified with Francie, her passion for reading and writing, her sense that they somehow offered her a way out. I may also have seen in her parents' marriage something akin to my own mother and father's marriage. My dad was not as dreamy and damaged as Johnny, my mom not as disappointed and damaged as Katie. But still . . . yes . . . their tensions (and yearnings) were completely recognizable.

9

Human Comedies

NOT ALL—maybe not most—of the problems addressed in movies of this moment were as complicated as those worked through in *A Tree Grows in Brooklyn*. Some of the best movies presented us with very simple issues, more conveniently within the range of childish sympathies. A boy's horse gets sick, his dog gets taken from him; we could, as we would now say, feel their pain, even though *My Friend Flicka* took place in far off Wyoming, *Lassie Come Home* in still more remote Yorkshire.

Possibly one took these two movies so particularly to heart because both starred Roddy McDowall. This was a great age of child actors—O'Brien, Garner, Elizabeth Taylor—all of whom were more naturalistic than their 1930s predecessors. But none was more believable than MacDowall.

He was, I guess, small for his age, because even though he was about five years older than I was, he was generally cast as my contemporary. He was also English, which caused him to struggle with his accent when he played an American like Ken McLaughlin in *My Friend Flicka*.

But that was a minor inconvenience compared to the authenticity of his playing. Many years later Pauline Kael would refer to his "magical seriousness," a phrase that exactly captures his salient characteristic. He was always a brave little boy and a grave little boy—a kid going about the hard business of growing up, alert and watchful but without any apparent desire to enlist unusual sympathy in what is, after all, a normal process.

Yet he seemed to be speaking directly to me in ways that most movie characters did not. In *My Friend Flicka* he was, like me, an only child and he was, also like me, a kid often lost in his own thoughts—not so much rebellious as isolated by his dreaminess.

Early in *Flicka*, Ken's father, Rob, played by Preston Foster, reads him his report card. All his grades are failing, and he has received a zero in English composition because he got to staring out the window and never put anything down on the page before the bell rang. Unless he somehow makes up the work, he will have to repeat his grade when school starts again in the fall.

I was just a year away from such a threat—after having scribbled all over my arithmetic workbook instead of neatly doing the problems. Already the "no" box on the "Working to Capacity" line of my report cards was always checked.

Yet there was good stuff in both of us. People always mentioned that at the parent-teacher conferences. It just needed to be brought out. "Discipline" was a word I often heard. As did Ken.

In order to instill that quality in the lad his (seemingly) hard-assed father insists that he spend a couple of hours a day studying in his room—with all of summertime Wyoming outside beckoning to him. When he does get free, he manages accidentally to stampede the horse herd, almost sending the hard-pressed ranch's only assets over a cliff.

His mother, played by Rita Johnson, insists that responsibility will cure him of his inattention. She prevails on her husband to give the lad a colt of his choice to care for and raise. The boy, naturally—and much to his father's dismay—picks a filly with dubious blood lines—a good sire, but a dam who has been touched by a strain of wildness. She is thought to be a jughead, untrainable. He names her Flicka ("girl" in the Swedish spoken by one of the ranch hands) and he slowly gentles her.

Unfortunately she has hurt herself trying to break through a barbed-wire fence. Her wounds infect, she sickens disastrously, and the father orders her destroyed. The ranch hand delays the execution. That night the boy slips out of bed and finds Flicka lying in a stream, trying to cool her fever. He slides into the water and cradles her through the dawn.

This ordeal makes him ill, but the horse is now able to stand with the aid of a sling, though the father remains determined to put her down. He, however, turns out to be not such a hard-ass after all. He is touched by her brave struggle and ends up guarding her through another night, eventually killing the mountain lion that has been stalking her. His son hears the shot and believes Flicka has been destroyed. He accepts that necessity. He is on the way to manhood, a role that is full of sad, stern dutifulness.

When he is well enough, though, his father carries him down to Flicka's pasture and there is the horse, well and handsome and trotting up to the boy, trotting up to a happy ending.

My Friend Flicka is a movie without visual or rhetorical flourish. Even the beauty of the Western landscape is unstressed. It simply exists as a stage for useful instruction. The conflicts in the McLaughlin family are unambiguously but unsentimentally marked out. The father, we learn, was a West Pointer, which accounts for his stiffness. The ranch is in financial trouble, a point made more emphatically in the Mary O'Hara novel—which, with its sequels, quickly found a place on my shelf—than in the film. He is stubbornly trying to make a go of horse ranching—you can see where his son got his determination to stick with seemingly lost causes—when everyone says he should be in cattle.

But he is gruff without being cruel, and his wife is gentle without being simpy. Over the needlework that keeps their rough old clothes in repair, or preparing healthy breakfasts that can sustain a man through a long day in the saddle, she murmurs patience, faith in her son's potential.

The movie shows ranch life as hardworking and taciturn, with room only for brusque and sidelong sentiments. Even when the colt is under a death sentence we are not encouraged to blubber over her fate. We have previously seen a horse die in this movie, and no great fuss has been made of it.

Kael says this is "one of the rare children's movies—old or new—that doesn't make you choke up with rage." That may be because it was not particularly conceived as a children's movie. It was just an inexpensive program picture of the kind studios routinely made in those days for anyone—man, woman, or child—who happened to drop into the neighborhood theater when the bill changed.

Lassie Come Home had a more overtly sentimental agenda, enhanced by the fact that Eric Knight, author of the book on which it was based, was killed in the war just before the picture was released. This gave MGM the chance to post a sober dedication to his memory in the main titles. It also had an unmistakable metaphorical resonance for its wartime moment. But again, it has McDowall's redeeming presence, and also that of Donald Crisp, an actor of similarly thoughtful reserve, playing his father.

The story, set in the last years of the depression, finds the Carracloughs—father, mother, and only child—living in a stone cottage near a Yorkshire village. The father, Sam, has long been out of work. The family's only asset is Lassie, a handsome and highly intelligent collie. Every day, as school is about to let out, she trots over to meet the Carraclough's son, Joe (McDowall), and accompany him home. The townsfolk literally set their watches by the dog's daily journey.

But there is no choice; Lassie must be sold so the family can survive. The local nobleman, the Duke of Rudling (Nigel Bruce, typically kindly and slightly befuddled), buys her. These passages of the dog's sale, her parting from Joe, her desperate attempts to reunite with boy—the duke's kennel master is stupid and mean-spirited and does not take kindly to Lassie's digging her way out of her cage or jumping the fence to keep her daily appointment—are even now unbearably poignant.

Finally, the duke, his niece (Elizabeth Taylor in her debut), the dog, and his keeper remove to Scotland for the summer. There Lassie languishes—until Taylor "accidentally" frees her and she begins the odyssey that consumes most of the movie's running time. She fords lakes and rivers, suffers hunger, thirst, and torrential storms, is shot at by poachers, takes refuge with a kindly old couple and with Edmund Gwenn's itinerant Tinker, whom she helps fight off robbers (his own dog, the brave, tiny Toots, is killed in the fray). Finally, in a mighty leap to avoid dog-catchers, she sprains a leg but still manages to limp home.

It's a journey of some six hundred miles, in the course of which several people recognize that Lassie, for all her affability and helpfulness, is a creature on a mission. Which is rewarded. The duke sees that her loyalties cannot be deterred, so he fires his kennel master, hires Sam to replace him, and rich and (formerly) poor live happily ever after.

The wartime metaphor is obvious: long, perilous journeys can be survived. We can—some of us—come home, no matter what the odds. The movie is the better for never mentioning its implied message. It is also the better for the refusals in McDowall's and Crisp's playing.

The latter is firm and sad. He has no choice but the painful one of selling the dog. He can only offer his son the cold comfort of utter necessity. The mother, well played by Elsa Lanchester, makes good-riddance noises, but you can see her heart isn't in them. As for Joe, he occasionally weakens in his resolve to accept the enforced separation from Lassie, but never for long and never weepily, angrily, hysterically. When, in the course of Lassie's odyssey, we cut back to the pining boy, he is in a rather delicately stated depression. He's all right, but he's not all there.

For example, there's a birthday scene in which the parents give Joe a fine pencil box which they obviously can't afford. They make him guess what the gift might be, and the wild hope that perhaps they have arranged Lassie's return springs up in the boy. The pencil box is a poor substitute, but he does his best to appreciate it. "It's champion, dad," he says.

The movie is like *My Friend Flicka* in that its sentiments are simple and true—hard times may make for hard lives but need not necessarily harden our hearts. It is also like it in that California locations stood in for authentic locales. But that really didn't matter. Unlike so many movies nowadays made for the family trade, it offered no special effects, no alternative realities. It needed only to touch authentic ground somewhere to make its main point, which was that our only entitlement is honorable toil and the modest satisfactions it purchases.

When the Carracloughs are robbed of those rights, the toll is palpable: Crisp's heaviness when he returns home after another unsuccessful search for a job; his wife's testiness when she is obliged to offer Joe bacon drippings instead of jam for his teatime toast.

It is possible nowadays to see the Carracloughs as English variants on the "greatest generation" theme—decent people doing what they must do in order to survive, inuring themselves against hardship, choking back the softer sentiments. But one can also simply like them for their uncomplaining ways, the manner in which they show their unhappiness but speak only rarely and haltingly of it.

WE HAD A DOG. He was an affable, not-too-bright black cocker spaniel, whom we never succeeded in training to heel and who was thrown into anxious frenzies by thunderstorms. I am ashamed to say that he was named, by my mother, Little Black Sambo, after the irredeemably racist children's book. I did not even dimly perceive there was anything wrong with that.

But then, I did not understand that Amos 'n' Andy were black men. I thought they were just funny guys, with funny accents, who ran a cab service in a mythical place called Harlem.

Sambo was a birthday present, given, I suspect, in somewhat the same spirit that Flicka was given to Ken McLaughlin— as a way of teaching me responsibility. It didn't exactly work out that way. He was a sweet-spirited little guy, full of a sort of panicky affection which, eagerly panting and drooling, he offered equally to everyone in the family.

But it was my father, not me, who bonded most closely with him. It was he who did most of the dog walking, saw to his shots and grooming. When Sam's end came, when I was in high school, it was my father who made the last trip to the vet's with him. I mostly did the ear-scratching and ball-tossing.

Curiously, Sambo one day revealed, quite unwittingly, the

tensions our family mostly kept buried. It was early on a summer's evening. I was idling around our front steps while my father was walking the dog. There was an open field across the street and down the block where we played sandlot football and baseball. A fairly steep bank, five or six feet high, separated it from the sidewalk. Sambo liked the scents up there, and he was amiably pursuing them when my grandfather turned the corner of Milwaukee Avenue and headed up our street.

I headed down the block to meet him. Sambo spied us both, barked a greeting, and tugged sharply at his leash. My father lost his balance and was pulled down the bank, briefly losing his grip on the leash as the dog bounded streetward. Dad recovered and gave the dog a smart smack with the leash. He yelped. Grandpa yelled. Dad yelled back.

"You damned young pup," grandpa cried—meaning my father, not the dog. More words were exchanged. My father's position basically was that the dog was our dog and grandpa should butt out. I fell into tearful panic and ran home to mother. I had never seen these two men be anything but polite to each other.

Grandpa stalked on to our house. Dad stalked on up the street. I ran after him, begging him to apologize. He was still steaming. But eventually he returned. "If I said anything, dad . . ." "That's all right, Eddie . . ." Peace was restored. Sambo curled up on the sofa, oblivious to the trouble he had stirred.

As I look back it seems to me that the dog, like all the rest of us, was trapped in the tightness of our family and showed his confusions more openly than the rest of us could. We didn't even have what the McLaughlins and the Carracloughs had to relieve their pressures—the vast and beautiful landscapes of Wyoming and Yorkshire where they could lose themselves in untamed beauty. We stepped out of the house onto sidewalks, every crack of which I knew.

WE HAD a country place too. But it was a little bit like the dog: not entirely satisfactory. No one—except occasionally, and out of grandpa's hearing, my father—mentioned its many inconveniences and inadequacies as, for two weeks and three or four weekends every summer, we grimly attempted to relax and have fun in Fulton, Wisconsin.

Fulton was an unincorporated village about seventy miles from Milwaukee. We drove to it on two-lane country roads. We always stopped at a roadside spring in Genesee Depot for a drink of water. From that wayside you could see the roof and chimneys of the summer house Alfred Lunt and Lynne Fontanne maintained there. I had no idea who they were, except that they were famous stage actors and spent their summers far from that fame in bucolic, starless Wisconsin, where Lunt had been born. Later I found out that the likes of Noel Coward and Gertrude Lawrence visited them there.

During the war you would sometimes see prisoners of war, with the letters POW stenciled on their shirts, being marched under guard along this road. They did farm work. They seemed as exotic, as out of place, as the Lunts.

Fulton was situated halfway between Evansville and Edgerton, those lodestars of my grandfather's youth. It had a one-room schoolhouse and a small church facing each other across a semikempt green. There was a country store—O. P. Murwin and Sons, General Merchandise—and the Yahara ("Catfish") River curved through the town passing beneath two iron bridges. An electrical substation sat across the road from our house, its generator powered by the flow of water from a mill pond fed by the dammed river.

Our house—actually, of course, it was my grandfather's, admired by him since boyhood—was two stories, green-shingled with white trim, with three pine trees towering over it. It was electrified, but that was the extent of its amenities. It had no phone, furnace, or running water; we pumped water from the well that stood under an arbor, halfway between the kitchen and the barn.

That water was not potable. Drinking water was carried out from home in jugs that formerly contained Coke syrup and was kept "down cellar," where it was cool and damp. I didn't like going there because of the nasty, musty smell—which could not compare to that of the toilet. It was in the barn and was basically of the outhouse variety. It stank horribly despite the chemicals grandpa dumped down it every day.

My grandparents slept in separate bedrooms upstairs—two weeks of relief from grandpa's snoring, according to grandma. My mother, my father, and I retired every night to cots on a sleeping porch, where it was nearly always cool and often rather unpleasantly damp. The power station hummed us to sleep every night, and thunderstorms frequently woke us. Two or three times a summer, they drove us indoors.

I awoke every morning to the smell of grandma's boiled coffee. She would make a hearty breakfast, and then we would all be shooed outside to the barn, where there was a glider, a workbench, and not much else. We were not allowed to return to the house, which my grandmother spent the rest of the day furiously cleaning. If I had left a book inside I would knock on the kitchen screen door and she would say, "What do you want, Dick? Don't come tracking in." She would then fetch whatever I needed, grumpy at this interruption of her ritual purifications.

In the mornings I would read in the sun near the pump. Then I might shoot at a coffee can hung on the barn wall, using my Red Ryder B-B gun, which I was not allowed to shoot in the city. Grandpa kept a shotgun in the barn. He would occasionally take it down and shoot at the birds in the pine trees. "Damn grackles," he would mutter.

Sometimes I would shoot some baskets at the hoop tacked shakily to the back of the barn. Or toss a football or baseball around with my father. Grandpa would do gardening chores, and I would occasionally tend my victory garden. I raised bumper crops of carrots and radishes. In the late morning my father and I would drive into Edgerton to buy the state editions of the Milwaukee papers.

At noon, two or three of us would wander up to Murwin's to buy lunch—some bologna or mortadella or swiss cheese, bottles of pop, fresh Wonder Bread a couple of times a week. Our tables were nail kegs lined up in front of the barn glider.

In the afternoons my parents would sometimes "go antiquing," and I would accompany them. They encouraged me to collect old military hardware—powder horns, mainly, but also a sword or two. I even had a flintlock rifle. All this stuff was obtainable for a few dollars apiece in those days, and it would stir my interest for a few minutes. Mostly, though, I was hot and bored on these trips.

Once every summer we would make a full day's journey to Janesville and Beloit, nearby cities with populations of 20,000 to 25,000. My father had a client in Beloit whom he felt obliged to call on—mostly, I suspect, to spare himself a day in Fulton. Each city had bookshops where I browsed. In one of them the manager observed to me that Alfred A. Knopf published the handsomest volumes. I had never before thought about such matters as binding and typography.

Some afternoons my father and I would go to the park in Edgerton, where we replenished our water supply from a tap. A tank was parked there as a sort of war memorial, and I would clamber around on it.

The park also had two tennis courts that were never in use. There my father taught me the rudiments of the game I still love. He had been a player good enough, in his day, to survive a round or two of the state tournament. But in one of his many sacrifices to family harmony he had given up tennis for golf, which he disliked, because for a time that was my grandfather's game.

Sometimes on these trips my father would reminisce about his boyhood summers, which he had spent on Lake Pewaukee, outside Milwaukee, swimming and sailing and socializing with the other well-to-do young people. He would wistfully contrast that life with what Fulton offered. You couldn't swim in the river—the bottom was too muddy—or even fish in it, since it contained mainly catfish, which had not attained their recent fashionability and were deemed inedible in our house, though the locals seemed to like them.

There was, naturally, more anger on this subject than my father dared show. How he must have hated these vacations: the knee-to-knee closeness with in-laws he saw too much of anyway; the sleeping arrangements that precluded sex; the restless driving about in search of diversion; perhaps, above all, the frustration over the fact that he could not afford to provide his wife and child with vacations of our own.

A few minutes before six every night we would set out for "The Girls." These were the spinster Raymond sisters, Edith and Louise, and their permanent house guest, the yet more elderly Nan Wallen. The Raymonds had gone to grade school with grandpa, still owned the family farm outside of town, and during the depression had begun offering country-style meals to people from the surrounding towns, out on their weekend drives. This they no longer did, but grandpa paid them to provide our evening meals.

The food was hearty and plain—chicken, roasts, lots of vegetables from their farm. The boredom for me reached exquisite heights on these occasions. But they were, I think, the high point of grandpa's day. For in the girls' dining room he was the local boy who had made good in the big city, and he was encouraged to expatiate on political questions—local, national, international.

He didn't know anything but what he read in the news magazines and his books-of-the-month, but he could pull this information together into forcefully opinionated packages. The girls were, I think, Republicans, but they listened respectfully to the challenges he offered their decorous conservatism. I generally slipped out of the room between courses and sat on their side-porch glider.

Sometimes I was joined there by Colonel Wallen, who came every summer to visit his sister. He was a retired army officer, a stern, silent, white-haired man with a splendid handlebar mustache. We did not speak, we just rocked gently while we awaited dessert. I think the colonel slightly cramped my grandfather's style. In his taciturn soldier's way, he was, I think, mildly contemptuous of grandpa's civilian prattle.

The colonel was an intriguing figure. He lived in Baltimore and still consulted, during the war, with the army on mysterious matters. At this time, late in life, he obtained a Ph.D. in Greek literature from Johns Hopkins. One year he showed us his thesis, a slender volume filled with impressive quotations printed in Greek. Most important to me, though, was the fact that as a young officer the colonel had done this remarkable thing—he had participated in the pursuit of Geronimo and his renegade band.

He did not mention this to me. His kindly sister, a bent, wrinkled, dark-complexioned woman, brought it up one time.

She had long ago visited her brother at some fort in Arizona and there had seen the great Apache warrior in captivity. She described his extremely long fingernails and sent shivers through me.

Odd to think that one could have a living link to Geronimo. Odd to think that at the soldier's home in West Allis, where I was occasionally taken by my mother, who did some charitable work there, you could see a handful of Civil War veterans, standing shrunken in their blue Grand Army of the Republic coats, wearing their medals, at the evening retreat.

COMPARED TO the vast array of electronic entertainments available to my grandchildren, these fascinations don't sound like much. But figures like Colonel Wallen or O. P. Murwin of the general store stirred my imagination. Ollie's son, Chet, actually ran the store, but the old man was always around. He had a club he liked to show me and far-fetched tales of long-ago encounters in which he used it to good effect on unruly customers. I didn't believe him. But I didn't quite disbelieve him, either. It didn't matter: the very language of old men like Ollie Murwin, rich in disused slang, hinted at the enigmas of a past not yet entirely disappeared.

The interpenetration of early and late twentieth-century ways was particularly vivid in Fulton. We had a radio to gather around at night. There was a movie theater in Edgerton that we very occasionally attended. We got about smartly in our well-tuned cars. But some houses were still lit by kerosene lamps. The few phones in town were party lines and had to be cranked in order to gain the operator's attention. Some farmers still plowed their field with draft horses, just as Edward G. Robinson did in

Our Vines Have Tender Grapes, a movie purporting to be about farm life in Wisconsin.

It comes as close as any fiction I know to capturing the quality of life we tasted every summer in Fulton: a couple of bright, restless kids (Margaret O'Brien and Butch Jenkins) filling their dull days as best they can while their parents eke out livings on marginal farms. The film begins with the kids idly shying stones at a squirrel, which O'Brien accidentally hits and kills, much to her consternation.

I had a similar experience. One day Dickie Berg, who lived across the street, and I were shooting my B-B gun at some birds in the fallow field behind our house. I killed one of them, and my response was exactly like O'Brien's—tearful agitation followed by long guilty thoughts. Innocents taking the lives of innocents—it is a poignant thing. I have never since aimed a gun at a living creature.

The movie, which was written by the ever-busy Dalton Trumbo, is languidly episodic. The kids squabble over some roller skates that O'Brien's character receives as a birthday present; they have a humble Christmas redeemed by the warmth of their many friends; she is awakened by her father in the middle of the night to see a circus pass through town, and he bribes a handler to let an elephant pick her up with his trunk; she and Butch are almost killed when their improvised boat (it was actually a wooden bathtub) is caught in a nearby river's spring flood.

The film's climax is a fire that consumes a proud, rich neighbor's fine new barn (and his herd of prize cattle, trapped in the blaze). At church the next Sunday, James Craig's "editor" (he owns the local weekly, reveres the simple life, and is having trouble getting the smart new schoolteacher from glamorous Milwaukee to share his small-town life), calls for donations to help the afflicted farmer. Everyone hesitates until O'Brien offers her pet calf to him. The floodgates of generosity then open—and the schoolteacher sees the virtues of the simple life.

It's a typical Trumbo trope. When he wrote movies in those days, his communism often manifested itself as communitarianism. For him it often took a village to solve a problem, whether it was the small Chinese town rescuing the Doolittle raiders in *Thirty Seconds Over Tokyo* or the group of female war workers sharing sugar rations and nylons in *Tender Comrade*.

That seemed fine to me. It was fine with everyone in those days. For it was made to seem a traditional American response to trouble, not a radical one. And our small towns—the occasional *Kings Row* or Sinclair Lewis novel to the contrary notwithstanding—remained, in popular culture, permanent bastions against the false glamour and slippery values of the big cities.

EVEN PRESTON STURGES, the most sophisticated filmmaker of the moment—maybe of any American moment—understood that. For some reason I saw none of his movies when I was a child—he was a taste I acquired later—but his two movies about small-town life revolve around the fundamental good nature and common decency of their citizens asserting itself, albeit it with comic crankiness.

The first of them, *The Miracle of Morgan's Creek*, is the story of a ditsy small-town girl, Trudy Kockenlocker (Betty Hutton), who goes out with a soldier, suffers a blow on the head that renders her partially amnesiac, and ends up pregnant. She claims she married the guy, but she can't remember where or what his name was (Private Ratskiwatski is the best she can do) or even what he looks like. She tries to get mild-mannered 4-F Norval Jones

(Eddie Bracken) to be his surrogate. That doesn't work out, for various farcical reasons. But on Christmas Eve Trudy delivers sextuplets (topping the famous Dionne quintuplets by one), and celebrity trumps tragedy.

The picture made the Breen office squeamish, but it succeeded with most critics and with the audience. We learn from Diane Jacobs's fine biography of Sturges that even General Eisenhower got a kick out of *Miracle*. What's interesting is that in the hubbub surrounding the picture's production and release, no one—not even the Catholic censors, preternaturally alert to impiety—noticed that it could easily be read as a sly retelling of the Christmas legend.

Ratskiwatski remains as invisible to everyone but Trudy as the Lord himself was to everyone but Mary; we are entirely reliant on her word about his immanence. Norval is, of course, the clueless but complaisant Joseph. The (multiple) births occur on Christmas and constitute a miracle comparable in modern terms to that of the Savior's delivery in a remote stable. In this scheme the world press's gaga response is the equivalent to the Magi; the gifts it bestows on this "holy" family are indeed more valuable than any the Wise Men offered—the forgiveness (and the forgetfulness) that is so often modern celebrity's by-product. What more appropriate place for all this to occur than a small American town, perpetual avatar of our innocence?

Hail the Conquering Hero is more perfectly crafted than *Miracle*. Sturges himself said it contained fewer "mistakes" than any of his films. It offers Bracken as Woodrow Truesmith, son and grandson of great war heroes, who has himself been discharged from the Marine Corps after a month's service because of hay fever. He is ashamed to return to his hometown, Oakridge, writes a letter to his mother suggesting a dangerous secret assignment that will prevent further communication, writes another letter to his girlfriend breaking off their engagement (he pretends to have found someone more glamorous), and settles down to a job in a shipyard.

At a bar one night some Marine veterans of Guadalcanal (led by that Sturges favorite, the incomparably choleric William Demarest) persuade him to don a uniform, grab some medals, and return home a "conquering hero." They assure him that the gag is harmless, just something that will restore his spirits and relieve his mom's anxiety.

But a careless phone call alerts Oakridge, and Woodrow returns to a huge celebration—and an invitation to run for Mayor. The town buys and burns the mortgage on the family home, and his girlfriend (wonderfully played by Ella Raines, as a flat-voiced realist, very like Veronica Lake in *Sullivan's Travels*) forgives him. Woodrow, however, is the true smithy of his soul; he confesses all at a town meeting. And is rewarded for his courage with everyone's admiration. He will get the girl—and the mayoralty—after all.

The comedy is wonderfully rambunctious, full of sharply played Sturgesian types—the nonsensically prating mayor, his feckless son, his sardonic adviser. Sturges loved our provincialism but refused to sentimentalize it. He would crowd his frames with his superb stock company of grotesques. He would play long, strolling scenes where, virtually without cuts, people—especially his boys and girls—earnestly, goofily talked through their dreams and desperations. By these means he captured, better than anyone, a country on the cusp of modernism, looking back longingly, looking forward nervously, uncertain whether traditional values or their opposite would prevail.

Sturges heard America squawking and caught in those

voices not just a comic tone but a moral question. He had been raised largely in Europe by an aesthete mother and had returned to his native land with an ear eagerly attuned to its idioms. He would often set his people to arguing over grammar and usage, because I think he heard something endangered in our language—something cranky, individual, old-fashioned that was threatened by the onrushing glibness of the newer rhetoric, driven by advertising and public relations (see *Christmas in July*, which is precisely about this subject).

NO ONE ELSE in the mass media perceived that threat. So far as the movies—or the *Saturday Evening Post*—were concerned, small-town America was the undying symbol of our stability.

In 1943 two movies, *The Human Comedy* and *The Happy Land*, used virtually identical devices—a ghost and an approximate reincarnation—to make this point. The former, based on a story by William Saroyan, who also turned it into a best-selling novel, is narrated by the dead father of the Macauley family—typical Americans living in typically American Ithaca, California. Played by Ray Collins, this ghost keeps a wry, forgiving eye on the family's doings and even appears in a few scenes with them, visible to the audience but not to his relatives.

The Happy Land, written by MacKinlay Kantor, another popular fictioneer of the time, is about a small-town druggist (Don Ameche) who loses his son, Rusty, in the war. He is bitter and inconsolable. But at his darkest hour his grandfather, a Civil War veteran (Harry Carey), returns from the dead to show him all the good things Rusty died defending. These immemorial entitlements include the right to join the Boy Scouts, play football, picnic in the nearby woods, graduate from high school.

These kindly spooks suggest, of course, an unshakable continuity between past, present, and future, a continuity that not even death can sunder.

But in case you have any doubts on that matter, both movies introduce surrogate sons to carry on the tradition. In *The Human Comedy* the eldest Macauley son, Marcus (Van Johnson), is a soldier, the kind of lad who leads his lonesome barracks comrades in consoling song—folk tunes and hymns. He makes particular friends with Tobey (John Craven), an orphan lad, filling him full of the details of family life in Ithaca. We understand that Marcus is foredoomed—all that goodness must be unjustly rewarded.

It falls to Homer Macauley (Mickey Rooney), who works as a delivery boy at the Postal Telegraph station, to bring home the War Department telegram informing his mother of Marcus's death. But as he approaches the door, there stands the orphan, whose knowledge of Ithaca and the Macauleys' life there is encyclopedic. He is Marcus's perfect replacement. He's even better than Marcus in that he can marry his sister, Bess (Donna Reed). Homer is so taken by Tobey's appearance that he puts the fateful telegram in his pocket and escorts him into the house, into the family's continuing life.

Something similar occurs in *The Happy Land*. After his trip through town, down memory lane, the druggist encounters a sailor (Harry Morgan) who was one of his son's shipmates. He tells him that the last time he saw Rusty he was struggling to carry a wounded man up a ship's ladder. Had he not been so burdened, he imagines Rusty might have made it to the deck and safety. On the other hand, what else would one expect of a Boy Scout and a football player who always put the team first? He died—no question about it—defending the values he had absorbed—no conscious learning required—in this little Iowa town.

Needless to say, the druggist invites the sailor home. The movie ends with them sharing a glass of his homemade Loganberry wine.

Death, where is thy sting? Grave, where is thy victory?

THE CONSOLATIONS and continuities proposed by these movies were sneered at by sophisticated critics, but in truth they played on authentic sentiments. Or, at the least, on generally un-examined premises. We spent our summers in Fulton because of them.

The facts of our case, discovered by me imperfectly and in-crementally over the years, are these:

Around the time I was born, my grandfather's smooth rise in his law firm was stopped—stopped short of a partnership, stopped short of the respect and prosperity that would have come with it. Beyond the fact that he had had some undescribed falling out with one of his firm's principals, I was never able to discover exactly what occurred.

But it was then that he bought his country house with an eye to converting it to year-round use and practicing law in Edgerton. There was a modest library of untouched law books in a small room off the kitchen. The story I heard as a child was that the stress of his big-city career had proved hard on his health.

This was plausible. The fantasy of a retreat to one's uncom-plicated roots is—or used to be—a common one. When I be-came a professional journalist in the fifties, it seemed that almost every older man I worked with entertained the dream of buying a small-town weekly and settling down to an autonomous proprietorship far from the big city's pressures. None of them fulfilled that dream.

Neither did grandpa. I don't know why, since none of the inconveniences of country living daunted him. He had been using outhouses since he was a boy.

Perhaps he clung to the hope that the breach at the firm could be healed. Perhaps the good salary and the prestige of his association was a factor. Maybe he could not bear the shame of so public an admission of failure. Possibly he did not like the idea of living away from daily contact with his daughter and her family.

I wonder if, perhaps, he saw the handwriting on the wall. People still live in small towns, of course, but in dwindling numbers and with no effect on how the nation—it's become more of a media community, hasn't it?—thinks and feels.

Now corporations like Disney create old-fashioned small towns out of whole cloth—virtual stage sets on which to enact empty nostalgic scenarios. Promotional literature speaks of "A place where the biggest decision is whether to play Kick the Can or King of the Hill. A place of caramel apples and cotton candy, secret forts and hopscotch on the streets."

If you choose to live in Disney's Celebration (Florida), you had better love Kick the Can. For when you sign your deed you also cede all meaningful political decisions to the ruling corporation. It is a place where a lawyer would have nothing to do but draw wills—and possibly handle a few divorces.

I FOUND OUT a little more about the mysteries of grandpa's career when I was in high school. The circumstances were comic-melodramatic. I was the editor of the *Cardinal Pennant*, the school yearbook. One day I discovered that, behind my back, the publication's faculty adviser, a geography teacher named A. J. Drost, had conspired with some of the staff to gather and publish baby pictures of prominent seniors. They had not told me because they knew I would think it a really dumb idea.

Mr. Drost was a man without children of his own, and so he put a certain obsessive interest into the *Cardinal Pennant*. It was, as people often said, "his baby." I challenged him about the pictures. He remained adamant. Hot words were exchanged. I quit.

I'm pretty sure I thought I was acting like a movie hero, risking all for principle. I didn't see that this fight predicted dozens of others I would eventually have; journalism's love of baby pictures—I'm speaking metaphorically, of course—has always stirred my contempt.

I reported my moral triumph at home. And the worst family storm of my life ensued. My mother yelled furiously at me for a long time. Then she fell into a withering silence. This was a Friday. She did not speak to me all weekend long. It was like one of those sitcom incidents. "Ask him if he's done his homework," she would say to my father, in my hearing, and he would dutifully repeat the question. Or, "See if he wants more mashed potatoes."

I tried to reason with her. I tried to joke her out of her mood. I appealed to my father for intercession. Nothing would placate her. On Monday I slunk into Mr. Drost's office, apologized, and got my job back, but never my pride in it.

But that's beside the point. In the course of her rage, mom asked me, "Why do you think your grandfather is a bitter old man?" This was news to me. He never gave the impression of harboring dark secrets.

I asked what she meant. She covered her tracks. "Something

at the office—some stupid principle he stood up for." She would say no more. Decades later I again asked her what had gone wrong for him. She claimed not to remember.

Maybe by then she really had forgotten. But I suspect she still had not come to grips with his dashed dreams and perhaps a few of her own. In any event, this professional failure explained a lot about him.

There was, for example, the matter of his "rests." For a few years, when he appeared for his nightly visits, he would immediately lie down on our living room couch, tent his fingers on his chest, and close his eyes. The radio could be played, but I was given to understand that he was not available for conversation. After a half-hour he would arise and resume normal social congress.

I was told that these silences were decreed by "doctor's orders." So was the single postprandial cigarette—a Marvel, extracted from a pack with a rooster on it—that he smoked as joylessly as if it were a pill he was ordered to take.

These therapies were supposed to steady his "nerves." People's "nerves" were often under threat in those days, and it was thought to be in bad taste to inquire how, exactly, they were frayed.

In time the rests and the smokes were abandoned. Grandpa took up lawn bowling. Its canny, Scottish calculations seemed to have a soothing effect on him. More important, he threw himself into Masonry.

I have reason to be grateful for that passion, since it diverted his attention from me. He was out at mysterious Masonic gatherings a couple times a week and became a thirty-third-degree Mason—an honorary degree that entitled you to wear a lapel pin, which he always did. He also became the right honorable grand commander of something called the Knights Templars. It was a statewide office. To its functions he wore a bemedaled blue uniform, a ceremonial sword, and a cocked hat adorned with white feathers. He looked like the ruler of the Queen's Navee.

The year he headed the Knights Templars, the entire family attended their annual review in the Milwaukee Auditorium— bands, drill teams, the works. Grandma had a new dress and wore her fur piece. Masonry's great occasions salved her social ambitions; she would spend weeks planning what to wear to the them, consulting with my mother and various functionaries at Schuster's.

A white formal jacket was purchased for me to wear, and there are newspaper pictures of us sitting in the best box seats, looking solemn. The governor of the state dropped by to pay his respects.

Looking at these pictures now, a line my friend Jane Howard, the writer, once purred as she took some snapshots of my own brood comes back to me: "Last tragic photos of the nuclear family."

There's a picture of grandpa and me. He is pointing something out to me, and I am following his finger with my eyes. He is wearing his fancy hat. My hair is cut "straight across the front," as mom always instructed the barber. I hated that haircut; it was so babyish. Mom insisted it was a practical necessity, because my hair was fine and unruly. Later, and well into adulthood, I wore an ugly crew cut, which made me look like a Nazi noncom.

Grandpa stood to take the salute as his troops passed in review. At first I was thrilled by the occasion, being the center of all that attention. Then I became bored and restless. What my father thought, decked out in his rented formal wear, I do not know. He had resisted grandpa's entreaties to join the Masons. Later on I would do the same.

Still later some Catholic and Jewish women I knew would

mention hurrying fearfully past Masonic temples when they were girls. They had been told the Masons would abduct them and subject them to unspeakable rituals.

I BEGAN TO UNDERSTAND that there was something not quite right about grandpa's obsession with me. As a teenager I became dismissive of his opinions, advice, and dogged attentions. I am sure I must have hurt his feelings. But he was ever patient and somewhat annoying in that mode, something like a jilted lover who refuses to get the message.

When at last I moved away to New York to begin my adult life, I became angry with him. I spoke of him contemptuously to my friends. When he died I did not go home for his funeral.

I thought I had become his opposite. I have joined no social or fraternal organizations. I have only a sardonic interest in politics and rarely vote. I am anti-religious. I avoid the countryside on vacations. I am now a grandfather myself, and though I adore my grandchildren I see less of them than I might and try not to interfere in their lives.

On the other hand, I have his taste for abstraction. I grumble as he did about things like bad driving and errant forward passes. I am all thumbs when I confront machinery. I am often shy and abrupt in company and have no use for "twaddle." I have conducted my career rather cautiously. Such successes as I have enjoyed have been rather like his—not all that that they might possibly have been.

IN THE YEARS before he died I used to see Roddy MacDowall in Orso's restaurant in Los Angeles. I knew him slightly, and we always exchanged pleasantries. As an adult he had become a reliable character actor, particularly good at conveying a silky sort of menace. He had also grown up to be a famously convivial and widely loved figure in show business. He was always the center of a happily chattering group.

Had I known him better I might have told him how the kind of sober, solitary kid he had once played had influenced my taste for self-containment, for keeping to myself the things that mattered most. But the opportunity never presented itself. And, besides, that extraordinary child had apparently outgrown his exemplary self, had become what most of us become, an ordinary man making a living, in the process doing as little harm, as much good, as possible.

10

Every Time We Say Goodbye

EXCEPT FOR our trips to Fulton, we went nowhere during the war. Gas rationing and overcrowded trains were the excuse. But even without the war we would have stayed close to home. That's the way we were.

We were caught in the diurnal as well as the quotidian, though we instinctively understood the calendar to be wrong. We knew then what we continue to know; that January First is a purely arbitrary and largely irrelevant interruption of America's true annual round, which begins immediately after Labor Day, when, the year having petered out in August's swelter and torpor, we are reenergized by the beginning of the school year. It's a fresh start that is, if not bred in the bone, at least taught—and never forgotten—by the new pencil box, purchased as a treat for enduring the boredom of late-summer shopping for knickers and hi-tops.

The Washington Grade School, where I was enrolled two years before the war started, and from which I was graduated in January 1945, eight months before it ended, was well appointed and carefully tended. It was a yellow brick building on Sixty-eighth Street, three long blocks (up and down a hill) from our house.

Entering it the second day after Labor Day you always found the hardwood floors newly scraped and polished, redolent of fresh varnish. It had a gym, a music room (where I never learned to carry a tune), an art room (where I never learned to draw), a welcoming library (where I liked to help shelve books), and an audio-visual room, where once a week we were shown an Erpi Classroom Film.

The Erpi logo featured a globe spinning above a motto that grandly promised to bring the world to the classroom. Actually what these shorts brought to the classroom were glimpses of well-known actors and actresses earning day rates in the years before they were touched by stardom. I remember the stir in the room when Alan Ladd suddenly appeared in one of the Erpi offerings.

When I was in the sixth grade I learned to operate the 16 mm projector and became a member of the squad permitted to run pictures for our own and other classes. This was the first time I involved myself in a nonpassive way with the movies. At the time, of course, it meant only a chance to skip the odd hour of classwork.

The school was not burdened with obligations to social services. In our middle-class world there was no need for hot breakfast programs. Extracurricular activities were entertaining and gently instructional; they were not compensations for failures of the larger social order.

The school sponsored a Cub Scout pack, to which I briefly and indifferently belonged, though I liked wearing the uniform, which was blue with yellow trim, vaguely reminiscent of the cavalry uniforms we saw in Westerns. In the winter an athletic field across the street from the school was flooded and frozen and turned into a skating pond, which wobblingly I circumnavigated, ashamed of my weak ankles. In the spring there was an after-school softball league. Being left-handed, I played first base.

Sooner or later, though, the school always betrayed the bright promise of September and settled into its unexciting routines. Our projects matched the months: decorating the classroom windows with pumpkin cutouts for Halloween and turkeys for Thanksgiving, getting up a Christmas pageant and making presents for our parents (my best was a multi-hued clay turtle paperweight I gave my father). In February we contemplated the lives of Lincoln and Washington, and once we had a debate about who was the greater. I argued for Washington and won. In April we colored Easter eggs as an art project.

THE SUMMER BEGAN officially on Memorial Day, a couple of weeks before school ended. My grandfather and I would load a few flats of geraniums into the trunk of his Buick and drive to the cemetery outside Evansville, where his family and his wife's family were buried. Grandpa always called the holiday "Decoration Day," and that's what we did—decorate the graves with the flowers he had brought.

It was a pleasant occupation. First the dead plants from the previous year were dug up. Then we would fill our sprinkling can from a nearby spigot, using the water to make a muddy base in the newly vacated holes. We would gently tap the new plants out of their earthenware pots, pat them into place, and then douse them with more water.

It took a while. Many Hendrickses and Purringtons rested here. We would lean back against the gravestones to eat sandwiches from our lunch bags, and grandpa would talk about growing up on the nearby family farm—the long walks through the snow to the one-room school, the buggy rides to town, the infant illnesses and deaths brought to mind by some of the graves we were decorating.

In the early afternoon we would drive by his old farm, still operating, past the one-room school he had attended (also still functioning), and stop in Fulton to assess what damage the winter might to have done our summer place.

The property always looked fine to me. But grandpa would find a few items to discuss with Johnny Berg, the caretaker. After that we would drive home, tired and content, obscure duty sucessfully discharged.

ON OUR BLOCK we were, in our sporting activities, always true to the season. In the summer we played curiously squeezed games of baseball on the empty lot on the corner, which was too long and narrow for the game. Its proportions were better suited to the touch football we played there in the fall. We never played football in the summer or baseball in the fall.

In the winter, after school, we played basketball on the driveway in front of Kenny Siegesmund's garage. We must have cut comical figures, lumbering around in the fast-closing darkness of a January or February afternoon, our moves rendered slow and ungainly by sweaters, snow jackets, heavy pants, and boots.

I remember the cold gritty wetness the ball acquired from dribbling and bouncing in the melt water of the driveway and from being knocked out of bounds into snowbanks. I remember the chilled stiffness of my chapped fingers and hands, the painful slap when the ball was passed to me, the rasp in my throat and lungs as, gasping for breath in the chilled air, I worked the ball toward the basket or went up for a rebound.

There were, of course, days when there were not enough players available even for a game of horse at Kenny's house, let alone a football or baseball game. Then one was thrown back on one's own resources. I might put on a fielder's glove and go around to the back of our house to fling a tennis ball high against its wall (being careful to miss various windows), then racing to catch it, pretending I was an outfielder, playing in games where, uncannily, every ball was hit to my position.

Sometimes I would repair to the yard by the side of our house and play in a solitary, imaginary football game, slashing off tackle or around end, eluding (or sometimes being hit by) opponents who existed only in my own mind. Talk about comical sights—a lone little boy, racing in maniacal circles (as it would have seemed to a passerby), throwing a football high in the air and then racing underneath it to make a spectacular catch, then falling in a heap as he was blindsided by an entirely invisible defender.

I carried this habit of creating imaginary games over into the games of catch my patient father would play with me after dinner in the summer. In those twilights I learned to handle my first baseman's clawlike mitt with a certain nonchalance. But what I really liked to do was pitch, and so after about fifteen minutes I would change gloves and toss a few imaginary innings, working my way in and out of imaginary trouble (left-handers are, of course, wild).

The summer school vacation, which lasted something like ten weeks, the long twilights of its days lengthened by daylight savings time (a controversial wartime novelty in Wisconsin, where the rural population hated to milk their cows in morning darkness), imparted a languor to our activities as we stretched them out to fill the endless days and weeks. On rainy summer days we sometimes gathered on the Nelthorpes' screened front porch for cards or Monopoly. The eldest Nelthorpe girl, Nadine, then in high school, had astonishing legs, long and shapely. She wore short shorts to show them off, and she entered our furtive sexual imaginings—mine anyway.

Her sister, Nancy, was in my grade—a pretty, lively girl, dark-haired, dark-eyed, like the rest of her family, which included a rather saturnine older brother who sometimes played in our games but generally held himself aloof from the younger boys. Their father, Blackie, was perhaps the most glamorous of our fathers: the golf pro at Westmoor Country Club, thus the only professional athlete we knew. He got his name in the paper occasionally when he played in tournaments. One year he ventured as far as Chicago and the Tam O'Shanter Open, then one of the major stops on the touring circuit, where he did all right.

Chores, errands, homework, parental plans, the sniffles could prevent a kid quorum from gathering. More dramatically, one could be quarantined for mumps or measles or chicken pox. The family doctor would notify the health department, and then a nurse would appear, look at your spots or lumps, and tack a red sign to the front door, warning the world that an infection was contained within. You were confined for two weeks, the last week of which you always felt fine; the symptom would disappear, and you would start driving your parents crazy since the new books you had been given to pass the time would have been consumed, and the new toys and games were by this time a bore.

Once there was a polio scare, and all of us, all perfectly well, were quarantined and nightmarishly restless. Nancy Nelthorpe and I took to meeting in the backyard of the Thomases' house, which stood between our homes. We felt smart and wicked at this evasion of authority.

Our little gang had its squabbles, of course—"safe"-"out"

arguments when we played baseball, for example—or sudden exclusionary moments when, spontaneously, the group would decide to "ditch" one of its members for the afternoon, deliberately "hiding out" from the victim, giggling and shushing one another in someone's attic, basement, or garage. But there was no particular malice in these actions.

They just blew up and blew over—unacknowledged attempts to create some drama in our lives.

ONE WARTIME SUMMER, in a heavily wooded empty lot, some of us made a camouflaged dugout with a fairly elaborate system of trenches snaking out from it. There, for a time, we played war games.

I was equipped with a plastic helmet liner (war surplus), a Boy Scout canteen, and a quite authentic-looking wooden model of a Garand rifle, standard issue for World War II infantrymen. Insufferably self-important as usual, Larry Morgan appointed himself commanding officer, and after a few weeks I deserted rather than remain under his orders. Soon enough, everyone abandoned the game. Fall rains turned our fortification slimy and chilly—more realism than we wanted.

And besides, we were singularly lacking in enemies, try as we might to imagine them streaming over the grassy field that our redoubt commanded. All we had created was a mini-Maginot Line and a sitzkrieg.

The sandbox in my backyard had a more consistent appeal. Combining toy soldier forces with a friend, one could spend whole days digging trenches and building fortifications out of wet sand reinforced with stones and gravel from our driveway, deploying our troops in them and then launching artillery barrages—more gravel, accompanied by guttural sound effects—

lobbed across no-man's land (like real generals, we had a tendency to fight past wars).

"All my pocket money went into armaments," Wilfrid Sheed recalled of his boyhood in wartime England. It is perhaps a measure of our distance from danger that they did not consume more than half my budget. Supplemented by parental lend-lease, it was enough to muster a good showing of toy soldiers and the support equipment they required—field artillery, tanks, trucks, and so forth. The Tootsie Toy people had a nice line of this materiel, cheaply available at the dime store.

I sometimes reinforced my troops with the smaller, more carefully painted and more exotically uniformed lead soldiers that came from Britain in long, narrow boxes. (It is interesting that they kept manufacturing them during the war and exporting them to the United States. Was it part of their propaganda effort?) My parents didn't approve my deployment of these more finely made forces in sandbox wars. They were expensive, a little bit rare, and could be lost or broken outdoors; in their minds these tiny fusiliers and guardsmen were for display only. And sure enough, Larry Morgan (who else?) and I got into a two-day engagement in which many of my elite troops were lost or wounded beyond repair. After that, removal of these soldiers from the house was forbidden.

Still, as I look back I am surprised at how little the war imposed itself on our play—reveries and fantasies are different matters. For, in peace or war, little boys always used to play war games, and popular culture, before Vietnam, encouraged them to fantasize military glory. We probably would have been playing soldiers no matter what was happening elsewhere in the world, just as we went on with our other, more peaceful activities despite the war. They were all part of a traditional childhood narrative, unchanging in its fundamental ways.

BUT IF we were stuck, we knew too that the world beyond us was coming unstuck. We could see that the war was democratizing travel—if not for us then for millions of others. The idea grew in us—or was it only in me?—that there were some places where people doubtless spoke in movie dialogue and dressed and ate and got about (we almost never took taxis, for example, or rode in airplanes) in ways that were exotic to us. Our time to roam more restlessly must, it seemed to me, inevitably come.

That was an important, maybe eventually a ruling idea for me. Until the war, everyone except the rich and well favored were pretty much trapped where they were born, or very near to it. There was by this time a vast literature of provincials who got out—the Lost Generation and all that. But it took talent to do that. Or, at the least, a belief in the idea that living well was the best revenge, whatever that nice, empty phrase may actually mean.

During the depression, of course, there had been a huge free-floating population of men seeking work—one or two even appeared at our door—part of a more desperate internal migration. But now, suddenly, it seemed that everyone was bopping around the country, the world: fourteen million men and women under arms eventually; millions more heading for the defense plants or government jobs both near and far. It was the last great age of railroading, the first great age of air travel.

ONE SUMMER MORNING Larry Morgan appeared at our door, bearing the news that troop trains would be coming through town. He was rounding up a group of kids to go down to the station to witness this spectacle.

How he knew this to be occurring—surely it must have

been classified information—I do not know. But having nothing better to do, five or six us made the long trek down to The Village and hung around on the platform of the little one-room station there. For a long time we saw nothing but freight trains lumbering by. We put pennies on the track to be crushed into coppery blobs by their passage. We began to doubt self-assured Larry.

But then the railroad signals beside the track clattered. Their semaphore arms raised or lowered—I forget which. And suddenly a long train, moving at high speed, appeared. It was loaded with uniformed soldiers. We waved. Some of them waved back. You could see that the cars were tightly packed. The train disappeared. But shortly thereafter another, exactly like it, high-balled through.

We waited another hour, but no more troop trains appeared. We wandered home thoughtfully. These were the Milwaukee Road tracks, leading eventually to the Pacific Northwest. These guys would perhaps fight the Japanese in the Aleutians or in China-Burma-India, the CBI.

I thought of the soldiers cramped and upright in their day coaches for at least another two days and sympathized with their discomfort. I thought too of the unknowns they would soon face—a sea voyage, a landing on some strange island. I may have envied them the distance they were being carried.

All those millions of young Americans being transported, en masse, in their innocence, to the far corners of the world, to witness things no one in their hometowns had ever seen, to witness things that I, more than a half-century later, and well enough traveled, have never seen. What an amazing thing it was—an unprecedented (and quite unintentional) act of mass education.

Those young men borne westward into the night had all

had their lives grievously interrupted, were about to place them at mortal risk, in return for which they were offered this modest increment of sophistication. I'm sure, at the time, it did not seem worth it to them. Yet we as a nation would never be quite the same again—quite so provincial, quite so prejudiced, quite so stuck in the mud.

By the time we were waving those soldiers off to their destiny, I dimly sensed that someday I would unheroically emulate them. I don't know how I knew this or why I knew this or when it came upon me. It was simply an assumption that stole over me—as it has over the protagonists of a thousand bildungsromans, a genre that, curiously, I rarely read, preoccupied as I have always been with my own version of the tale.

MILITARY TRAVEL was obviously touched by ambiguity. You might want to get up and get out, but not because you were ordered to do so. And surely you did not want to exchange your life for the opportunity. I remember a line from some war correspondence. "See Naples and die," it said, quoting an old travel slogan. It added, "Many did."

Portents of doom aside, we perhaps understood that even though those guys on the trains might get a twenty-four-hour pass before they shipped out, they would most probably do nothing more than wander aimlessly about some port of embarkation, looking for nonexistent action. We had seen them on the streets of downtown Milwaukee, grimly seeking fun. We saw them in movies that stressed the poignancy, brevity, and contingency of the romances they found.

It was touring actors and singers, briefly playing Milwaukee, who brought the most potent hints of a glamorous life elsewhere. For example, the Metropolitan offered *Tannhäuser* at the Milwaukee Auditorium, and I begged to go. Lauritz Melchior starred. Singing opposite him was Margaret Lawrence, who had been stricken with polio and played her role in a chair (wheeled or not, I cannot say). Everyone was impressed with her bravery, her insistence on not abandoning a glamorous career hard won.

I got bored pretty quickly. But still . . . up late on a school night, doing something no one else my age was doing. You have to give my parents credit, earnestly bending their twig.

The first professional play I saw was *Life with Father*, at the decrepit Davidson theater, which shamed Milwaukee almost as much as Borchart Field did. Something would also have to be done about the performing arts after the war. We encountered a friend of my father's in the lobby. He said he had gone to college with Carl Benton Reid who was playing the title role. He said he was going out to dinner with him after the show. I was impressed. These people were knowable, they had touchable (therefore reachable) lives.

Three or four times a summer I was taken to the Emil Blatz Temple of Music in Washington Park, for a concert under the stars. The large band shell had been a gift to the city by the brewer, who was often in attendance, called upon to take a bow. The orchestra was conducted by one Jerzy Bojanowski, heartily disapproved of by Richard S. Davis, the *Milwaukee Journal*'s cranky, witty music and drama critic (an early role model for me), and, for some reason, by my mother. It was thought, though, that his name attracted the city's Polish minority, its largest, and perhaps it did.

The concerts, which featured prominent singers of the day—John Charles Thomas, Nelson Eddy, Jeanette MacDonald—were always well attended. My particular favorite was Paul Robeson, whose former career as a Rutgers football player was always pointed out to me. His offstage career as a militant Stalinist was unmentioned—perhaps because at the time it was generally unknown. A tradition at the Emil Blatz Temple of Music was at some moment in the evening to douse all the lights and ask members of the audience to raise a match or cigarette lighter. The effect was of thousands of fireflies glowing simultaneously. Robeson seemed to take a particular, childish delight in this display.

One time the last surviving child of "The Fighting Sullivans" appeared, wearing her WAVE uniform, speaking inspirationally of her brothers' sacrifice as she aided a war bond drive. The Sullivans, five lads from Waterloo, Iowa, were one of the war's instant legends. All of them had volunteered to serve in the navy, insisting they be assigned to the same ship. When it went down, all of them went with it.

As far as I know, none of them did anything particularly heroic, but the thought of losing five sons all at once was a terrible one—much discussed at the time. Even my mother, who was a resolute optimist about the war news, grew uncommonly grim when she thought about the Sullivans and their mother's unimaginable loss. Their deaths led to a change in military regulations—siblings could no longer serve in the same unit—and ultimately to the motivating plot device of *Saving Private Ryan*.

I believe we had already seen the movie based on this story, *The Sullivans* (latterly retitled *The Fighting Sullivans*), when the sister appeared at the Music Temple. It is disconcerting to reencounter it now. That second title was meant to be double-edged; the Sullivans fought for their country, of course (although we see little of them in action), but they also fought endlessly among themselves. The movie makes the point that when their country was in danger, they set their squabbles aside and bonded against the common enemy.

The movie wants desperately to be charming about kids

growing up in a small town—the stray dog they adopt, fun at the old swimming hole. But it isn't. There is something mean-spirited about their pranks, particularly in the way they attempt to sunder the youngest boy's relationship with a girl (Anne Baxter) somewhat above him in class. Their Irishry is petty and unfunny, and the actors playing them, both as kids and adolescents, are notably unwinsome.

The reaction of their parents (Thomas Mitchell and Selena Royle) when they get the bad news is incomprehensible. He gulps a couple of times and goes to work—he's never missed a day as a freight conductor on the Illinois Central and is not about to; she gives the officer (Ward Bond) who carries the fatal telegram a friendly cup of coffee. As the father's train chugs out of town he sees his ghostly sons waving to him from a water tower. The boys are last seen as spirits, ascending to heaven—Dutch rubs through all eternity.

An argument from realism could be made for this movie. Maybe the Sullivans were as unpleasant as they were portrayed; that would make their sacrifice (they die trying to rescue a wounded sibling on their sinking ship) the more remarkable. But the film's intent is otherwise; it is meant as yet another celebration of small-town (and working-class) virtue. How it came more to resemble "The Greatest Man in the World," James Thurber's marvelous story of another brave Iowan, Jacky Smurch—the anti-Lindbergh, an aviation hero so feckless, so anti-social that the establishment murders him—remains a mystery.

Applauding the Sullivans' surviving sister, so tiny, vulnerable, and brave on that faraway stage, we did not think about how she was, in some sense, being exploited by her government. Nor did we dare think that she was at least out of Waterloo, staying in hotel suites, ordering room service. We were not yet cynical about celebrity.

CONSIDERING the burden of her loss, you would not have dared to call her lucky. You might, however, have called *me* lucky. For I was beginning, in my little way, to expand my horizons. By now, for example, I was allowed to spend some summer afternoons at the "downtown" (that is to say, first-run) movies all by myself while my mother shopped at the Boston Store or Gimbel's.

Normally these theaters were reserved for special treats—a birthday or a good report card. But a mom in summer is occasionally a desperate creature. So I would be given some change, enough for admission and a trip to the candy counter, and parked for the afternoon in one of the theaters on Wisconsin Avenue, Milwaukee's main thoroughfare. This was perfectly safe, for ushers constantly patrolled the aisles, and, anyway, matinees in hardworking Milwaukee were virtually unattended.

The oldest of these venues was the Alhambra, intended originally as a vaudeville house and running toward seediness when I was a boy. The Strand, which was the first downtown theater specifically designed to show movies, was the least imposing of the first-run houses. The Palace, built around the same time as a vaudeville house, had a steeply raked balcony, rather vertiginous in its effect. My grandfather fondly remembered playing hooky from work to see the young Will Rogers there. The grandest theaters were the newest ones—the Wisconsin, the Riverside, and the Warner. The former were French Baroque in manner, the latter was basically Art Deco, but with all sorts of eclectic encrustations.

Not that I knew anything about the styles they echoed. All I could see were vaulting lobbies and grand staircases sweeping up to their balconies. And, of course, cavernous auditoriums (the

Wisconsin had more than three thousand seats, the Riverside and the Warner more than two thousand).

The Riverside tended to play negligible B pictures between stage shows that starred the big bands—Tommy Dorsey, Benny Goodman, Gene Krupa. Ozzie Nelson's band featured his wife, Harriet Hilliard, as its singer, and they did primitive versions of the domestic comedy routines they would soon bring to radio and then make famous on television.

I first encountered Sid Ceasar at the Riverside. He was working in *Tars and Spars*, the Coast Guard revue. He did a routine, also to become more famous on television, in which—hilariously—he played all the parts in a war movie, including the MGM lion. The show starred Victor Mature, who played a genially self-satirizing version of himself as an egocentric movie star.

These afternoons were, I think, the best of a lifetime's moviegoing. In the emptiness of those vast, dark spaces, with the cool air—moviegoing in those days provided almost our only experience of air conditioning—gently washing over you while the images on the huge screens flooded over you, you felt an exquisite mix of feelings: of luxury and privacy, of privilege and autonomy. You were out in the world and entirely out of it. Most important, you were on your own recognizance, just like a grown-up.

Except once. One day when I was eleven, one of these outings was rudely disrupted by officious reality. I stepped up to the Wisconsin box office, confidently plinked down my quarter for a child's admission, and was informed by the woman behind the glass that I must pay the full fifty-cent price. No, I said, I was under twelve. You are not, she replied. I was astonished. I had never before been disbelieved by anyone.

We argued. I demanded to see the manager. A head usher appeared instead. He backed up his fellow employee. This was the unexpected downside of being "big for his age," as my parents liked to explain when other adults overestimated my years. Voices were raised. I came close to tears. An impatient line formed behind me. Finally I forked over my second, candy-counter quarter and entered the theater in sweaty outrage. Later, when I told my mother and father what had happened, they decided to arm me with a birth certificate. I carried it folded up in my wallet until I turned twelve, though I don't recall ever having to flash it.

But the picture quickly absorbed and deflected my outrage. It was *Wing and a Prayer*, about airmen on a carrier. The personnel included William Eythe playing a Hollywood star carrying his Oscar as a good luck talisman in his cockpit, and Dana Andrews as the squadron commander, patiently offering to play acey-deucey (I still wonder how the game is played) with a nervous flyer. Don Ameche was the flight officer, unforgiving in his demand for discipline, revealing the loneliness of command, the anguish of sending young men up to face death, only when he was alone.

Usually when one of these matinees was over I would meet my parents at my father's office, which was in the Wisconsin Tower. This I fondly imagined to be a skyscraper, because, unlike the other downtown buildings which were low and thick, its lines imitated those of the Empire State Building, images of which were everywhere—in movies, in the magazines, even in our school texts—and which little boys talked about constantly, wonderingly in those days. Actually, of course, the Wisconsin Tower was just a stubby imitation of Gotham Glamour, not more than twenty stories tall.

THE GRANDEUR (and whimsy) of the downtown theaters was, in its way, transporting. Nothing in grey, practical Milwaukee compared with them. I was beginning to understand that the allure of the movies matched that of these theaters in that they defied the dull physics that ruled most of our life. This was, I thought, a wonderful thing.

I have always resisted the idea that movies analogize comfortably to dreaming. Dreams announce their fantastic qualities much more openly; the cutting is more abrupt and crazy, the imagery more outrageous, the interpretations infinitely more ambiguous than anything the movies (Bunuel aside) usually offer. The best short definition of movies I ever heard was offered, almost as an aside, by Joseph Campbell in a lecture he gave not long before he died: "The genial imaging of enormous ideas." It seems to me that whatever was dreamlike about the movies was subsumed by their desire to maintain that geniality within a realistic context. Everyone's shoulder patches were utterly accurate.

IF THIS WAS a great age of travel, it was also, perforce, a great age of movie farewells—farewells that were inevitably touched by the possibility that they might be irrevocable. Take *Casablanca*. It is almost impossible to write about it freshly, for everyone, of every generation, has by now come to Rick's. They know what they think as firmly as we did when the movie first transfixed our squirmy little beings.

I heard about it the minute it went into release—something in the reviews or the ads or the talk made it seem important to see quickly. I begged to see it on its first run and was greeted with uncharacteristic dubiety by my mother. She thought it would be over my head. She quoted a friend who had seen it and had characterized it as "melodramatic." I didn't know what the word meant exactly, but it did not dim my impatience. I had to wait, though, until a Friday night at the Times, when Danny Seyfert and I at last beheld its entirely comprehensible glories.

It succeeds in large part because the writing is so good—smart and pacey, like that of a good screwball comedy, yet capable of embracing deeper emotions. It's often a hard, cynical, wisecracking movie, but it always rediscovers its immortal romantic center again, no matter how much it is temporarily unbalanced by other obligations.

I want to consider it simply and narrowly—as a movie about learning to say goodbye gracefully. That's something Ingrid Bergman's Ilsa doesn't manage at all well when she deserts Rick Blaine in Paris ("You wore blue, the Germans wore grey") in the flashback that explains his bitterness. The news comes to him in the form of a feeble note, delivered to the train station as he waits for her to join him on the last train leaving Paris before the German occupation. Its words are washed away by the rain, but even if he could have read it to the end, how could it possibly have conveyed the sternness of her duty to stand by her man, Victor Laszlo, the great underground leader?

We, of course, guess that he's not half as much fun in bed as Rick. Despite Paul Henreid's attractive playing, he is all politics, politics, politics, and thus it is easy to imagine a rather distracted, possibly neglectful lover.

Be that as it may, he clearly lacks Bogart's tough-nut composure. We know nothing about Rick and we know all about him; he plays mystery incisively—in a way that we suspect has been attractive to women other than Ilsa. But even though Rick has run guns for some lost causes, he is not a political sophisticate. He's just another inexplicably jilted lover who's still taking it hard as *Casablanca* opens.

He says he sticks his neck out for nobody, which makes him kin to all the selfish guys in all the grubby platoons in every theater of the war who need to be politically, idealistically educated. It may be, indeed, that the art of *Casablanca* consists of relocating him (not to mention a lot of other familiar war-movie types) away from the front, in a more glamorous place, where people dress well, eat well, and have time to exchange well-honed quips and elegant rue.

When Ilsa walks into Rick's "gin joint," it is clear to everyone that she loves him as much as he loved her—that it was only the overwhelming exigencies of anti-fascism that caused her defection. Now Rick has what she needs—the letters of transit that she and Victor must have to get out of town and carry on his fight. She will do anything for them—including a one-night stand with Rick. But wait—that's too cynical. What they really risk is conflagration, a reignition of romance that will burn away all idealism, return them to love's selfishness.

Rick, who is obliged "to do the thinking for both of us," now comes to understand that they would sooner or later be destroyed by their lack of an appropriate *weltanschauung*. The vagaries of world war have given them the opportunity to say goodbye properly—with regret for what might have been, but with memories ("We'll always have Paris") to sustain them forever. So he tells her all that and puts her—tremulous under her big hat—on the night plane for Lisbon with Victor, his romantic sacrifice rekindling his lost idealism.

In the entire history of the movies there is not a better farewell than *Casablanca*'s. The dialogue is perfectly placed, at a point maybe just over the edge politically, but capable of being underplayed, which it is. The lighting and editing are superb—the impatient cough and sputter of the plane's engines starting up come at exactly the right edgy moment, the swelling and murmurings of Max Steiner's score are expertly judged. We forget, sometimes, how important technique is in putting over Hollywood's dicier moments. Michael Curtiz may not have been an auteur, but his timing here, and throughout this picture, is impeccable. This is the way we'd all like to say goodbye, able to walk away from these little deaths with our heads high, full of brave renunciatory thoughts. "It is a far, far better thing that I do . . ."

I SUPPOSE it is the element of choice that lends *Casablanca* its poignancy. Rick and Ilsa could have made a separate peace, could have opened a new Café Américain in some pleasant neutral capital. That was not an option available to Robert Walker. He was twice a very nervous soldier—a humble, vulnerable, radically innocent G.I. whose time out of war is severely limited by orders that are blind to the needs of the human heart.

His farewell to Jennifer Jones in *Since You Went Away* is a famous one—emotional high point of the movie, centerpiece of a dozen subsequent documentaries about World War II. What's good about it is its hysteria. There are no stiff upper lips here. They're both nuts with loss. He's on the train, she's running along beside it—they're both yelling promises of faithfulness. He's passing her his most precious possession—an heirloom watch his estranged grandfather gave him. We all know that his character, William G. Smollett II, is going to die in this war, die proving that he is not the softy his grandpa (Monty Woolley) thinks he is. His duty is to prove that sensitive guys can be heroes too.

He exists, however, in an odd context. After *Gone with the*

Wind, its producer, David O. Selznick, spent the rest of his professional life trying to duplicate its huge (and, to me, entirely inexplicable) success. This largely took the form of inflating modest little projects to unnatural dimensions. *Since You Went Away* was meant to be a simple tribute to that "fortress" (as a preamble describes it) of democracy, the American home. But it got away from Selznick. It is over three hours long mainly because Selznick, acting as his own screenwriter, requires all that time to maneuver his characters into positions in which they enact the most familiar tropes of "serious" Hollywood drama.

Selznick was a man born and raised in the picture business and had never penetrated a typical American home; the only reality he knew was Hollywood's. So he had no choice but to substitute its clichés for felt or observed reality.

His "fortress" belongs to the Hilton family. Dad is away at war (and is eventually reported missing in action). His wife, Anne (Claudette Colbert), anxiously mourns his absence in private, puts a chipper face on in public, and worries about money. Besides Jones there is another daughter, Shirley Temple, who is slightly boy crazy. Uncle Tony (Joseph Cotten), the Hilton family's best bachelor friend, drops by improbably often for a man on active duty far away. He'd like to fuck Colbert but is too decent to try. There's a black maid (Hattie McDaniel), ungrammatical but full of loving common sense, and a bitchy, gossiping neighbor (Agnes Moorehead) who is revealed to be a hoarder. There's a bulldog who attaches himself to Colonel Smollett, the boarder the hard-pressed Hiltons have taken in, who despises the dog almost as much as he does his grandson, whose sin is that he flunked out of West Point.

One of the film's oddest aspects is its lack of geographical grounding. You don't know in what part of the country the Hiltons live. They appear to be suburbanites, but we don't know what kind of city their suburb is attached to. We guess it must be fairly sizable—a place Colonel Smollett can do his valuable, if undisclosed, war work, a place Tony can easily visit on his frequent leaves, a place that can sustain everything Selznick needs for his drama—heavy war industry, an air force base with a gigantic hangar suitable for conversion to a huge dance hall, a train station spacious enough for Jones's and Walker's long goodbye, a veterans' hospital where, before the picture is over, Jones takes up with a shell-shocked soldier (she is clearly drawn to the psychologically damaged).

But these locales are as generic as the people and the problems Selznick places in them. In other words, he offers a totally Hollywood approximation of middle-class life—the Hardy family goes to war. It delivers its beats—sad, inspirational, comical, romantic—on a movie schedule, without reference to life as people actually live it. This lack of specificity guaranteed the perfection of our detachment.

One suspects that Selznick was trying to do for the American home front what the Academy Award–winning *Mrs. Miniver* did for England's. But bad as that movie is, it at least offered Mr. Miniver's service at Dunkirk, the lady of the house capturing a downed German flyer, their home struck by a stray bomb, the death of their son's fiancée by similar aerial accident. Paradoxically it found a certain crude honesty—all right, maybe it was just catering to a little boy's need for deadly risk—in these moments. The Hiltons' troubles are more muted. Mainly we get to see trembling chins, forced humor, brave reactions to the bad stuff happening off-screen.

We are permitted a moment's wild, subversive hope that Jane Hilton will be discreetly deflowered by Smollet/Walker. It would be a perfectly plausible contribution to the war effort, and Selznick supplies the moment—a last walk in the country before he must leave for war. A rainstorm comes up. A barn is handy. Wet clothes really ought to be shed. But the moment is devoted to wistful talk. The storm passes, and it's train time.

Poor Walker/Smollett. Not only does he die, but he dies a virgin. It was a fate we sometimes discussed of a lazy afternoon, and though what loss of one's virginity actually entailed was a mystery to many of us, we knew it was the most important business we needed to attend to before we confronted death.

But never mind. The Walker-Jones love scene is like all the movie's other big scenes. It could just as well be worked out in an opposite manner. They develop as they do because Selznick was so nakedly playing to our cheapest, most predictable expectations.

Just how the farewell sequence broke through is something of a mystery. Maybe it was driven by sexual frustration—their failure to consummate when they had the chance. Maybe it worked because Jones and Walker, who had been married, were in the midst of a separation (she was taking up with Selznick at the time), and something of their private anguish leaked into it. Or maybe it was simpler than that. They were among the most overtly neurotic performers in movie history up until that time— nervous, overthinking, never quite comfortable and settled in any role. Perhaps they drew on their imperfectly suppressed tensions and anxieties for the scene, and the director, John Cromwell, just let them rip.

IT IS PERHAPS a measure of how loco Robert Walker was that Judy Garland, this movie era's other great head case, could be made to look relatively sane in his company. She was *The Clock's* sensible, slightly bemused small-town girl in the big city. He was the rube soldier in New York on a forty-eight-hour pass. In that time period they meet in Pennsylvania Station—he literally runs into her and breaks the heel of her shoe—court, marry, have second thoughts, but then reconcile as they part. It is an absolutely wonderful movie, the anti–*Since You Went Away*.

Probably it is the movie that turned my escapist fantasies definitively eastward, though I'm not completely certain of that. All kinds of wartime movies, in many veins, ranging from *The Fallen Sparrow* to *Laura* to *The Lost Weekend*, painted a darkly glamorous portrait of the big city. I know now that these were backlot visions of New York—as indeed *The Clock* was. But they were suffused with the longing that the West Coast expatriates felt for the city they had left behind to pursue their movie careers—a compound of dress, decor, moral challenge, and sleeplessness—that was more important than set decoration.

The Clock, I suppose, was a lucky accident—as most good American movies tend to be. A couple of other directors had been assigned to it before it passed to Vincente Minnelli. I got to know him later, and he told me, as he told others, that what needed to be done with the script was to make the city a character in the movie—a third point in the triangle of which the Walker and Garland characters were the other two.

In his handling of it, New York is an untrustworthy character. Sometimes its citizens help bring the lovers together. Sometimes its institutions pull them apart. As he steps out of Penn Station to catch his first glimpse of the city, Walker's Cpl. Joe Allen sees skyscrapers, shot in raked angles, towering forbiddingly over him. Later, after he and Garland's Alice Mayberry have gotten to like each other, they are separated in the subway, where the trains rumble through at desperate speed and menacingly preoccupied crowds drive them apart. Still later, racing a montage of ticking clocks to get their marriage license before closing time at the city clerk's office, the timepieces become malevolent menaces to young love. Their wedding itself, with their vows drowned out by passing elevated trains, is a nightmare. Their wedding dinner is in a hash house, their wedding night is passed in a charmless hotel room, overstuffed with heavy furniture. In these passages Minnelli's vision, as it often did, comes closer to surrealism than that of any other American director.

On the other hand, the movie is mediated by friendly New Yorkers: a woman with a German accent helps Joe make a date with Alice as he runs alongside a bus carrying her away—translating the shouts only she can hear above the traffic noises. And then there's James Gleason's winsome milkman, who gives them a ride in his horse-drawn truck and takes them home for breakfast with his wife (who was played by Gleason's real-life wife). It is their faithfulness and good nature that inspires the two kids to their hasty marriage.

Marriage in wartime was a subject much discussed, in private and in public. The topic offered a real romantic agony. On the one hand, people sympathized with the yearnings of young people about to be torn asunder by wartime exigencies. They deserved, many believed, their brief moment of happiness. Maybe that's all they would ever have.

On the other hand, they were cautioned about the consequences of rushing into things—unwanted children, postwar divorces. "Marry in haste, repent in leisure," my mother always said. It came to this: should one shed caution, grab what happiness one could on an accelerated schedule? Or should one wait and see?

The Clock is alert to both possibilities. Minnelli himself was bisexual, so he was inherently dubious about marriage. On the other hand, he married several times and was at this time in love with his leading lady. They had had an affair while they were making *Meet Me in St. Louis*, and it resumed on this picture. You can surely argue that many of its best qualities derive from his ambivalence.

Alice and Joe are seemingly en route to annulment when it is time for them to return to Penn Station so Joe can catch the train that will carry him into action. They pass through a crowd of similarly separating couples. We hear the variety of promises they make to one another, some of which are transparently false. When they move to Joe's platform the sequence is beautifully shot—with a strong, shadowy emphasis on barred gates closing on the departing soldier, Garland peering desperately through them as he disappears. She turns to leave, and Minnelli pulls back higher and higher in the magnificent reconstruction of the station MGM made on one of its soundstages. Eventually Garland's figure is lost in this larger crowd. We understand that her little story is no more important than their little stories. We understand, as well, that the story of Joe and Alice's story is not over, that it is in fact only beginning.

Maybe he will die in the war. Maybe she will think again in his absence. Maybe they will be spared the time, later, to get to know each other and make a more rational decision about their future. But that's not important. What is important is that no wartime movie more sweetly caught the contingent mood of the moment, the way people were obliged, by desperate circumstances, to improvise their fates, make choices when the most salient facts of their circumstances were hidden from them.

Somehow I caught the slightly subversive drift of the movie, which was like *Meet Me in St. Louis* in that it suggested, without particularly accenting, the dark undercurrents flowing beneath our American ordinariness.

Minnelli, I must say, was a strange bird—almost completely unable to articulate his aims yet also capable of very detailed, largely visual inventiveness. Himself the product of small-town America, he caught in his best work the kind of provincial yearnings (and anxiousness) that were beginning to rattle me. Somehow—it was largely a matter of style—he was able to unsettle and to glamorize simultaneously. It is what movies are supposed to do. And rarely do.

The ambivalence of *The Clock*'s farewell—its undercurrents of haste and doubt—is masterful. Curiously, I found an echo of it in my own life.

IT HAPPENED when I was in the sixth grade in 1944. Our teacher was a woman named Carla George. She was tall, slim, raven-haired, perhaps more sophisticated and ambitious—or maybe just more restless—than the other teachers. She had once taken a Lurline cruise to Hawaii and had met Lana Turner on the voyage.

Miss George and I had an edgy relationship, since, as noted, I did both well and badly in school. It was in her class that I scribbled incoherently all over my arithmetic workbook and was threatened with demotion.

I hated Miss George at that moment. But I realize now that her impatience stemmed from concern that some potential of mine was about to be lost through laziness and inattention. I also realize that she stirred something in me sexually.

One Friday, at the end of the school day, she called for attention and made an announcement. She had, she said, applied for and been accepted as a Red Cross worker. She would be leaving in a couple of weeks. She said she hoped she would get an overseas assignment.

We were stunned. Teachers simply did not leave in midsemester. Life's little routines were not disrupted in this abrupt fashion—not in that time and place. There were many questions from the class. In the midst of them I broke into uncontrollable sobs. No one else did. My outburst was as astonishing to me as it was to the others. Miss George seemed to understand what I was feeling. She hugged me. I faithfully executed my arithmetic assignments from that day forward.

She kept in touch with us for a while. Eventually we learned that she was stationed in England. The local weekly printed a picture showing her in a trimly tailored uniform and Red Cross hat. It was pert, but her handsome, slightly hawkish face was set in a determined expression. Her air was that of women in those magazine ads of the time, which showed members of their sex cheerfully yet soberly taking up unprecedented tasks.

Years later, when my byline began appearing regularly in magazines, she encountered my mother at some DAR conference. She encouraged Miss George to send me a letter. In it she said she had met an American officer in England and married him. After the war they settled in a quiet town in Michigan, her taste for adventure safely and apparently fully satisfied. She expressed pride in my accomplishments. I guess they were something like what she had in mind for me.

Her own accomplishment was not a small one. I have no idea what measure of patriotic idealism went into her decision. Or what measure of desperation went into it, for it may be that the war represented a last best chance for her to escape the smallness of life as we knew it. Or, conceivably, she was simply escaping impending spinsterhood. She may even have been escaping from a love affair gone wrong or sundered by wartime impositions.

About all that I knew (and know) nothing. We were not encouraged to think about such things. We imagined schoolteachers living in rented rooms or small apartments, soberly listening to H. V. Kaltenborn or "The Voice of Firestone" while they graded papers or worked on their lesson plans. And I suspect many of them—children of the depression, glad to have respectable jobs and fearful of losing them—actually did endure lives as circumscribed as that.

In any case, we did not imagine them as sexual beings—going dancing, having a drink, taking moonlit drives with the top down. In our minds such activities were simply not permitted them. And in fact they would have been frowned upon by the adult community, which expected the teachers it employed to "set a good example." Our school board, for instance, forbade their smoking in public.

If any of these young women did kick up their heels, they did so with great discretion. So Miss George's spectacular defection from routine was consequential. Whatever need or ambition she sought to fulfill was something the rest of our community did not feel (or could not acknowledge).

It was as if she stopped going to the movies and entered one, became a player instead of a spectator. I know that some of the tears I shed when she announced this intention were for myself, for my inability to imitate her.

11

"Lost in Always"

I AM STANDING on a corner, across the street from the Washington School. New snow is falling lightly, dusting huge mounds of the stuff, left over from earlier storms, that had been shoved to the curb by the plows. Some of these rise—lumpy, crusty, soiled—to my shoulder, the icy detritus of a typically hard Wisconsin winter.

It is cold on the corner but not subzero, as it often was in January and February. Under a hooded parka I am doubtless wearing my usual school clothes—hi-tops and corduroy knickers, a sweater and a flannel shirt. Over the parka is a white, webbed, over-the-shoulder belt, to which is attached my badge of rank—signifying that I am a lieutenant or perhaps even a captain of the Safety Cadets, which as a sixth-grader I had automatically attained (everyone got a brief turn as commander of this troop).

On this afternoon I was supposed to supervise the none-too-perilous crossing of Sixty-eighth Street by the "little kids" (as we "big kids" always called them). These members of the lower grades were dismissed from school before the rest of us were, so my task got me out of about a half-hour of class time.

I did not have much business that day. Because of the weather's slight inclemency, most of the little kids were picked up by their mothers and didn't need my help to cross the street. So my duty was lonely—though I don't think I would have used that word to describe my condition. What do privileged eleven-year-olds know about loneliness?

In this case my idling mind somehow turned to the mortality of my dog, Sambo. I began multiplying his actual years (four) by "dog years" (seven) and worked it out that he would probably be around for another eight or nine years. I then began figuring my parents' and grandparents' remaining span. I gave them all the benefit of the doubt—correctly so, in that they all turned out to be long-lived. I then turned to myself, paying particular attention to the possibility of making it to the millennium. Of course, I didn't think of it as the millennium—just as the round-numbered end of a century that had not yet reached its halfway mark. It seemed entirely possible to live to be almost sixty-seven.

This was reassuring to me, as the entire exercise was. Sambo excepted, we all appeared to have plenty of time left to us. If I felt any sadness at all it was that the dog was likely to miss a great deal, especially the many successes I imagined I would some day attain—first on the gridiron, then in some other dimly imagined form of public life.

For by then I knew that I wanted to be well known, acclaimed in some way, though for what I hadn't the faintest idea. I merely understood that the anonymity of this place, whatever other pleasures and comforts it offered, was not for me. Some day I wanted someone to write a biography about me. Or better still, make a biopic (though that term had not yet been coined) based on my life.

This, however, is beside my present point. Which is that this was the first time I ever confronted—however optimistically—mortality. I naturally understood that death was something everyone worried about. It was why Sambo was always on a leash outdoors. It was why I had only a sidewalk bike. It was why my mother stood tensely in our living room window, her face anxiously scrunched, when my father was fifteen or twenty minutes late coming home from the office.

What I did not understand then, and would not understand for decades, was that mortality is the only worthwhile subject. The mystery beside which all others pale. The goad which renders all others paltry. The distinguished thing we seek to elude by distinguishing ourselves and leaving something tangible and admirable behind.

I did not understand how much hard work would have to go into achieving that end, how much pleasure would have to be sacrificed to this goal—a lifetime of loathsome homework, as it were. Being adored as I was, I assumed that everyone would take me as my grandfather and parents did, as naturally brilliant. Or maybe, standing as I was on the cusp of the celebrity age, I perceived that lots of people seemed to get famous and lead lives of apparent wealth and ease without working very hard. They seemed always to be entering or leaving nightclubs. Or, in the case of movie stars, going to the races at Hollywood Park or merely lolling by their swimming pools or tennis courts.

WHAT IS ODDEST about that slightly silly boy standing dutifully in the swirling snow is how radical his innocence is. I don't mean that he should immediately have set aside *The Keystone Kids* for *The Brothers Karamazov*. Or even that he might at least occasionally over the next few years have spared a few more minutes from his busy life for the intriguing topic that blew up and blew away so quickly on that winter's afternoon. What I'm thinking is that at the time he was living amidst death on a scale unprecedented in human history and had no conscious knowledge of that remarkable fact.

Close to 55 million people died in World War II—perhaps more than that. No one knows for certain. We don't even know when to begin counting, since there were so many rehearsals for the war. We certainly can't calculate all its unrecorded deaths, history's road kill, occurring out of sight of the graves registration units. In the few minutes I stood on my corner, dozens of people died—in Europe, in the South Pacific, somewhere in the vast, tormented world.

But no one toted up these numbers—not in any form of public discourse to which I had access. The *Milwaukee Journal* published local casualty lists, and the wire service stories on distant battles mentioned casaulties—generally "light" or "moderate" on our side, "heavy" on the other side. But no one ever added up, say, the combined losses of the Blitz, Pearl Harbor, and Stalingrad. Those of D-day and the Battle of the Bulge were never combined with those of Iwo Jima and Okinawa. Nothing, of course, was said about the firestorms that had already devastated Cologne and Hamburg and would soon wipe out Dresden—those mad decimations ordered up by strategic bombing's truest believer, Arthur ("Bomber") Harris, commanding the RAF's heaviest squadrons of destruction. The man simply loved to see vast cities burn and crumble, vast populations reduced to little pools of bubbling protoplasm.

Hiroshima and Nagasaki had not, at that point, been targeted, but we can imagine Bomber Harris happily anticipating such attacks. We cannot for a moment imagine him sparing a thought for the terrible toll his war took on truly innocent populations. Two years after the war, Hannah Arendt wrote: "The problem of evil will be the fundamental question of postwar intellectual life in Europe—as death became the fundamental problem after the last war."

I think she perhaps misstated the issue. Death was still, I think, very much a part of the equation. I would define evil as the taking of innocent lives without thought or hesitation and from a distance at which the victims remained anonymous—statistical rubble.

Perhaps I could not have imagined such thoughts as I kept my chilly, silly vigil, but I have to say that one reason I could not was the utter failure of our leaders or our media even to hint at such dreadful matters. The linkages between death and duty in popular culture were always inspirational. Each engagement won by the Allies was viewed as a step toward the ultimate victory, which was never in doubt. Even the battles we lost were seen somehow to contribute to that satisfying end. Naturally, inevitably, deaths occurred in our fictional narratives. They could not be entirely ignored, even by a popular culture determined to put a cheerful face on every aspect of the war. But no one on our side ever died absurdly or "in vain." And no death among our enemies was ever unjustified.

Before and after the war James Cagney had frequently paid for his life of crime with his own usually colorful, often lengthy demise. Now, in *Captains of the Clouds* and *13 Rue Madeleine*, he could sacrifice himself for a better reason. John Wayne, Humphrey Bogart, Errol Flynn, Gary Cooper, many another leading man joined him in a warrior's martyrdom that was rarely mute, and often enough not entirely final. In the movies a busybody afterlife was always an option.

SOMETIMES you didn't have to die in order to be reborn. Amnesia, for instance, offered splendid opportunities for reincarnation on the cheap.

The illness reached near-epidemic proportions in wartime movies, most notably in *Random Harvest*. In it we find Ronald Coleman's World War I vet, known only as Smithy, silent in a mental hospital, unable to remember any of his life before a shell shocked him into silence. His fate is likely worse than death—a lifetime in this twilight zone.

But one day he wanders away from the hospital, out into the small town's Armistice Day celebration. In a tobacco store he meets a music hall performer named Paula (Greer Garson), who loves him at first sight, takes him in, cares for him. They retreat to an idyllic country cottage. They marry, have a child, and he begins a career as a writer (though, without the writer's capital of memory, one wonders what exactly he finds to write about). Alone in Liverpool, looking into a newspaper's job offer, he is involved in a traffic accident which restores him to his prewar self but causes him to lose all memory of Paula and the life they shared.

He is, in fact, Charles Rainier, rich and wellborn, with an unsuspected talent for business—he vastly expands the family's manufacturing interests. We are startled to discover that the new tycoon's executive secretary is—yes—Paula, who saw his picture in the paper and applied for this frustrating job. Their child has conveniently died, and Paula is now going under the name of Margaret Hanson. She is a model of efficiency, though we wonder about resumés and birth certificates. Didn't anyone in interwar England do background checks?

Never mind. She does not reveal her identity. Once Charles enters Parliament he proposes a marriage of convenience—separate bedrooms, of course, as Paula attends brilliantly to their glamorous social life. But it is empty emotionally, and they are on the brink of separation when, settling a strike in one of his factories, which happens to be in the town where he and Paula met, Charles's memory begins to return. They meet again at their dear cottage, as unchanged by the passing years as their love.

The movie does not explain why seeing some streets of which anyone, amnesiac or not, would have only the dimmest memory would trigger Charles's recovery, while intimate, daily contact with a woman he once deeply loved does nothing to stimulate recall. This is perhaps because the real business of the movie is to reassure its audience that a "return from the dead" (that phrase and variants on it are repeatedly used to describe Charles's condition) is possible. Indeed, he is reborn twice, both times in agreeable circumstances, as *Random Harvest* glides slickly, soberly past our realistic reservations. We can't help but think that if love can trump metaphorical death, it might have a similar power over the real thing. In *I'll Be Seeing You*, Joseph Cotten as an amnesiac soldier and Ginger Rogers as a convict on parole heal each other's psychological wounds. On the premises of *The Enchanted Cottage* a plain girl and a disfigured war hero magically triumph over their physical defects and are permitted to see one another as beautiful.

A FAVORITE inspirational device was a letter or some sort of imagined conversation between the ghostly fallen hero and the son—it was never a daughter—he has never seen.

These encounters generally came at the end of the movie, and *Tender Comrade* offered perhaps the most lunatic of them. It's a home-front story about the courtship and marriage of

small-town childhood sweethearts played by Ginger Rogers and
Robert Ryan. She is pregnant when he goes off to war, but takes a
job as a welder in a defense plant and moves into a big old house
with other female war workers to save money. We might note
that as she settles in with the girls she delivers her infamous line
about how sharing and sharing alike is the American way. This is
the moment that Rogers's mother, Leila, a right-wing crazy, cited
at the House Un-American Activities Committee hearings in
1947 as an example of how Communists—the film was written
by Dalton Trumbo—slipped their nefarious propaganda into
movies.

Her instance was ludicrous, of course. But in a strange way
Mrs. Rogers was not entirely wrong. Trumbo, as we have seen,
was discreet in his propagandizing, especially after he moved to
MGM and become Hollywood's highest-paid screenwriter. But
in this film, directed by Edward Dymytrk, also at the time a
Communist, he achieved what is surely the height of popular-
front sappiness.

Rogers's character has her baby just days before she receives
the War Department telegram regretting to inform her of her
husband's death. She grasps a framed picture of Ryan in one
hand, their baby in the other, and "introduces" them to each
other: "Little Guy, this is your father. Chris, this is your son. You
two are never going to meet. . . ."

Her speech consumes some five minutes of screen time and
is occasionally interrupted by idealistic voice-over quotations
from Ryan's earlier dialogue. Its conclusion goes like this:

> He didn't leave you any money. He didn't have time, Chris boy
> [the child is named after his father]. No million dollars or
> country clubs or long shining cars for you, little guy. He only
> left you the best world a boy could ever grow up in. He bought

it for you with his life. That's your heritage. A personal gift to you from your dad. And one more thing: as long as you live, don't let anybody ever say he died for nothing. Because if you let them say it, you let them call your dad a fool, you let them say he died without knowing what it was all about. [The father's voice-over interrupts: To be free, to live with you, with enough food, in our own house—I guess that's what the war's about.] He died for a good thing, Little Guy. And if you ever betray it, if you ever let it slip away from you, if you ever let anyone talk you out of it, or swindle you out of it, or fight you out of it, you might as well be dead, too. So hang on to it, sweet. Clutch it to you with those tiny little fingers. Grab on to it, Chris boy. Grab it right out of your dad's hands. And hold it high, hold it proud. . . .

What can one say about this kind of writing? That no one in human history ever talked like that? That its platitudes about country clubs and long shining cars entirely lack realistic traction? Beyond that, you have to wonder who these mysterious swindlers are—guys in long shining cars from the country club, no doubt. Now, as he approaches retirement age, has he, in memory of his father, refused to keep his own car shiny? Or refused to participate in the 401(k) down at the plant? Or given his inevitable, doubtless unheroic, stepfather a lifetime of hard times?

All right. No one could see the richness and materialism of postwar America, the immunity it granted all of us from Trumboesque thought and rhetoric. On the other hand, there is a serious disconnect between the humble war aims expressed in the voice-over—"to be free, to live with you, with enough food, in our own house"—and the new widow's grand assertion that her husband's death insured his son of "the best world a boy could ever grow up in."

Having said that, though, I have to admit that tears flowed when I first heard this speech. I have to admit, more shamefaced, that a slight, hateful catch came to my throat when I reencountered *Tender Comrade*. "Strange how potent cheap music is." And what chin music was cheaper than this?

Passage to Marseilles uses this device more stolidly—an actual letter, left behind by the dead hero, is read out at the end of this grimly romantic film. It is possibly movie history's greatest festival of flashbacks, layer upon layer of them, though the script, written by Casey Robinson (one of Warner's most reliable constructors of complicated narratives) and Jack Moffitt, is never confusing.

In their story Claude Rains, as a liaison officer with a Free French bomber squadron in England, recounts the odyssey of one of his gunners, Humphrey Bogart's Jean Matrac, to an inquiring journalist. Before the war Matrac was an idealistic French newspaper editor, crusading against the appeasements of the Daladier regime. For his pains, a mob destroys his paper's plant, and he is arrested on a trumped-up murder charge and shipped off to Devil's Island for fifteen years.

He leaves behind a pregnant wife (Michelle Morgan) and takes with him a half-mad hatred of "beautiful, decadent" France. With four other prisoners, supposedly French but actually speaking in a loopy variety of generically "foreign" accents— we didn't make fine verbal distinctions in those days—he escapes through the swamps and puts to sea in a canoe. After twenty days without food—but not looking especially the worse for wear—

the voyagers are picked up by a French tramp steamer. It is captained by the Belgian actor Victor Francen and includes on its supposedly all-French passenger manifest the English actors Rains and Sydney Greenstreet, playing a proto-fascist.

Greenstreet sees the escapees for what they are—desperate men with dangerous pasts. Rains sees them for what they claim to be—patriots who, their crimes aside, are willing to fight for their country. When France falls, the captain changes course for England, Greenstreet's character briefly seizes command of the ship, a traitorous radio operator sends out their position, and a German bomber attacks. Both the would-be collaborators and the attacking plane are defeated in a melee well staged by—who else?—Michael Curtiz.

The important, the unprecedented thing about it is the remarkable moment where Matrac cold-bloodedly machine-guns survivors of the crashed plane. The captain is horrified. But Bogart shouts, "Look about you captain"—referring to the dead and wounded littering the ship's deck—"and tell me who are the assassins?"

But still. In all the movies of World War II this is the only example I have ever seen of what would be, by any standards, a prosecutable "war crime" committed by our side. At the time, church groups protested it, and the scene was apparently cut from foreign-release prints at the insistence of the Office of War Information. But it remains a shocking and psychopathic moment.

It is, however, very much in Bogart's character. He never gave a performance more clenched with suppressed rage. In reality, one has since learned, he was pissed off at Jack Warner, with whom at the time he was feuding. But sullenly fulfilling a contractual obligation, giving as little of himself as possible, his mood works for the movie.

Whenever we see him within the framing device of the Free

French bomber squadron, Bogart broods much but speaks never. It is only through highly improbable action that his softer side is shown. For every now and then he asks that his plane be diverted from its course, so that it can swoop low over the French farmhouse where his wife and son are living out the war in surprising comfort. He drops messages to them by canisters attached to tiny parachutes.

In many significant respects *Passage to Marseilles* knocks off *Casablanca*—same director, same leading man, some of the same supporting players. Its noirish lighting is similar, and so are its exotic-romantic locales. Most important, Matrac is caught in a conflict similar to Rick Blaine's: he's another former idealist whose principles have been shattered by events. You could, in fact, argue that in the later movie this condition is more richly justified. In *Casablanca* he was merely jilted by a woman. In *Passage to Marseilles* an entire nation has jilted him.

Passage to Marseilles may even have a slight edge in political sophistication; at least it mentions the actual name (Daladier) of a politician it deplores. And though it possibly overstates the prefascist condition of prewar France, it is more hardheaded about French politics than other movies of its time, which leaned toward the snuffling mode: "The last time I saw Paris her heart was warm and gay . . ."

The woozy scene in *Casablanca* where Victor Laszlo leads the denizens of Rick's café in the Marseillaise, drowning out the German officers singing their own national anthem, is typical of the way Frenchmen were presented in movies—defeated on the battlefleld but never in their gallant hearts. Only *Passage to Marseilles* suggested the defeatism and appeasement of France's prewar leadership. Naturally it does not take up the extensive collaboration (and anti-Semitism) of wartime France, which has since preoccupied so many historians.

But the rather desperate complications of its plot lack the more straightforward inevitabilty of *Casablanca*'s, and of course the dialogue entirely lacks that film's wit and rue. Especially in its ending, *Passage to Marseilles* signally fails to match the toshy elegance of the earlier hit. It wants to achieve a similar romantic renunciation, but there's little in the cool Morgan-Bogart relationship to work with.

So—arbitrarily—he gets killed in a bombing raid. There's no special reason for that. He might just as well have lived. But the picture must end sometime, somewhere. When Matrac is lifted, mortally wounded, from his plane, the canister containing a birthday message to his son is prized from his hand. After he dies, it is read out by Rains at his burial, with the sea cliffs above Santa Monica standing in for the rugged English coastline:

My Dear Son:

Today you are five years old and your father has never seen you. But someday in a better world he will. I write you of that day. Together we walk hand in hand. We walk and we look. And some of the things we see are wonderful and some are terrible. On a green stretch of ground there are 10,000 graves, and you feel hatred welling up in your heart. This was, but it will never be again. The world has been cured since your father treated the terrible abscess on its body with iron and fire. And there were millions of healers who worked with him to be sure there would be no recurrence. This deadly conflict was waged to decide your future. Your friends did not spare themselves and were ruthless to your foes. You are the heir to what your father and your friends won for you with their blood. From their hands you have received the flag of happiness and freedom. My son, be the standard-bearer for the great age they have made possible. It would be too tragic if the men of goodwill should ever be lax and fail again. Or fail to build a world where youth may love without fear and where parents may grow old with their children and where men will be worthy of each other's faith. Take care of your mother, Jean. I hold you in my arms. I love you both. May God keep you in love as I do. Goodnight and *au revoir* until our work is finished and until I see you. Remember: France lives. *Vive la France.*

Rains repeats the last phrase, promises this message will be delivered to Matrac's boy, and hands it over to a pilot, another of the Devil's Island escapees, standing by in his flying suit ready to pay this last homage to a fallen comrade. Taps. A volley. Fadeout.

That letter is not powerfully written, and Rains reads it matter-of-factly. But it strikes all of Trumbo's notes—the sacrifices unstintingly made, the notion that they will buy a better world for the children, the charge to kids to defend this future against someone or other—in a manly, dignified way.

It is strange that this dour and insanely complicated film remains so memorable to me. But it does. That's because of all the things I didn't know about at the time but that worked on me anyway: the energetic conviction of Curtiz's direction; James Wong Howe's moody, deep-focus cinematography; Claude Rains's intelligent civility as the audience's surrogate, that character, vital to traditional movie narrative, through whose eyes we apprehend the story.

I see now an interesting undertone in Bogart's performance that may also have worked on me. In later years it has pleased people to think of him as a character who prefigured postwar existentialism, and it is possible to see Jean Matrac as a Camus-like character, his newspaper as a prediction of Camus's wartime underground paper, *Combat*. The risks Matrac ran to tell the unwelcome "truth" to a hostile public were inspiring to me, already drawn, without quite knowing it, to journalism. So was the ambiguity of his relationship to France, mixing contempt and love but stopping short of total cynicism, which would come to define my adult relationship with my own country's political life.

At the time I thought Matrac's letter better written than it was. Now I see it as something like an editorial he might once have written for his newspaper—hasty, lumbering toward a rhetorical takeoff, but not quite catching the wind. Reconsidered, it seems just the sort of slightly abstract thing a politicized man would write as he struggles to express personal feelings that are not natural to him.

PUT SIMPLY, the wartime screen was a haunted screen: all those disembodied voices addressing us from the back of the beyond; all those ghostly figures ascending, through cloud effects, to heaven; all those wise immortals entering the action invisible to their mortal brethren but always full of the reassuring wisdom that one seems to acquire only in death.

The film most preoccupied—romantically, comically, dramatically—by the eschatological conundrum is *A Guy Named Joe*. It does not actually have any guys named Joe in it. The hero is Pete Sandidge, a hot and careless flyer played by Spencer Tracy. He's sweet-souled—he always has time to stop and chat with the kids who hang around the airfield in England where he's stationed—and Irene Dunne's Dorinda Durston, a ferry pilot, loves him dearly, though he takes her rather too much for granted. But his habit of not flying by the book, of banging up his airplanes, finally results in a transfer to a remote outpost where his dull duties consist of patrolling for nonexistent enemy incursions.

One day, though, he spots a German convoy, and of course

he attacks instead of waiting for reinforcements. He crashes his plane into a capital ship, dies, and goes to pilot heaven. There the commanding general (Lionel Barrymore) in effect insists that he earn a new kind of wings—angel wings. This he can accomplish by helping a good but green young pilot, Van Johnson's Ted Randall, learn his wartime trade.

Pete rides with him on his missions as a sort of invisible copilot, whispering advice in his ear. The kid becomes a splendid pilot. What Pete doesn't count on is that Dunne, though still mourning Pete's passing, will be drawn to the youngster. The action has by now switched to the South Pacific, where Pete remains rebellious about his ghostly duties. Then Ted is assigned to what appears to be a suicide mission—blowing up a Japanese fuel dump. But Dorinda—not about to lose another lover—steals his plane and flies off to what everyone but the audience is convinced will be her doom. We know that Pete is aboard, and we know he will talk her safely through the mission and return her to his rival.

In Dalton Trumbo's script, directed by Victor Fleming, we are never permitted to doubt that Pete's cranky insolence must finally yield to his fundamental good nature. Or that Dunne's character will somehow know—without being able to prove it—that a loving, ghostly hand was guiding her at her moment of mortal peril. Or that in this war, although the good may die young—well, anyway, youngish (Tracy was forty-three at the time, Dunne forty-five and a bit matronly to be the twenty-seven-year-old Johnson's lover)—they do not necessarily fall completely silent. Or completely useless.

A Guy Named Joe is a widely beloved movie. Steven Spielberg modernized and remade it (unsuccessfully) as *Always*. People continue to care for the original, I think, because its romanticism is not too pumped up. The naturalistic writing and playing keep the film—hard as this may be to believe—within a good-natured, even plausible realm. It is rarely preachy, even when Barrymore is instructing Tracy in the ways of responsible immanence. It suggests that good men enlisted in a just cause can never really be lost, that service to a total war did not necessarily have to stop at the grave.

IT'S A PRETTY THOUGHT. And it is given weight by the fact that we were dealing with this harsh fact: that the war was taking so many men before their time. We were obliged to mourn lives that were essentially unlived, lives that would never fulfill their promise. This is a consequential and devastating matter. You cannot, perhaps, blame the movies for their desperate scramble to offer some sort of consolation for it.

I think the best Hollywood had to offer in this regard was *Pride of the Yankees*, Samuel Goldwyn's biography of Lou Gehrig, the baseball player who was felled in his late prime by ALS, the disease to which his name remains, even now, attached. It was made in peacetime, released during the war's first year, and is in many ways a silly movie—featuring a scatterbrained romance between Gary Cooper's somewhat rubeish Gehrig and his sophisticated bride, Eleanor (Teresa Wright). It even takes time out for specialty musical numbers by Veloz and Yolanda and Ray Noble's band.

But it does not funk Gehrig's illness or his famous farewell. Of course it could not: his "luckiest man on the face of the earth" speech was simply too well known and too well judged to be toyed with. Nevertheless the sequence is beautifully underplayed by Cooper and well directed by Sam Wood. In particular, Cooper's painful, silent walk-off through the shadowed dugout into the tunnel leading to the locker room—leading to the final, inconsolable emptiness—is superbly understated.

Granted we do not actually see Gehrig die. Granted too, he was an aging athlete, his achievements on the ball field largely past him by this time. Granted, finally, he had time to prepare himself for death before he made this last, proud appearance, a benison not available to, say, a fighter pilot shot from the sky.

But even so. . . . There is a dignified, anti-mawkish acceptance of mortality in this passage, a sense, perhaps, that the screenwriters, Jo Swerling and Herman J. Mankiewicz (fresh from *Citizen Kane*, which is, of course, an extended gloss on a dying man's last mysterious word), had read their Housman: "And silence sounds no worse than cheers / After earth has stopped the ears."

It is doubtless too much to ask of wartime movies that they fully acknowledge the absurdity and panic of sudden, youthful death. That was for a later time—for *Bonnie and Clyde* and *Chinatown*, for *Pulp Fiction* and *Fargo*—though I do think that the way death is now portrayed in our best movies is one of their great improvements upon the past. But it seems to me that the imposition of heroic meaning upon it—not to mention their many promises of an agreeable and useful afterlife—is, when all is said and done, the salient defect, the great lie of wartime movies. Acceptance—dutiful, dignified, silent (or at least monosyllabic) was the mode not taken.

I know of only two movies that make no attempt to console us about battlefield losses. These are *They Were Expendable* and *The Story of G.I. Joe*, completed while the war was still on, released shortly after it was over.

The former is, in my estimation, John Ford's best movie, the one in which he fully controls his propensity for raucous sentiments, vulgar music, lame lower-ranks humor. It is about the torpedo-boat squadron commanded by John Bulkely (called Brickley in the film and played by Robert Montgomery) that spirited MacArthur and his family away from the Philippines in 1942. Mostly, though, it is about loss borne in utterly uncomplaining, manly fashion. One by one the squadron's boats are destroyed, their crews decimated. John Wayne, playing the hotblooded second in command, "Rusty" Ryan, falls in love with a nurse on Bataan (Donna Reed), who is killed in a Japanese attack. He bears that blow with the same silent fortitude the rest of the command bears its losses.

Finally, having retreated halfway across the Pacific, Brickley, Ryan, and a handful of survivors are preparing to fight as infantrymen on an island about to be overrun. The two officers, however, are ordered to Australia, perhaps as a reward for their efforts on the MacArthurs' behalf. They climb on the last plane leaving an island about to fall to the Japanese. That means that two officers with lower priorities will have to be bumped from the flight. Which means, in turn, that they will probably sooner or later die—in the immediate fighting or in a Japanese prison camp. They arise without complaint, there are some murmured "good lucks," perhaps, one thinks, a slightly guilty look on the faces of the lucky ones. But that's all. Orders are orders, duty is duty.

The Story of G.I. Joe is even more taciturn. It is the story of Ernie Pyle (Burgess Meredith), the war correspondent who became famous by telling the war's story through the eyes of enlisted men. William A. Wellman, the film's director, admired the unassuming Pyle almost as much as the men he wrote about did, and the film is animated by his affection. By the time it was released, Pyle had been killed on Ie Shima, among the men who were his subjects, and that added to the impact of the film.

But what is most moving about the film is a fictional lieutenant played by Robert Mitchum. He's a GI's officer, looking out for his men at the risk of his own life. The last we see of him he is writing letters of condolence to next of kin, getting a little drunk in the process, and saying to Pyle: "They're the best, Ernie, the best."

The next we hear of him, he's dead, a body slung over a pack mule in the back of the shot, heading for the rear as his weary troops shamble forward, up the boot of Italy. Again, there is no hint of transfiguration. He's just another anonymous number in the casualty report. But he is also one of the most memorable figures in Hollywood's war; the role made Mitchum, who spent most of the war playing small parts, a star.

Perhaps it is significant that these movies—together with Lewis Milestone's more (unfortunately) "poetic" (but still anti-heroic) *A Walk in the Sun*—were made so late in the war. Perhaps by then Hollywood was beginning to discover the right diction for its war. Perhaps it sensed that its audience was beginning to suspect its embrace of the uncanny in resolving so many of its narratives. I really don't know.

BUT I do know this: that whatever we, as kids, knew about death we learned at the movies. It was a subject barred elsewhere. In children's books, death was never discussed. On the radio, the serial nature of the kid shows demanded that their villains live on and on to haunt the heroes. The self-contained crime-stopper shows did just that—they stopped crime short but without, as a rule, definitively stomping it to death.

In the comics the rules were different. The bad people were often grotesques—see in particular Batman and Dick Tracy. Since they were subhuman anyway, it was all right for them to die grotesquely: their passings were often portrayed as black comedy.

So, almost by default, it was the movies that were obliged most often to face up to death. But the kind of starry martyrs we have been discussing were a minority: most of those who died on camera were extras and small-parts players, whose deaths went largely unmourned. Everyone else was too busy taking the hill or beating back the counterattack.

This convention remains with us in today's action movies, where the passing of hundreds, even thousands, of victims goes unremarked by the critics of media violence. They instead focus their outrage on those few movies—*Pulp Fiction* is a good recent example—in which the startlement and terror of sudden death are made palpable, profoundly painful, deeply discomfiting to the audience.

Serious movies, movies that make a moral point with which everyone agrees—*Schindler's List, Saving Private Ryan*—are exempt from these strictures. Logically, of course they should not be. What does a child know about the higher morality? The horrors of a concentration camp or of D day are bound to disturb him as much if not more—given the vivid brilliance of Spielberg's filmmaking—than anything he might see in *Scream II*.

This was obviously not an issue during the war. Because Hollywood and the Office of War Information and our own needs conspired to make us look away from death, soften its impact in all the ways I've been discussing. The whole point was to make it seem not final for the people we cared about, to give them some sort of noble out-clause.

THIS VIEW was supported by such religious training as I had. Which wasn't much. We attended—in those days mainly on

Christmas Eve and Easter—the Congregational church. It was the most cheerful and dispassionate of denominations. Our minister was an Englishman, the Reverend Henry James Lee—"the Domini", as my grandfather always called him. Grandpa went more often to church than we did—though I was obliged to attend Sunday school every week for years—and regarded the minister "as the finest pulpit orator I've ever heard." He was a round-faced man with slicked-back black hair, and he certainly had a mellifluous voice.

But Sunday school bored me senseless, and I thought Henry James Lee was a windbag. He personally prepared us for confirmation. Mostly we had to memorize the books of the Bible and be able to recite the Ten Commandments; he never raised any of the really interesting theological questions. Before I could be confirmed I had to be baptized in front of the whole congregation, because my parents had somehow neglected that obligation when I was a baby. It was a public humiliation I begged, without avail, to be spared.

Childless, "the Domini" hadn't the slightest idea how to talk to children. So religion, as it was presented to me, was an inconvenience and an irrelevance. I did not know, because no one made the connection, that the only worthwhile business of religion—"That vast moth-eaten musical brocade," in Philip Larkin's phrase—was to help us pretend that our inevitable extinction was not as final as it might seem, that our spirits, at least, would not forever "be lost in always," another of Larkin's terms.

What WASP religion put up against the endless darkness and silence were pink clouds, heavenly choirs, busybody angels, and a God who appeared to be rather like my grandfather—strict yet generous and forgiving. It was a pretty fantasy but not a very sturdy one, considering the hard reality it was supposed to oppose.

For a long time I did not see that what wartime movies offered, when they could not escape confrontation with death, was
confirmation of that same fantasy. Talk about the genial imaging
of enormous ideas!

Most American movies tended to avoid direct expressions of
religious belief. It is true that a number of European underground fighters sought sanctuary in churches. And who can forget William Bendix's hysterical invocation of the Deity in
Guadalcanal Diary, when a group of Marines is trapped in a
bombardment? But on the whole God was invoked in a nonde-
nominational way. He was on our side, naturally, but his voice
tended to come to us not from on high but as an expression of
the people's will.

Take, for example, the sermon in the bomb-damaged village
chapel at the end of *Mrs. Miniver*. Mostly this "Domini" stresses
that this is a "people's war," fought to free us "from the tyranny
and terror that threaten to strike us down." He adds: "It is our
war. Fight it then. Fight it with all that is in us." As he speaks,
massed Allied bombers—God's own avenging angels— are
glimpsed through the chancel, opened to the sky by German
bombs.

In 1942, obviously, this minister was not addressing his own
parishioners. As a result of air raids, they already knew war's
deadly costs—though why the Nazis were wasting so many
bombs on this remote garden spot is one of those unanswered
movie mysteries. Rather, the minister is speaking to the American audience, who were implicitly inspired to analogize these
raids on this "quiet corner" of England with the attack on Pearl
Harbor on a sunny, peaceful Sunday morning.

Analogy was Hollywood's great weapon when it came to
wartime religious statement. It permitted the Jewish moguls to

address their audience's religiosity without compromising their own. Speaking to a Christian country, whose core belief was in a martyr who was resurrected and ascended to eternal life, the movies secularized that belief, presenting us with dozens of guys named Joe who recapitulated that eschatology without saying a conventionally pious word about what was going on. This was a holy war without a lot of holy words.

Which suited my own tenuous belief system just fine. What did I know? Or maybe the better way to put that question is, What did I care?

I did not even take advantage of "released time," an hour or so once a week, when the other kids were excused from school to go to "Bible Class" at their churches—a practice later struck down by the Supreme Court. It struck me as a nuisance, especially when I discovered that the few kids remaining in the classroom could spend the time goofing off.

My late wife, Carol, who was raised a Catholic, sometimes said that one of my troubles as a writer—maybe as a person— was that I never had anything worthwhile to rebel against. I needed an intrusive, hectoring, all-encompassing religious institution to drive me into guilt-ridden frenzies of disbelief. I think she was right. It was too easy for me to go along with this wishy-washy Protestantism, if I so chose. Or to go away from it, as eventually I did. It really has not made any difference in my life.

I BEGAN to absent myself from religious belief when I was about twelve years old. Sweet Aunt Nell, one of grandma's sisters, died—quite suddenly, so far as I knew. She had a house across the street from Camp Randall Stadium in Madison, and gave us lunch when we went to the Badgers' games. She always baked homemade doughnuts for me, and proudly belonged to a Dickens society.

There was a funeral in Evansville, my first. I didn't have to be told to sit still; solemnity was so obviously called for. But I was startled—embarrassed really—when Nell's husband, my Uncle Max Fisher, a wiry little house painter of acerbic temperament and a favorite relative of mine, broke into loud, wracking sobs during the minister's eulogy. It was far out of his character as I understood it. But in that howl of pain I finally began to get it: the void, the emptiness that death leaves behind, from which most of us recover; the utter silence and loneliness of the grave, from which no one recovers.

Did I fully understand all this at Aunt Nell's funeral? No, of course not. But I was beginning to get the distinctly unconsoling idea.

It is perhaps worth noting that the Reverend Henry James Lee died in an auto accident when he was vacationing in his native England. It was said that he became confused driving on the wrong side of the road after so many years in America. I wonder what his last thought was as he confidently entered "always." Surprise, I'll bet—have bet—at the absence of angels. At the enveloping darkness, the resounding silence.

12

The Best Years of Our Lives

IN THE SPRING of 1945 I moved on from the Washington School to Longfellow Junior High. It shared facilities with the town's high school, which had a gym and an auditorium, both of which could accommodate the entire student body of either institution. The buildings of the two schools were connected by an underground tunnel, and the size and bustle of the place at first disconcerted me. I thought I would never be able to manage the crowds, the clangor of bells signaling the end of class periods. For a few days I mourned, absurdly, for my lost childhood. But soon I settled in.

In April we mourned President Roosevelt's passing at a school assembly. In May we marked V-E day at a similar gathering. When the atomic bombs were dropped on Japan, we were on summer vacation and had to come to grips with the unimaginable on our own. On August 14, the day hostilities ceased, factory whistles sounded all over town.

On its front page, after the Hiroshima bombing, the *Milwaukee Journal*, as usual looking for a local angle, ran a picture of a huge conventional bomb casing, which the caption said was made at Allis-Chalmers in West Allis, which in peacetime made orange-painted farm equipment. The bomb dwarfed the guy standing next to it to suggest its scale. We later learned that the A-bombs were nowhere near this big.

But how quickly we put the war out of mind. Bob Hanel came home limping slightly, as I recall, but with his good nature intact. Bob's dad, who taught shop at one of the Catholic high schools, had fashioned a little shrine on the stairs leading up to Bob's bedroom. It was a polished wooden niche, containing a statuette of the Virgin Mary and a metal plate made from the shrapnel that had wounded Bob, identifying the time and place (Saipan) it had happened. Mr. Hanel had showed it to my father and me one evening, proudly imagining his son's delight when he first caught sight of it. I'm certain Bob did not disappoint him.

My father threw himself into the campaign for the war memorial. Perhaps unsurprisingly, it did not attract the kind of support its proponents had imagined. Perhaps the plans—a library, a civic center containing most of the municipal offices and services under one elegant roof—seemed just a little pretentious for our conservative community. It was sometime in the sixties, I think, before the memorial was completed in a form somewhat less grand than originally planned.

Everything would turn out to be less grand than originally planned. I could not see that at the time. Few did. But World War II was the last great narrative in which, in some way or other, we could all find our place. The postwar world was basically a long, stumbling retreat from coherence of that sort. Robert Skidelsky writes that in that era we suffered a "collapse" of "the view that history has a 'meta-narrative' linking the past to the future which can be rationally discerned, and in the light of which explanations can be given and tasks undertaken."

EARLY IN 1946 my father took me to a parade on Wisconsin Avenue. It was part of a national "Don't Buy Another Depression" campaign, the emblem of which was an apple, the fruit sold on street corners by men out of work in the 1930s.

I didn't much care about that. I wanted to see the parade because it included one or two huge balloons of the sort featured in the Macy's Thanksgiving parade. Get it? Big inflatables warning us against inflation.

The parade's other attraction was its grand marshal, Jim Thorpe, the great Indian athlete. Everyone knew he had been screwed by the Olympic committee, which had long ago made him give back his medals when it discovered he had made a few bucks playing semi-pro baseball. We were hostile to the hypocrisy of the rich nitwits who ruled amateur athletics, sympathetic to this obviously honorable and simple man. Perched atop the back seat of his open convertible, he waved genially to us.

But the crowd was small, the parade short, the day cold, with snow flurries. Naturally, everyone went ahead and bought lots of new stuff anyway, initiating the postwar boom that has never really ceased.

I didn't particularly notice our prosperity. I accepted it as a given. Which has remained in place for the rest of my life. I never fully participated in it—not in the way so many people did. But at least I never went broke, either. Still, the big surprise to my economic innocence was how much time I have spent in life worrying about money. I can't tell you how many hundreds of legal pads I have covered with figures—projected income, projected expenses—as I tried to calculate a freelance writer's erratic cash flow. I can't tell you how much crap I have written because, studying these figures, I guessed—usually correctly—that I would need the dough.

ALSO IN 1946, wartime's last picture show appeared—*The Best Years of Our Lives*. It is, of course, the story of how three servicemen (one each, neatly enough, from the army, the air force, and the navy), meeting for the first time when they hitch a ride to their hometown on a military aircraft, make their adjustments to peacetime.

It was instantly beloved—a huge, multi-Oscar hit. It remains so for most people. I think of it as the last great wartime lie, a fantasia of good feelings, as eerily out of touch with human reality as, say, the people of *Since You Went Away* had been two years earlier.

It is conscientiously produced by Samuel Goldwyn. Robert E. Sherwood's script is well enough realized by the director, William Wyler, and Gregg Toland's deep-focus photography subtly intensifies the film's realistic air. But it is only an air. The film historian David Thomson calls the movie "undeniably honest and touching." I think it the opposite—undeniably lying and sentimental.

Not that Sherwood deliberately prevaricated. He had won three Pulitzer Prizes for his impeccably liberal-minded (now almost forgotten) plays in the prewar years, spent the war years writing speeches for Roosevelt, and won a final Pulitzer for his joint biography of Roosevelt and Harry Hopkins. His screenplay assumed that everyone had by now internalized the political values he had so long espoused, that American life was now mainly a question of minor behavioral adjustments within the framework provided by those values. We had, he implied, fought a war for them, and they would now supply a permanent American consensus, a permanent American coherence.

But this was wishful—not to say wistful—thinking. As Robert Warshow observed at the time, none of the issues the film took up was overtly (or intractably) political. All are shown to be soluble by the common sense and common decency of its leading characters, who never have an ideological thought or discussion.

It is doubtless unfair to criticize the movie for its failure to imagine the cold war, McCarthyism, the Silent Generation, the pietism of Norman Vincent Peale, the quietism of the Organization Man. Or, most significantly, the unending postwar struggle for racial justice (no blacks are visible in the film). Sherwood was not, after all, a futurist. On the other hand, he might have guessed that something would go wrong since something always does.

He did imagine that a class system of sorts pertained in the mythical Midwestern city (said to be inspired by Cincinnati) where the film is set. But no one is the least oppressed by it. Rather the opposite. Such modest ideological freight as the movie carries is borne by Fredric March's Al Stephenson, who is oxymoronically both a liberal and a banker, a man who served as an enlisted man in the war—no "wangling a commission" for him. It is not explained how his family maintained their spacious apartment while he was earning sergeant's pay. We only understand that he acted on principle, and they went along with him.

Dana Andrews's Fred Derry is harder to place sociologically. He was an officer and a bomber pilot during the war, which implies college education, middle-class aspirations. On the other hand, his parents are shown to be trashy, and he is married to a slut (Virginia Mayo) who loved his fly-boy's uniform but not the honorable man inside it. She's now carrying on with a wartime slacker, and poor Fred must return to his humiliating prewar job as a drugstore soda jerk. He wears a little white cap and jacket instead of his flier's hat with a twenty-mission crush in it.

The working class is represented by Homer Parrish, who is

artlessly played by Harold Russell, a real-life veteran who lost his hands in the war. He obviously has the most serious readjustment problem. He fears being so visible a cripple and tries to drive his girl friend, Wilma (Cathy O'Donnell), away. He thinks her love must have turned to dutiful pity.

But everything works out for all of them. Al has a spot of trouble at the bank, where he insists on granting loans to vets based on character rather than collateral. But he persuades his bosses that his is the right policy. Fred gets fired from his terrible job (for punching out a patron who questions our war aims), dumps his awful wife, but gets a better job and a better woman (nice Teresa Wright, the banker's daughter). Homer finally accepts Wilma. At the end of the movie all these good people forgather at Homer and Wilma's wedding, where he demonstrates his dexterity with his hooks by using them to slip the ring on her finger. See—all you had to do was try a little tenderness.

It was what we had not yet learned to call a feel-good movie. And I'll concede that the grown-ups needed to feel good just then, with war and depression survived, sober lessons learned from them. But I didn't. In fact the comfortable—not to say semi-comatose—world of *The Best Years of Our Lives* was exactly the world I wanted to escape.

It required only thirteen years for someone neatly, perfectly, to subvert *The Best Years of Our Lives*. In 1959, in *The Magic Christian*, Terry Southern imagined his impossibly rich and wickedly transgressive hero, Grand Guy Grand, buying up such release prints as remained of *The Best Years of Our Lives* and inserting a near-subliminal shot of Russell's hooks disappearing up O'Donnell's skirt.

Many years later there was a more poignant postscript. Harold Russell had won an Academy Award for *Best Years* and published an autobiography (*Victory in My Hands*). He became what we would now call a motivational speaker. He appeared at one of our school assemblies, and I still remember that as we applauded him he clasped his hooks above his head—a gallant reference to the prizefighter's traditional gesture of triumph.

But things went sour for him. In 1992 he put his Oscar statuette on the market because he needed the money. Perhaps what he feared and fought in the movie had at last overwhelmed him. Perhaps what the war had cost him was too vivid, too discomfiting a reminder of sacrifices we preferred not to think about as we grew fatter and richer.

The Best Years of Our Lives marked the end of our wartime earnestness. It was the last movie to insist that, whatever sacrifices we had made, they would be rewarded with a better postwar life for the survivors.

The movies did not abandon World War II as a subject. For decades it remained what it was (until quite recently, with *Schindler's List* and *Saving Private Ryan*)—a background for pure, morally weightless adventure. I did not notice this. I'm not certain I particularly noticed anything about the movies in the early postwar years, though I kept going to them.

I especially liked *film noir*, though the genre had not yet acquired its frenchified name. I liked its rain-wet streets, its blinking neon signs, its cynical dialogue, and its most basic trope—damaged guys being lured into insanely complicated criminal adventures by women using sex in a new movie way, overtly manipulating their victims. There was a dark glamour in these films that was very strange yet curiously plausible. Very un-Wauwatosa.

But the truth is, in these years I was otherwise engaged. Mainly I was engaged—without at first consciously knowing it—in becoming a writer.

In junior high I remained the kind of student I had always been and in fact always would be—good at English and social studies, bad at math and the sciences (and languages, to which I now wish I had paid attention). There were also some new and loathsomely irrelevant challenges—the required shop courses (mechanical drawing, metalworking, woodworking), general science, that sort of thing.

Here is a story that has always, for me, perfectly exemplified my comical situation: Woodworking was taught by Mr. Engeseth, a wiry little Scots bachelor who carried his change in a drawstring leather pouch. One day, watching me ruin the third or fourth piece of wood I was trying to run through a band saw in aid of a birdhouse I never finished, he cried out to me in anguish: "Schickel, you're not a real boy."

He was both right and wrong. I was a real boy in many respects. I liked sports and goofing off. And I was beginning to like girls. But I didn't give a hoot about this stuff, which, I have to admit, the more struttingly macho guys sailed through.

I couldn't imagine what use it would ever be to me. Same with math. I knew even then that all I'd ever have to do in life was add, subtract, multiply, and divide. Had I known that in a few decades they would invent hand-held calculators, I probably wouldn't have bothered to learn even those simple skills. All through junior high and high school I begged the other guys for help when it came to equations, theorems, and the ablative absolute.

My strange mixture of grades—high in the courses I liked, abysmal in those I abhorred, caused worried comment at school and at home. Concern about my future was often expressed.

What did I think I was doing? What college would possibly admit me? How would I ever earn a living? I dunno, I would mumble, promising with patent insincerity to do better next term, which I never did.

But, as I've said, in same dim, incoherent way I did know what I would be doing if I ever managed to grow up. The trouble was, there was no one in the entire community who could possibly have given me practical advice about how to become a writer. So I kept my ambitions to myself.

IT WAS IN sports that I did my best to be a real boy. I was an inept substitute center on the junior high basketball team (total scoring over two seasons: three points), a first-string center-linebacker in ninth-grade football, and a third-stringer for two seasons on the high school football team. I wasn't much better at football, though I was stronger on defense than offense. As a line-backer you sort of freelanced around, making opportunistic tackles. Offense was more like math. You had blocking assignments I could never quite remember, and you had to move on a snap count that sometimes eluded me.

Beyond that, I didn't like the towel-snapping, dumb-joking camaraderie of the team, even though my good buddies Ned Kurtz and Jack McCrory, both steady, reserved guys, also played. Something in that sport—possibly the way it pushes male bonding to the flash point—makes morons of us all, players and fans alike.

And yet, old as I am, I remember in my bones the profound satisfaction of a good tackle, the fresh, clean smell of the frosty ground in early November, the catch in one's throat as the chilly night air settled over the lighted practice field. I carry a tiny scar near my right eye, where some cleated foot kicked me as I downed someone in some game that was, at that point, long lost to us (I would not have been in the contest if we had still had a chance to win).

In both sports I played behind massive Art Mathias, with whom I had been competing since first grade. He was an artless, rather phlegmatic boy, better at basketball than football. He turned lobster red as he chugged up and dawn the court, using his size to bully his way to an all-time suburban conference scoring record in high school. He went on to Northwestern on an athletic scholarship but never made it in the Big Ten.

He made it in life, though. I kept inquiring about him in later years. But Lary Elliot, who had remained in the Milwaukee area and is the high school pal with whom I am in the closest touch, professed to know nothing of his fate. Then, at my fiftieth high school reunion, there Art was—still physically imposing, still quiet. He told me that after college he had taken over his father's plumbing business and had even stayed on in his father's house, eventually expanding it to accommodate his own expanding family. He had prospered and had become an alderman. Retired, he remained active in volunteer work. I found, now that ancient rivalries were stilled, that I liked him enormously—a composed, thoughtful man who had devoted his life to practical, useful work. I thought that in some ways he had done better than I had, volunteering for nothing except my own advancement. It saddened me to hear, within days of writing this paragraph, that he had died.

MY FALLING OUT with Mr. Drost dampened my enthusiasm for the yearbook: I became a sort of ghost editor, sulkily seeing the book through the press. In my senior year I began spending time on the high school paper, the *Cardinal News*. It was edited out of Mr. Regensdorf's room, just up the stairs from Mr. Drost's lair.

Philip Regensdorf was one of the two teachers who definitively changed my life. In my senior year I could sometimes admit that well, maybe, you know, I might like to be a writer someday. Nothing fancy, you understand—sports reporting, maybe. I read some books on newspapering—most notably Stanley Walker's *City Editor*, which was filled with helpful advice about clear, concise writing yet was touched by a sort of raffish, big-city glamour. I could imagine myself writing on deadline amidst the hubbub of a metropolitan newsroom, a cigarette dangling from my lips.

This was not something Mr. Regensdorf could imagine, though he surely did nothing to discourage my fantasy. He was a marvelous man and teacher. I suspect he had wanted to be a college professor. He kept his master's thesis, something about the use of metaphor in Spenser's *The Faerie Queene*, in his bottom desk drawer. Every Friday he read us something from an anthology of good American prose. That's where I first encountered Jackie Smurch. It was his remark that the *New Yorker* was "my one indispensable magazine" that led to my lifelong subscription. Most important, he patiently read and criticized the stories I began writing in those days. I remember his words of praise for one of them: "This is the real stuff."

Dapper and cool in his well-cut suits, obtained on his employee's discount at Schuster's where he worked nights and weekends as a floorwalker, he stood out from his more rumpled colleagues. Stood out from them, too, in his ambitions. While I was still in his class he abruptly quit teaching—another Carla George experience for me—and accepted an executive position with the store. It was a decision conditioned, I'm sure, by the depression and the hopes it dashed, the fears it engendered. He was positioning himself to participate in our burgeoning postwar prosperity. Farewell, *Faerie Queene.*

That was not an option for Julia K. Henninger. She was more openly passionate in her love for English literature, breathy and excitable as she parsed Keats or Wordsworth for her largely indifferent classes. She also had psoriasis, which caused her to scratch at herself while lecturing. A lot of people laughed at her. But I didn't. And neither did a girlfriend of mine. We responded to her desire to enflame us. We invented a romantic past for her—maybe a lost love, an airman, perhaps, downed over the trenches in World War I, whom she still mourned in the silence of her lonely room.

That was, I'm sure, pure fiction. But there was nothing fictional in her ambitions for Mary Jean and me. We were her acoloytes, defending her against the boobocracy and its casual slurs. We would sometimes visit her in her neat little apartment. We took seriously her recommendations for additional reading. We discounted the sometimes comic effects she created with her helter-skelter ways.

And we stayed in touch for years, for she was a lifer. She continued teaching until she reached retirement age, and lived on to a considerable age, writing me the occasional encouraging note when I became a professional writer.

I don't think there has ever been an American writer's memoir that does not feature English teachers like these, keepers of a flickering literary flame on some windswept provincial plain, waiting for someone to stop and warm his or her longing at their little fires. I owe these two people more than I can calculate. At a crucial moment they replaced my grandfather's less focused regard for good writing, directing my attention to specific examples of aspiring prose. Implicitly they suggested that the limits of my talent might be a little farther out than I imagined.

More important, their encouragement was objective, not obligatory, as it was with family. They constituted my first tiny audience. And somehow—quite unconsciously at first—I gathered from them the peculiar notion that if you wrote a lot, to the best of your ability, you could swell this crowd and, by so doing—yes— cheat death by insinuating yourself in their collective memory.

It is preposterous, of course. Absurd. Irrational. Especially for a talent that turned out to be as minor as mine. But there it is—not surely the only reason I have written so much, but a reason nevertheless. The hope of achieving a touch of some very modest, rather short-lived immortality always lurks in a dim corner of my mind. I imagine some graduate student of the future, coming across a citation of something I wrote in a bibliography, looking it up and using it in his or her thesis. I like that sneaky thought. I think that kid I once was, standing on his snowy street corner, contemplating the great nothingness for the first time, would like it too—not at all what he imagined, but, what the hell, you take what you can get—in death as in life.

AT THE END of my first senior semester Mr. Regensdorf invited me to become coeditor of the newspaper for my final semester. He told me, though, that I couldn't do that and play football too.

Ostensibly this was a hard choice, but I don't recall hesitating long over it. I knew where my future lay. My mother, needless to say, was greatly relieved.

At the *Cardinal News* I wrote everything—editorials, news stories, and, yes, reviews—school plays, community concerts, even television programs. I gave a snotty notice to the senior class production of *You Can't Take It with You* and was briefly, enjoyably, a pariah in certain circles.

Mostly I wrote heedlessly. I liked showing off. I liked pissing people off. When the topic was serious I wrote pompously. My last editorial for the paper was a solemn welcome to the second half of the century written in January 1951, just before I graduated. But it did win a prize in a competition sponsored by the Quill and Scroll Society, an organization devoted, if you can imagine such a thing, to improving the standards of high school journalism. The society also granted me a journalism scholarship to the University of Wisconsin.

SUCH MODEST TRIUMPHS did not count where I most wanted them to count—with girls. I nearly always had someone I was "dating." But I got nowhere with any of them. I was too enthusiastic, too romantic. I wanted this part of my life to be like a movie. If I actually got to kiss one of them good night, I immediately began imagining some sort of *grande affaire*. I would become possessive and broody and moon over them. They would, sooner rather than later, grow skittish.

I think I interested some of them; I was not, after all, a total dope. On the other hand, they did not quite know what to make of overpassionate me. I suppose every adolescent male they encountered was equally full of free-floating libidinal energy and had to be closely managed once the car was parked on same secluded cul-de-sac, the sweater raised, the bra strap loosened. But the other boys had predictable futures—law, medicine, their father's business—and the effect of marriage to one of them (and I do believe these girls were thinking about that) could be predictably calculated.

That was impossible with me. I spoke of things they could barely imagine—New York and a writing career, the details of which were vague and murky. Surely that scared them. They were already lost to predictability. Meantime, where did he think he was going with that hand?

Nowhere, really. It was easily disciplined. We published the *Cardinal Pennant*, the yearbook, out of a room adjacent to Mr. Drost's classroom. It was filled with cabinets in which he stored maps for his geography classes—each containing a series of long, flat drawers, reaching to eye level. We would pull these out and rest our publication's layout boards on them for study.

One time my hand was resting on one of these pulled out drawers when a young woman—her name now lost to me—joined me in contemplating one of our designs. She was a semester ahead of me, a senior soon to graduate. She had her own car and was pretty in a fresh, chunky sort of way. She thrust a small, angora-clad breast against my hand. I thought it was an accident. But no, it stayed there. I felt it rising and falling as she breathed.

We were alone in the room. It would have been easy to convert seeming accident into stirring incident. I couldn't do it. Because I couldn't believe this was happening to me. A week or two later we went riding in her car and stopped somewhere for a soulful talk. She is, for me, the girl on the ferry boat that Mr. Bernstein glimpsed once and never forgot.

Later that spring I met a girl I won't name. She worked on the *Cardinal News* and was also a semester ahead of me in school. She was smart, slightly depressed, mournfully pretty, and, like me, not fully in tune with the humming high school universe. We began to date. I think we fell in love—I, doubtless, more than she. But she was as curious and horny as I was. We did not go "all the way." Yet I did things with her in my parents' car that I have not done with any woman since—pious refusals all mixed up with perverse curiosity.

We broke up during our first year in college at Madison.

But we stayed friends. And one afternoon she came over to my apartment and cheerfully, belatedly took my virginity. She had long since lost hers. For years thereafter, when we had nothing better to do, we would meet and make good-natured love.

I MOVED to Madison in a January snowstorm. It was merely typical, not symbolic. I quit journalism school as soon as my two-year scholarship ran out. I already knew that I was supposed to double-space my copy, and it had nothing else to teach me.

I also quit my fraternity as soon as I could. It had been my last attempt to be the lad my parents wanted me to be, and I pledged a "good" house—SAE. I hated it instantly. It was filled with suburban fatheads, determined to become exactly what their fathers had been. In the interim they played bridge, drank (and puked up) vast quantities of beer, and mauled sorority girls. No Jews or blacks were admitted to these revels; the brothers were noisy in their prejudices.

I moved out of the house and stopped attending meetings in the middle of my sophomore year. Since you were not allowed to quit the fraternity—it insisted our brotherhood was lifelong— I had to be expelled. I wrote a letter giving the brothers ample cause to do so, and they obliged me.

My true fraternity was the *Daily Cardinal*, the student newspaper. I'd been recruited to it by a guy named Jerry Schecter, who was its executive editor. We'd met on a student ship going to Europe when I was nineteen. Freddy Leysieffer, my dorm roommate and best friend from high school, and I were spending the summer wandering the continent. Schecter was working his way across the water by editing the mimeographed ship's newspaper. He was, however, prone to seasickness, and Freddy and I ended up doing a lot of the work—especially on the voyage home, when we encountered a hurricane. With decks awash, we managed to get out a reassuring storm extra while Schecter took to his bunk. It is maybe the only thrilling journalistic experience I ever had. The captain invited us to his cabin for cocktails after the storm passed. He felt our efforts had had a calming effect on the passengers.

BACK ON CAMPUS I wandered over to the *Cardinal* one day. It was so shorthanded that I had a byline on its lead story in the next morning's edition. From that day forward I was completely hooked. I virtually lived at the paper for the next two years, studying there, eating at the Italian Village next door—my first experience with pizza. When I left the fraternity I moved into an apartment on Francis Street with Schecter and Dick Carter, a saturnine small-town boy who, like me, was slightly an odd man out at the *Cardinal*, which had for some time been managed by New York Jews.

Or, to employ the campus genteelism, "Easterners." They were too liberal for the McCarthyite Republicans who filled the paper's board, but they were stuck with them. The board could not recruit a competent staff from its frat boy–sorority gal peers. The paper, which had to support itself without university subsidy, was failing—we had to cut our issues from five to three a week—and itself became a center of campus controversy.

We knew what the problem was: we needed to cover the bread-and-butter issues—intramural athletics, fraternity elections—better than we did. But we didn't have the staff to do it. This made our "radical" editorial positions stand out starkly. We were thought to be irresponsible ideologues, though of course we were really just traditional liberals, living off the dwindling New Deal legacy.

It was absorbing to be embattled. Campus politics and journalism became the equivalent of what sports had been in high school—something that took up too much of my time but which it was hopeless to resist. Maybe the best part was putting the paper to bed, standing over the compositor's stone after midnight, under bluish light, scribbling the last couple of headlines, working with the printer to adjust and hammer dawn the front page as the linotypes clunked and clanked, spitting out the last lines of a story.

That duty attended, I would retreat to my office, pound out a story for the *Milwaukee Journal,* whose campus correspondent's job I had inherited from Schecter when he graduated. It was my first paid journalism, forty to fifty dollars a month in accumulated space rates. I would rush my copy to the Western Union office not far from the capitol, toss it to the sleepy telegrapher, growl "NPR Collect" (for night press rate) at him in my best foreign correspondent's tone, and totter home to a bed from which I could rarely move before ten o'clock the next morning.

Stan Zuckerman (another "Easterner" and my new roommate) and I were running the paper now, while amiable Roger Thurrell (the *Cardinal* board's safe choice as editor) wrote editorials supporting the blood drive or urging a high-spirited homecoming rally.

Predictably my grades slipped, classes were cut (especially those before 9:45 in the morning), assignments were carelessly done. I had to quit my English major because I didn't have the time to plow through vast nineteenth-century novels. I switched to Poli Sci, where the reading lists were less demanding.

I began thinking about becoming a political reporter, mostly because I wrote so much about Joe McCarthy, who was our defining issue. He was, of course, Wisconsin's junior senator, a shabby drunk as we now know, and, like all bullies, a coward.

For despite the fact that the University of Wisconsin was a notoriously liberal campus, he never attacked any of the locals.
Among his doughtiest opponents were the *Milwaukee Journal*
and the *Madison Capital Times*, against which he sneered and ful-
minated but never ranted of subversion.

Those newspapers, like all the rest of us, kept chipping away
at McCarthy, disproving this or that unprovable allegation. But
we didn't make much headway. That's because, I now think, we
misconceived the issue McCarthy presented. He and his kind
were not so much a political threat as a cultural one. He was really a primitive postmodernist. Diving into his huge, battered
lawyer's briefcase, pulling out some spurious document that
"proved" Soviet penetration into one or another government
agency, he was inventing non-narrative politics.

Until the 1950s each new American political generation had
woven a piece of its own devising into a historical tapestry which
had as its hopeful theme our halting progress toward some
doubtless imperfect but still worthwhile enlightenment. This was
a murky but somehow dimly perceptible tale. McCarthy, however, dumbly perceived that tapestries were out. The characteristic art form of the age was the collage.

McCarthy made of his crazy collection of snippets and doo-
dlings an anti-intellectual politics, against which rational argument was largely useless. This decline in traditional political
narrative naturally coincided with the decline of traditional narrative in everything else—poetry, painting, the novel, the theater,
even movies. The aim of this art is the striking image, not the
stirring thought. None of us noticed this at the time. It was all so
new, so ill-defined. This was the postwar world the wartime
movies could not imagine.

McCarthy's imagery was finally undone by the equally
primitive but more powerful imagery of television—Edward R.

Murrow's devastating broadcast, the Army-McCarthy hearings. The senator could not stand up to the camera's intimate scrutiny. He lost legitimacy when the cameras searched his spirit and found anarchy's nervous giggle.

This was fine with us. We did not care about the means of his destruction, we only desired it. We did not see that this new instrument would soon be searching every public face, that its pitiless revelations of common humanity in the mighty would become the chief—quite irrational—means by which we selected our leaders, the chief means by which we chose among competing "ideas."

MY ANTI-MCCARTHYISM cost me the *Cardinal* editorship but left me feeling fine. Okay, my consolation prize, the executive editorship, was not exactly Devil's Island, but I imagine I thought of myself as brave Matrac, framed and tormented by adherence to principle.

On a trip home my grandfather counseled caution. He thought I might be endangering my future career—getting my name in the FBI files or some such. He startled my contempt, since I knew he loathed McCarthy too. But grandpa was not grandpa any more.

He still strode the streets brisk and erect, but he was semi-retired now, working out of a small office at his firm for those few clients who still valued his legal opinions. With his work diminished and with me away, he projected a slightly lost air. He continued giving me books. He hung about inconveniently, moonishly. I was impatient with him; he was maddeningly patient with me. I am not proud of my dismissals.

Then my grandmother fell and broke her hip. She entered a nursing home but remained confined to her bed. For a few weeks grandpa maintained the fiction that she would soon return home. But she did not, and it turned out that this old man, this model of opinionated self-sufficiency, could not function on his own. He could not so much as boil an egg or get his shirts to the laundry. Millie had spared him those chores all his life, and he was completely lost without her being up and fussily doing. He spent his last years perfectly healthy, sitting around with sick, dotty old folks. He always wore his suit and tie to distinguish himself from them.

He died in 1964. I'm ashamed to say that I refused to attend his funeral. I claimed I could not leave my family—we had a new baby, our first. I was wrong of course, in my refusal to mourn or forgive him. He could not avoid the passions that gripped him and forced him to grasp us more closely than he should have.

The *Milwaukee Journal*'s obituary of Claude J. Hendricks was of a respectable length. But it misspelled his name. I was not amused. He would not have been amused. He deserved better than the careless attentions of a distracted deskman.

IN 1954 I wrote a piece about the "Joe Must Go" campaign, an effort to recall McCarthy that almost succeeded, and sent it over the *New Republic*'s transom. They published it, paid $100 for it and gave me my first national byline. I was, I thought, on my way.

And I was. I published a number of pieces in small magazines while I was still in college. These appearances in publications they all glanced through, however dismissively, impressed the "Easterners," with whom I was now hanging. Not all of them were Jewish, and some weren't even from the East, but the group's prevailing accent and spirit were distinctly New York—a lot of their parents were leftish garment workers or teachers' union activists. But their radicalism was not entirely political. They read and talked far off all their syllabuses, and I had never seen their likes before. Their *spritzing*—at once sober and wacky—bedazzled my provincial innocence. And I was thrilled when I saw that I could keep up with them.

We hung out in the Rathskeller in the basement of the student union. Someone from our crowd would claim the big round corner table in front of the fireplace early in the morning and, though its population would shift, swell, dwindle through the day, we never abandoned it until late in the evening. We ate there, studied there, argued there. Carter and I even played chess there. I developed a taste for Jewish hubbub that has never left me.

I stayed on for a year after graduation, dodging the Korean War draft (eventually a kindly doctor gave me 4-F status), working desultorily an a master's thesis in American history. Most of the "Easterners" were graduate students in American history, a department that was then one of the university's great ornaments, and many of them later distinguished themselves in that field. But I knew, even then, that I would not. I needed more action. Brick-and-board bookcases were not for me.

POLITICS may have defined me as an undergraduate, but inevitably I was the *Cardinal*'s drama critic. I simply arrogated the job. I've lately seen two or three of my old reviews, and they make me wince. The delegation from the Wisconsin Players who visited me, begging for some rudimentary kindness, was entirely right.

But in those days I didn't understand what the function of reviewing was. I was still showing off—just as I had in high school. Maybe that's a stage in any reviewer's evolution. It was certainly something you saw in the way reviewing was then practiced, particularly on Broadway. Much of that writing was touched by a sort of phony subjectivity, in which you learned a lot about what the reviewer said was his state of mind, not very much about the play in question.

But these reviewers had power: they could close a show or make it a hit solely on the basis of their collective opinion. Nowhere else in journalism was there such a direct connection between an expressed opinion and a palpable result. I wanted to be among them someday—not that I had the faintest idea how to do so.

Besides, that was just a shady passing thought—not something I dared admit out loud. It seems odd to me that I so successfully evaded what now seems such a self-evident fate, which was reviewing movies. It was not that I was neglecting them. We went to the movies all the time. We talked about them all the time. And the movies of the immediate postwar period—until 1953, when ponderous CinemaScope came in and pretty much ruined American moviemaking for awhile—were on the whole quite good. Why, then, didn't it occur to me that they might be a subject I would be happy writing about?

Because, to put it simply, the intellectual and artistic communities were still exercising their contempt for the medium. The period was actually regressive in that there were no critics like James Agee writing about movies. Excepting a couple of items like Paul Rotha's *The Film Till Now*, there were not yet any serious books about them. And the universities, with a couple of faraway exceptions like USC, did not consider them a worthy subject for academic inquiry. It's hard to be serious about a subject no one else wants to take seriously.

The university itself offered not a single film course—historical, critical, or practical. It did, however, have weekend screenings in the student union's pleasant little theater. It played the Ealing comedies, the early David Lean films, and the canonical works of the 1930s—*Grand Illusion, Rules of the Game*. On Thursdays there was a series of more esoteric historical fare— mostly silents by Eisenstein, Griffith, Fritz Lang. Eventually we organized our *Ecstasy*-driven film society, where we pretty much booked what we most longed to see. It was at a meeting at our president's apartment that I saw my first copy of *Cahiers du Cinema*. Imagine that—a brotherhood of cinematic autodidacts. But we were so much more isolated than those Lucky Pierres, writing in a capital city where movies were actually produced, where at the least there was some kind of an audience for your musings.

This story typifies our situation: A guy I knew grew restless as a graduate student in sociology. He applied for admission to the film school at USC and was accepted. One August day he packed his car, enjoyed a sendoff party at the 602 Club (the bar that was our alternative Rathskeller), and headed west. Two or three days later he was back. Alone and brooding as he made his way across the Nebraska plains, he spun a decisive U-turn. Safe in the comforting confines of the 602, he muttered into his beer: "People like us don't go into the movies." He re-upped in sociology and got his Ph.D.

I understood completely. The journey from cinephile to cineaste was not marked out on any mental maps available to us. I wonder now how my life might have played out if, leaving Wisconsin in 1956, I had turned right at Chicago instead of left, headed west to Los Angeles instead of east for New York. But that was not really an option.

IN NEW YORK I worked as a reporter, a writer, and an editor on three magazines. I published my first book in 1960, mainly because the contract offered an escape from one of those publications (*Look*) that was making me crazy. Then I started freelancing. In 1965 I wrote my first movie reviews for *Life*. I have been reviewing films ever since. In 1968 I wrote my first worthwhile book about the movies. In 1969 I wrote narration for my first television program. In 1972 I added producing and directing to my television activities. In all I have written thirty-one books and have made a similar number of documentaries. Almost all of these endeavors have in some ways been about the movies.

I was lucky to come to movie reviewing when I did. In the mid-sixties the New York literati began reversing the situation that had pertained during my college years. They belatedly discovered that the movies were an "art form" and began nattering about them. If you happened to be reviewing them, and were not a total moron—or even if you were, come to think of it—the forums I have mentioned were suddenly opened to you. And others too—late-night talk shows, academic assemblages, church basements. If you were energetic and shameless enough, you could cut quite a figure around town.

Eventually I gained a certain fame from my activities, a modest prosperity, even a bit of authority. I think, over the years, I've become a better reviewer than I was when I started out. Without much conscious study, I now know quite a bit about movies. You hang around, you learn.

I sometimes find this odd. It seems to me a career ought to be created more intentionally, more self-consciously, than mine was. But maybe not. I recently read a review of some books by and about John Ruskin and came across this passage: "In a caveat to his future biographers, Ruskin cautioned that we are made into what we become only by these external accidents that are in accord with our inner natures." Clever slacker me! I found a way to turn my habit of skulking in the shadows of movie theaters into a respectable occupation.

I don't know what good it has done. Most of what I have written about, often enough in hot passion, has simply disappeared from everyone's memory. Who cares about what anyone thinks about old movies? Or, for that matter, last week's movies? My friend John Gregory Dunne looks upon my activities with the jaundiced eye of a novelist and screenwriter. Movie reviewing, he once said to me, "is not something you aim for; it's a place you end up." A very rich producer, in the process of a failed attempt to corrupt me, once said: "You know what your trouble is? You're a smart guy in a dumb job."

I think if I'd not written some of the books or not made some of the documentaries, I'd agree with both of them. You've got to do something to occupy the time between the cradle and the grave, and my choice has been neither better nor worse than anyone else's—just a little wider than that of most reviewers. John Dunne also once said to me that you get to do only four or five worthwhile things in life. I think that somehow I've managed that—to my own satisfaction, at least. If you think I'm going to name them, you're nuts.

13

The Evil of Banality

LARGELY LEFT OUT of this account of growing up are all the things that eventually make you a grown-up—marriage, children, grandchildren, divorce, deaths in the family. And, of course, details about the appointments and disappointments that constitute an adult's working life. All that is for another book. Or, more likely in my case, for no book at all.

This book, though, is not quite finished. That's because, during the period I was working most intensively on it, I was also doing a television documentary about the combat cameramen of World War II. I interviewed many of them—modest men who spoke evenly, contemplatively, about their experiences photographing, often at high risk to themselves, this or that small, deadly corner of a vast canvas of destruction. More important, I acquainted myself with hundreds of thousands of feet of film they shot.

Some of this material tugged oddly at memory. I seemed to remember fragments of their footage from the newsreels of childhood, vivid flashes of imagery that were deeply buried in my consciousness. After talking to these photographers, I found a curiously perfect match between their war stories and the films they made. There were no lies, no aggrandizements either of themselves or of the solders whose exploits they recorded.

This contrasted with the more famous footage shot during the war by Hollywood directors who made a number of longer documentaries. John Ford, John Huston, William Wyler, George Stevens—all of them at some point went bravely under fire, but none could resist shaping the material they and their crews shot into more heroic (and patriotically meaningful) narratives. To put it simply, they faked footage. Or, later, in the editing room, conflated disparate images in order to create more coherent (and uplifting) tales. They were much praised and honored for this effort. Oscars were passed out. Certainly at the time their work was inspirational to us at home. And it has had a powerful afterlife. Even as I worked on my film, more than a half-century later, people would confidently advise me that I must be sure to include this or that "unforgettable" shot or sequence from their documentaries.

But these movies now made me uncomfortable. Well made as they often were, their fraudulence now seemed particularly apparent; sometimes in the outtakes we found vivid proof of directorial manipulation. I preferred the rawness of the footage grabbed by the GI cameramen as they popped up, armed only with their Eyemos—cameras whose load was one minute of 35 mm black-and-white film—to record the scenes before them. These guys had no control over the uses to which their film was put. It was sent to the rear unedited. It was censored or passed by anonymous military functionaries. It was seen or not seen— American casualties were not even hinted at photographically until late in the war—on an almost whimsical basis. But this material was truer to the chaos and terror of combat than the more formally controlled, consciously shaped footage of the Hollywood operatives.

It became emblematic for me, for it is clear to me that, after a long period of forgetting, we have arrived at a point where we are falsifying anew, in ways not so different from those employed in *The Battle of San Pietro* or *Memphis Belle*—our recollections of war. The more I thought about the ways we are now remembering the war, the more I began to think that we are still caught in an old groove, our perspective essentially unchanged even though some sixty years have passed.

I'M GLAD, naturally, that we are not finished with World War II. It remains the central event of the twentieth century—my generation's century, if you will, the event that permanently defined and shaped us, no matter how much longer we live on into the twenty-first century.

Some of the reasons we keep returning to World War II are quite simpleminded. There is, for instance, the steady march of round-numbered anniversaries—the 50th of D day, the 60th of Pearl Harbor, and so on. There is a natural human tendency both to nostalgize and glorify the events that occurred on these historic dates. This tendency is reinforced by the lure of always suspect commerce—the special magazine issue, the visually arresting, intellectually empty picture book, the television documentary that spins by too simply and too fast.

Amidst these occasions there have, of course, been celebratory products that we must take a little more seriously—Stephen Ambrose's histories of the war from the GIs' point of view, *Flags of Our Fathers*, *Saving Private Ryan*. These works propound a fundamental American decency and dutifulness that is both poignant and indisputable—though not quite the whole story.

This spirit of celebration is also reinforced because the generation that fought World War II is passing from the stage. More than half of the sixteen million men and women who served in the American armed forces during the war have died. The rest are dying at a rate of eleven hundred a day. There is a desire to honor the fighting men of World War II while substantial numbers of them are still alive to hear our encomiums.

It is said, on every hand, that the war they fought was our last "good" war, possibly our only good war. This characterization derives from one simple yet enormous fact—the Holocaust. Democracies had faced bullies before, national leaders who had exploited their own people and cruelly assaulted others who stood in the way of their territorial ambitions and dictatorial dreams. Indeed, genocide was an issue in many a conflict both before and after World War II. But no one had ever seen behavior so monstrous, so beyond civilized comprehension, as Nazi Germany's. And never had our nation been obliged to confront anything like it so directly, at such cost.

Yet, curiously, mass recognition of this enormity has come well after the fact. It is true that the photographic evidence of the death camp horrors shocked the world when they were liberated in 1945. It is also true that *The Diary of Anne Frank* was published in the Netherlands as early as 1947. But the pictures were more or less forgotten for many years, and it was not until Anne Frank's diary was published in English in 1952—followed by its dramatization in 1955—that it began, rather slowly, to make its immortal impact on human consciousness.

George Stevens's 1959 movie version of the *Diary*, however, was a ponderous failure. Insofar as popular culture was concerned, the matter of the Holocaust more or less rested there for a long while—unless you wanted to count *The Night Porter*. Mostly the agony of European Jewry was conveyed through literature—reportage, memoirs, scholarship, and the occasional documentary like *The Sorrow and the Pity* and *Shoah*. This work, not much of it wildly or immediately popular, has nonetheless slowly leached its way through layers of indifference.

We are at last fully sensitized to the Holocaust—though not yet to the scarcely less heinous crimes of our other major wartime enemy or, for that matter, those of our wartime ally, Stalinist Russia. But, yes, in the last two decades, from say, *The Tin Drum* to *Schindler's List*, movies and the rest of the popular media have quite powerfully begun to communicate the full extent and horror of German crimes against humanity. There is a determination that they never be forgotten. One thinks of Steven Spielberg's Shoah Foundation, trying to capture on videotape the recollections of every living Holocaust survivor. Or of the very moving Holocaust Memorial Museum in Washington, D.C.

It is from this vast effort at remembering that what we have come to identify as the "Greatest Generation" derives its claim to greatness. In itself the phrase is no more than a peculiarly vapid example of the evil of banality, a television anchorman's doubtless sincere attempt to tag a group with the highest accolade our society has to offer—a catch phrase.

But heroism—"greatness," if you will—must, I think, include self-, social-, and perhaps world consciousness. And that, as we have seen, is precisely what the generation that fought World War II lacked. Surely it was an unlucky generation—hustled from depression to global warfare without a moment to catch its breath. Surely it was a dutiful generation. Its members stood where they were told to stand, advanced when they were ordered to, and died—many of them—because they were the right age for the killing fields.

On the other hand, as a Jewish war veteran said to me, "This generational thing is shit." He cannot forget the virulent anti-Semitism he encountered in the army. Or the discussions he overheard in which the question of how bad, really, it would be if the Germans won the war, was openly raised. Or the fact that an essentially anti-Semitic U.S. State Department callously prevented massive Jewish immigration from Europe in the years before the war.

Some of the cameramen I spoke with were too shocked to shoot when they encountered the death camps in the waning days of the war. Because nothing they had officially or unofficially heard or read prepared them for what their astonished and sickened eyes beheld. In short, they had been kept, quite willfully, in a state of innocence by those charged with the war's conduct and with the way it was presented to the mass public.

Arthur Schlesinger, Jr., the historian, served as a bureaucrat in wartime Washington, where he had an excellent opportunity to observe the way civilian leadership prosecuted the conflict. He writes: "Like all wars, our war was accompanied by atrocity and sadism, by stupidities and lies, pomposity and chickenshit." He is—as instinct and common sense easily inform us—quite correct.

Speaking purely of the propaganda Washington pumped out, we can perhaps be ambivalently forgiving. Mobilizing a mass society for unprecedented effort and sacrifice is never easy. And at the time, history offered few guidelines. In any case, calls to arms cannot, in their nature, be delicately nuanced.

But that was then, and this is now. And we find ourselves confronting, in the idea of the "greatest generation," a notion that is not essentially different from the wartime idealization of the triumphant, ubiquitous "common man" that ruled the rhetoric of the movies, radio, journalism, and popular literature of the time. To be sure, this later idea carries an implied criticism of several postwar generations. The idea is that they are too soft, too lost in materialism, too lacking in ideals to measure up to the hard, uncomplaining model of their forefathers.

It must also be observed that the patronizing "little guy" tropes that were the contributions of the Popular Front writers have been stripped from the more recent considerations of the war. So have the celebrations of democratic bonding in small warrior groups. There are, in Stephen Ambrose's works, few cynical outsiders who need to be integrated into the warrior group. And, of course, the "one world" promise—all flapping flags and a beamishly dawning sun—with which so many wartime movies concluded, is entirely missing from these more recent works.

But all of that aside, Brokaw and the rest are still in the business of celebrating the virtues of American ordinariness in the old-fashioned way. They implicitly posit some mystical connection between the dumb, dutiful decency of the average American and the great and necessary moral task they accomplished, which was, of course, the defeat of absolute and unprecedented evil.

The point is inarguable, I suppose, though it leaves out of the argument those dull, practical points that assured our victory: infinite superiority in numbers and productive capacity, and the safety of the North American continent as a staging area for war—our steel mills and aircraft factories could not be disrupted by bombing raids. It also leaves out the horrific reality of this war as it was actually prosecuted.

You can argue that war on the scale of World War II does not encourage fine—or perhaps even crude—moral distinctions. In his memorable essay "Thank God for the Atom Bomb," Paul Fussell makes this simple argument: Better them than us—*them* being the Japanese civilians at Hiroshima and Nagasaki, *us* being the American troops (Fussell, then an infantry lieutenant, among them) poised to invade Japan's home islands in the fall of 1945.

Drawing on a great and brutal war memoir by former marine E. B. Sledge, Fussell creates a sickening picture of marines "sliding under fire down a shell-pocked ridge, slimy with mud and liquid dysentery . . . into the maggoty Japanese and U.S.M.C. corpses at the bottom, vomiting as the maggots burrowed into their own foul clothing."

His point is simple: anything to bring fighting of that kind to an end. This war, like all wars, finally bleached morality out of consideration, just as the marines carefully bleached the skulls of their Japanese foes so that these prized souvenirs of combat would not openly stink of death. Of course such men sobbed openly when the atomic bombs were detonated. Those explosions meant their lives had been given back to them.

It was, as Fussell makes clear, for men who served farther behind the lines to debate the morality of the bomb. It has been for generations farther in the future to venerate these men as the "greatest generation." But what everyone can and perhaps should debate are the silences, evasions, and outright lies by which all of us, soldiers and civilians, young and old, were encouraged to support the war.

Those who were obliged to support it with their last full measure of devotion mostly died as soldiers from time immemorial have died—because they were in the wrong place at the wrong time. They went—if they had time to think about it at all—cursing God or fate. Or, more likely, calling poignantly for their mothers. They did not die murmuring inspiring thoughts to the folks back home. That only happened in the movies.

SAM FULLER, the movie director, was a veteran of some three years of fighting in the European theater. He landed on three D-day beaches, including Omaha. He once said to me that a soldier under fire has only one thought—"to live, live, live." He also made the point that we do not usually mourn the fallen very long. Their loved ones get up and get on with their lives very quickly—accompanied by increasing vague regrets. It is only officially and semi-officially that, well after the fact, encouraged by the media and the politicians, we remember to remember—as we have lately done. Finally, and most important, Sam always insisted that we are all heroes and that we are all cowards. The difference between the one status and the other is as thin as the paper on which citations for bravery are written up. It is all a matter of circumstances. And of chance. Sometimes our viscera instruct us that the best opportunity for survival lies in fighting. Sometimes they propose fleeing as the sensible course. These thoughts are scarcely original with Sam, though he did make several films that illustrate them, films that, one must say, were not wildly popular except among cinephiles drawn more to their vivid style than to their harsh substance.

War, we must acknowledge, has always been with us. And always will be with us. As it is conducted in the modern world, it cannot—all pious protestations aside—make distinctions between civilian casualties and military ones. Whether one survives in a war or dies in it is purely a matter of chance, a question of where you happen to be standing when the Daisy Cutter lands. Whether you are deemed a hero or a coward is similarly a matter of circumstance. All we know for certain is that if you are unlucky enough to be a fighting soldier, you will see, and very likely do, things that will shame your humanity and disturb your dreams for the rest of your life. It is no accident that the evidence presented both anecdotally and in psychological literature records a high rate of disturbance—drunkenness, familial abuse, dark silences—among the veterans of World War II. These conditions did not suddenly surface after Vietnam. It is equally no accident that existentialism, the philosophy that defines man purely as the sum of his actions within a Godless universe ruled entirely by chance, came into fashion immediately after World War II.

I am one of that lucky generation whom the war dead granted the luxury of philosophical debate. I can't say that I fully appreciated the opportunity. Like almost everyone else I knew—all right, Brokaw is right about that—I was too busy getting and spending to concentrate on the gift I was given. It is only lately that—by chance, of course—my mind has been more urgently directed to the questions that war raised, and more specifically to the ways we are being asked to remember it.

World War II now increasingly belongs to memory. Soon everyone who lived through it will disappear, and it will belong exclusively to the historians, trying to recreate the living texture of the time out of dry documents, fading photographs. There are only a few years left during which there will be enough of us to debate its conduct and its meaning. While there is yet time, while those of us who can remember the war are still alive in substantial numbers, it is important to get straight about it.

We need now to take better care of our wartime memories than circumstances permitted when the war was being fought. Certainly that's true of my generation, safe at home while the fighting proceeded. We were the first—but not the last—beneficiaries of this citizen army's exertions. Its members—for the most part draftees, we must remember, men without choice in the matter—were by chance called upon to defend their country. Equally by chance, they somehow brought to a belated end a vast evil.

This book has been much preoccupied with the kinds of lies we were told during the war, lies that coalesced around a "metamyth" of democratically parceled-out sacrifice in aid of creating a more perfectly democratic union, a more perfectly democratic world. Most of us no longer believe in that myth. When we encounter it, usually in a late-night television rerun of some old war movie, we laugh and shake our heads at the naiveté of, say, Humphrey Bogart's propaganda speech as we impatiently await its end and the resumption of the scarcely less mindless action.

That said, I continue to believe that World War II was a just war. At the time we officially and unofficially evaded and elided its highest moral purpose. Yet somehow we stumbled through it to the right, the necessary, conclusion. Whether in its conduct— and most specifically in the way our war "aims" were laid out for us by the mass media—it was a "good" war I am, obviously, far less certain. About whether we need now to dress the old clichés in "greatest generation" finery I am utterly certain. It travesties history and experience. It becomes a false and falsifying reference point in a world no less dangerous, no less ready for war, than it was more than a half-century ago.

I am now close to being an old man—probably I *am* an old man in everyone's eyes but my own. In any case, I am much closer to my death than I am to the hopeful, silly boy who is the subject of this memoir. I don't want to live the remainder of my life by the lies that sustained him. And I don't want to replace those old lies with new variants on them. In the end, at the end, we owe ourselves the truth. Not the whole truth—no one can encompass that. But as much of the truth as we can see and express.

Put the matter simply: If we cannot remember truthfully, we cannot think clearly or behave decently. That is one important thing a critic—that curious, not to say exotic, creature I have become—tries to do: recall honestly, so as to measure new experience in such light as memory can shed on the case. It is a subjective business, finally, therefore a suspect activity to some. But it is all I have to offer—a small and flickering light burning amidst all the false remembrance, forgiving sentiment, smug triumphalism that rolls in like the morning low clouds that form over a distant and mysterious sea, obscuring and distorting an already dimming picture.

I WANT TO THANK my agents, Don Congdon and Susan Ramer, for piloting this vessel through stormy seas to a safe harbor. The voyage was longer than we anticipated, but their patience and support never wavered.

Thanks also to Ivan Dee, my best publishing friend, for his enthusiasm and for his deft editorial pencil. He has made this book far better than it might otherwise have been. The same may be said of my life's companion, Barbara Isenberg, that model of tact, taste, and patience with an often surly author.

Finally, thanks to my daughters, Erika and Jessica, for producing this book's dedicatees. It seems to me that you're never fully grown up until the grandchildren arrive and you become aware of life's cycle renewing—but this time with no responsibility except to give advice no one pays any attention to, tell stories no one is interested in, and enjoy the unearned happiness of new company—eagerly bouncing, unqualifiedly loving, and, above all, entirely uncritical.

Index

Index

Index

Index

Index

Index

Destination Tokyo, 95; The Devil
With Hitler, 98; A Diary for Timothy,
148; Diary of Anne Frank, 296;
Disney movies, 16–19, 62;
documentaries, 293–296, 297;
Double Indemnity, 146; Dragon Seed,
79; as dreams, 229; Drums Along the
Mohawk, 45–46; Dumbo, 17–18;
Ecstasy, 144–145; Edge of Darkness,
85; emotional depth in, 71–76; The
Enchanted Cottage, 248; Erpi
Classroom Films, 213; as escape,
xii–xiii; Escape, 102; The Fallen
Sparrow, 98, 236; fantasy aspects of,
21; Fargo, 259; film noir, 273; Flags of
Our Fathers, 295; Flying Tigers, 85;
football movies, 22–24; For Me and
My Gal, 154; For Whom the Bell Tolls,
112–114; Gentleman Jim, 153–154;
Going My Way, 146; Gone With the
Wind, 143, 232–233; Grand Illusion,
290; The Great Dictator, 24–25, 97;
The Greatest Generation, 87;
Guadalcanal Diary, 264; Gung-Ho,
87; A Guy Named Joe, 256–258; Hail
the Conquering Hero, 201–203;
Hangmen Also Die, 105; The Happy
Land, 203–205; Henry V, 156–157;
The Hitler Gang, 115–116; Hitler's
Children, 99–101; Hitler's Madmen,
105–106; Hollywood Canteen,
129–131; honor represented in,
151–155; Hotel Berlin, 116; The
Human Comedy, 171, 203–205; I'll Be
Seeing You, 248; illness portrayed by,
258–259; In the Navy, 26; In Which
We Serve, 155; intellectual contempt
for, 289–291; Joe Smith, American,
64; Johnny Come Lately, 154; Journey

for Margaret, 171–172; The King in
New York, 25; Knute Rockne, All-
American, 22–24; Lassie Come Home,
185, 188–191; Laura, 236; legal
classification, 20; Lifeboat, 98;
Limelight, 25; Listen to Britain, 148;
The Lost Patrol, 94; The Lost
Weekend, 236; love of, 19; The Magic
Christian, 271; mass chorus scenes,
74–75; The Master Race, 110;
matinees, 125–127; Meet Me in St.
Louis, 170–174, 238; Memphis Belle,
295; The Miracle of Morgan's Creek,
200–201; Mission to Moscow,
107–108; Monsieur Verdoux, 25; The
Moon is Down, 85, 99; The Mortal
Storm, 102; movie magazines,
128–129, 132, 136–137; Mr.
Skeffington, 101–102, 115; Mrs.
Miniver, 141, 234, 264–265; My
Friend Flicka, 185–188; The Navy
Comes Through, 85; The Night Porter,
296; None Shall Escape, 116–117; The
North Star, 108; Northern Pursuit,
62; nostalgia in, 150–159, 170–174;
Objective Burma, 95–96; One of our
Aircraft Is Missing, 155–156; Only
Angels Have Wings, 90; Our Vines
Have Tender Grapes, 198–200; The
Outlaw, 143; Passage to Marseilles,
251–256; Pinocchio, 18; pinups,
135–137, 140; Pride of the Yankees,
258–259; Pulp Fiction, 259, 262; The
Purple Heart, 82; radio dramas of,
51–52; Ragtime, 72; Random Harvest,
136, 247–248; religion in, 146, 201,
264; The Reluctant Dragon, 18–19;
Road to Morocco, 26; Rulers of the
Sea, 21–22; Rules of the Game, 290;

Index

Index

Index

Index

A NOTE ON THE AUTHOR

Best known as a film critic for *Time* magazine, Richard Schickel is also the author or co-author of more than thirty books, most of them about the movies. They include major biographies of D. W. Griffith and Clint Eastwood, and shorter books about Marlon Brando, Cary Grant, Douglas Fairbanks, Sr., and James Cagney; a definitive study of Walt Disney and his works; and a pioneering consideration of the celebrity system. Mr. Schickel has also written, directed, and produced thirty television programs, many of them documentaries about film and filmmakers. He has been nominated four times for an Emmy, has held a Guggenheim Fellowship, and has been awarded the British Film Institute book prize and the Maurice Bessy award for film criticism. He lives in Los Angeles.